HANDBOOK FOR
HIPAA-HITECH
SECURITY

SECOND EDITION

MARGRET AMATAYAKUL, MBA, RHIA, CHPS, CPEHR, FHIMSS

AMA

AMERICAN MEDICAL
ASSOCIATION

Internet address: www.ama-assn.org

The American Medical Association ("AMA") has consulted sources believed to be knowledgeable in their fields. However, the AMA does not warrant that the information is in every respect accurate and/or complete. The AMA assumes no responsibility for use of the information contained in this publication. The AMA shall not be responsible for, and expressly disclaims liability for, damages of any kind arising out of the use of, reference to, or reliance on, the content of this publication. This publication is for informational purposes only. The AMA does not provide medical, legal, financial, or other professional advice and readers are encouraged to consult a professional advisor for such advice.

The contents of this publication represent the views of the author and should not be construed to be the views or policy of the AMA, or of the institution with which the author may be affiliated, unless this is clearly specified.

Additional copies of this book may be ordered by calling 800 621-8335 or from the secure AMA Web site at www.amabookstore.com. Refer to product number OP320612.

Library of Congress Cataloging-in-Publication Data

Amatayakul, Margret.
  Handbook for HIPAA/HITECH security / Margret Amatayakul. — 2nd ed.
      p. ; cm.
  Rev. ed. of: Handbook for HIPAA security implementation / Margret Amatayakul . . . [et al.]. c2004.
  Includes bibliographical references and index.
  Summary: "Handbook for HIPAA-HITECH Security details the final regulations brought about by HITECH changes to the HIPAA security rule and to the privacy rule as it applies to security. Learn practical and pragmatic ways to interpret the new regulations and ensure compliance"—Provided by publisher.
  ISBN 978-1-60359-801-9 (alk. paper)
  I. American Medical Association.   II. Handbook for HIPAA security implementation.   III. Title.
  [DNLM: 1. United States. Health Insurance Portability and Accountability Act of 1996.   2. United States. Health Information Technology for Economic and Clinical Health Act.   3. Medical Records Systems, Computerized—standards—United States.   4. Confidentiality—legislation & jurisprudence—United States.   5. Confidentiality—standards—United States.   6. Medical Records Systems, Computerized—legislation & jurisprudence—United States.   7. Security Measures—legislation & jurisprudence—United States.   8. Security Measures—standards—United States.   WX 175]
  344.7304'12—dc23 2012042212

BPO2:12-P-O23:12/12

CONTENTS

TABLE LIST

FOREWORD

Providing good security for healthcare information has always been difficult and complex. The Health Insurance Portability and Accountability Act (HIPAA) of 1996 implemented, and the Health Information Technology for Economic and Clinical Health Act (HITECH) of 2009 subsequently augmented, rules, regulations, requirements, audits, and enforcement activities that may involve sanctions and penalties for physician medical practices. HIPAA and HITECH provide a base level of what must be put in place to avoid civil and in some cases criminal liability and avoid the loss of public confidence in a medical practice or other healthcare organization.

HIPAA and HITECH security areas are complex. A solid understanding of health information security and privacy are needed. Unless you are already an expert on health information security and privacy, it is unlikely that you have the knowledge and experience that is necessary to achieve compliance with HIPAA and HITECH. *Handbook for HIPAA-HITECH Security*, Second Edition, provides the knowledge and guidance that will permit you to do so. In many practices the steps described can be accomplished without the need for external support or consultation.

Margret Amatayakul has done an excellent job of assembling an approach to HIPAA and HITECH security and privacy that is straightforward and practical for physicians. The book's organization is designed to yield a successful result. Each chapter deals with a particular topic, takes the reader through an explanation of the topic, and lays out the series of tasks that are designed to result in compliance.

A logical 10-step approach is laid out for addressing HIPAA and HITECH:

1. Create a culture of privacy and security awareness.
2. Ensure a solid understanding of the Security Rule.
3. Assign/affirm responsibility for information security.
4. Conduct/update a security risk analysis.
5. Develop/maintain an information security plan.
6. Select applicable vendors for security services.
7. Implement security policies, procedures, and services.
8. Document information security compliance.
9. Develop/manage ongoing security monitoring.
10. Incorporate security compliance into overall compliance program.

In this manner, Margret breaks this large and complex area down into very understandable parts. The key area of risk assessment provides a practical approach that can help you avoid getting trapped in the quagmire of analysis paralysis.

I am confident that *Handbook for HIPAA-HITECH Security* will be the physician's key resource to achieve compliance with HIPAA and HITECH.

I wish you great success.

Talmadge (Ted) Cooper, MD, FACMI
Associate Clinical Professor, Stanford Medical School
Past Chair, Privacy and Security Committee at Kaiser Permanente Northern California
Past Chair, Privacy and Security Task Force, Healthcare Information and Management Systems Society (HIMSS)

Information security awareness is increasing in health care, yet for many medical practices security still focuses primarily on the safety of the persons in the practice and its physical property and less on information security. A limited study of healthcare providers conducted in 2011 found that most respondents were aware of and reportedly had a strategy for addressing HIPAA privacy and security compliance, and utilized mainstream technical security controls (eg, passwords, backups, firewalls, and antivirus software), but "security culture-building measures and relevant training seemed inadequate."[1] The Healthcare Information Management and Systems Society (HIMSS) 2011 Security Survey, co-sponsored by the Medical Group Management Association (MGMA), found that one-fourth of practices have not conducted a security risk analysis, only half of respondents have an information security officer, only a quarter of those surveyed intended to purchase security technology in the following year, and 14% had at least one known case of medical identity theft reported by a patient in the previous 12 months.[2]

With complaints to the Office for Civil Rights (OCR) continuing to increase,[3] with breaches ever more profound and expensive (including a resolution agreement for $100,000 at a five-physician cardiology practice in Arizona),[4] with even the Centers for Medicare and Medicaid Services (CMS) having difficulty addressing breaches and medical identity theft among Medicare participants,[5] and with as many as 82% of respondents to the 2011 HIMSS survey reporting that their organization shares patient data in an electronic format with external organizations, it is imperative that the sophistication of our security environment increase.

As you read through this book, keep in mind this single theme: A practice worth creating is worth protecting! Physicians have long held privacy as an inalienable right for their patients. Security is a modern-day extension of privacy.

We all know we should lock our doors at night and password-protect our computer, but many of us are either less familiar with or at least less inclined to address a less visible door—the computer system that maintains your mission-critical health information. Could an intruder gain access through the Internet to confidential information about a patient or your practice? Do you know how much computer access to assign to a new hire? Did you conduct a background check, or just leave a message to call back with one of the three references on the resume? Do you encrypt e-mail, backups, and the laptop onto which you just loaded the monthly outstanding patient collection information to work on over the weekend?

Security begins with a strong defensive plan that is kept up-to-date as you acquire new information technology. A defensive plan that's right for a large physician group may be too

---

1. Mishra, S., et al. (2011). Security awareness for health care information systems: A HIPAA compliance perspective. *Issues in Information Systems*, Vol. XII, No. 1. Pp. 224-236.

2. HIMSS (November 11). HIMSS Security Survey. Available at: http://www.himss.org/content/files/2011_himss_securitysurvey.pdf

3. Office for Civil Rights. 2011. Complaints Received by Calendar Year. Available at: http://www.hhs.gov/ocr/privacy/hipaa/enforcement/data/complaintsyear.html.

4. Office for Civil Rights. 2012. Resolution Agreements. Available at: http://www.hhs.gov/ocr/privacy/hipaa/enforcement/examples/index.html.

5. Levinson, DR. (October 2012). CMS Response to Breaches and Medical Identity Theft. Department of Health and Human Services Office of Inspector General. OEI-02-10-00040.

comprehensive and expensive for a two-physician office. In *Handbook for HIPAA-HITECH Security,* Second Edition, you evaluate what's right for you. You learn how to evaluate your information assets, identify your strengths and vulnerabilities, and then build a defense strategy to protect those assets. But you'll do more than protect; you will also learn how to ensure availability of your data—which may now be residing somewhere on the cloud!

In designing the content of this book, I blended guidelines that would fit small and large practices. The Security Rule comes with a unique set of flexible and reasonable standards. While you must address each standard, your security design must be right for you.

HOW TO USE THIS BOOK

From a concise overview of HIPAA to section-by-section descriptions, charts, graphs, timelines, checklists, and case studies, *Handbook for HIPAA-HITECH Security* leads you into the core of HIPAA security, updated with regulations resulting from the HITECH Act in support of increasing utilization of electronic health records. What follows is a chapter-by-chapter synopsis of this book.

Chapter 1: Why Information Security Is Important

To start you off thinking about information security, you are provided with a big-picture view of why information security is important—for protected health information (PHI) as well as all other confidential information in your office. While the HIPAA Security Rule is the primary context from which to approach information security, additional regulations from the HITECH Act, guidance documents from the US Department of Health and Human Services (HHS), and industry best practices also are germane.

Chapter 2: Overview of HIPAA and HITECH

This chapter reviews the context in which the Security Rule exists within HIPAA, reminds you about the "mini-security rule" within the Privacy Rule, and describes the principles on which the Security Rule is based. It defines some unique security terms and concepts, reminds you about how the Security Rule is structured, and helps you establish a plan for security compliance.

Chapter 3: Your Approach to Security

Because so much has changed since 2005 when compliance with the Security Rule was first required, it is appropriate to take a fresh look at your approach to information security. Many offices have adopted an electronic health record (EHR) system that now represents a mission-critical component of your practice. This chapter helps you create a culture of privacy and security awareness and gives you tools to further your understanding of your information security needs.

Use this chapter to assign and affirm responsibility for security; conduct and update a security risk analysis; develop and maintain an information security plan; select applicable vendors for security services; implement security policies, procedures, and services; document information security compliance; develop and manage an ongoing security monitoring process; and incorporate security compliance into an overall compliance program.

Chapter 4: Organizing for HIPAA

No office operates in isolation, and this chapter provides security planning and documentation strategies to help you work with other covered and noncovered entities. This chapter defines organizational relationships including affiliated covered entities (ACE), organized healthcare arrangements (OHCA), hybrid entities, and other relationships in which security documentation is critical to compliance. A documentation management tool provides guidance on what policies and procedures to create, revise, or retire.

Chapter 5: HIPAA Security Risk Analysis

A risk analysis and risk management plan is the key to determining how you will identify and select controls to manage your security risks. This chapter links your risk analysis to a detailed plan that helps you manage those risks. If you prefer to read chapters out of order, do read this chapter before reading Chapters 6, 8, and 9.

Chapter 5 provides a flexible approach to managing each implementation specification in the HIPAA Security Rule. You'll find plenty of charts, templates, and assessment tools to help you analyze and manage threats as you move from an environment of suspicion to an environment of awareness and accountability.

Chapter 6: HIPAA Security Administrative Safeguards

For information security officials, this is the first of three nuts-and-bolts chapters that offer specific direction. Do you know what specific security controls are right for your practice? Would you know if they were working? The HIPAA Security Rule includes nine administrative standards and implementation specifications. With the exception of security risk analysis, covered in Chapter 5, and business associate contracts, in Chapter 7, this chapter describes the HIPAA Security Rule administrative safeguards in priority order for you to implement in your practice.

This chapter shows you how to evaluate each administrative requirement so that you can develop or amend your own policies and procedures, from security reviews to employee sanctions, contingency planning, and ongoing evaluation. You'll find useful charts, tables, and checklists to help you implement the administrative safeguards. Excellent real-life examples let you know how others have solved similar problems.

Chapter 7: Business Associate Contracts and Other Arrangements Standard

The identification of business associates and contractual arrangements with them to ensure a chain of trust when providing access to PHI have become increasingly important. Not only do offices have many more business associates than in the past, but today they often serve a much more integral part of your office functions. In addition, the HITECH Act is changing the relationship of the business to the HIPAA Privacy Rule and Security Rule. As of the writing of this edition, final regulations have not yet been adopted, but suffice it to say that managing your business associates and business associate contracts will only become more important.

Specifically, this chapter provides a model business associate contract, describes special considerations when acquiring information systems from vendors providing Internet hosting services and other shared services, discusses health information exchange (HIE) participation and health information exchange organization (HIO) agreements, and provides suggestions for managing your Web presence and social media usage.

Chapter 8: HIPAA Security Physical Safeguards

Many offices are increasing their physical security—not only as a result of heightened use of information systems but also to improve personal safety protections. Still, reviewing your physical security with an eye toward reducing risk of breaches of PHI from lost or stolen devices and media (including paper) should help you detect your vulnerabilities. A detailed summary of each physical safeguard standard and implementation specification will aid you in selecting the best physical controls for your environment. Case studies highlight physical safeguards that worked and others that didn't.

Chapter 9: HIPAA Security Technical Safeguards

In this chapter, you learn about each technology security requirement, how to implement controls to meet each requirement, and examples of best practices for physician offices. This chapter includes a library of information security language so that you can comfortably discuss technology with your information technology vendor. It also covers key strategies for addressing new requirements associated with, for example, e-prescribing of controlled substances, increased cell phone usage, and wireless networks.

Chapter 10: Practical Tips for Applying Security Controls

The last chapter discusses how to implement your security controls in order to comply with the HIPAA and HITECH information security requirements, including assuring you are able to demonstrate your compliance. This chapter helps you budget for your security controls; discusses options for managing security services and their implementation; stresses the importance of policies and procedures, training, documentation, and change control; helps you respond to an OCR complaint or audit; and provides tools to use in breach notification.

A Word About the Second Edition

Readers of the first edition may wonder what happened to the chapters entitled "Security Implementation" and "Special Considerations for Electronic Data Interchange and Electronic Medical Records." Much more emphasis on the implementation aspects of information security controls have been covered throughout this second edition. In addition, electronic data interchange (EDI) and EHRs, as well as completely new constructs of HIE, responding to complaints/audits, and breach notification, have become much more a way of life for many practices. These are no longer viewed as outside the norm; hence any "special considerations" have been integrated within each chapter as applicable.

Appendix and Glossary

The appendix provides a brief overview of the final Security Rule to help you understand how to read the rule. From time to time you may have questions, and the answers are often found in the regulations. Also, one of the most comprehensive security glossaries ever published is included in this book.

Compact Disk

A CD-ROM is also supplied with this book. It contains not only the Security Rule from the appendix but its Preamble, the Breach Notification Rule, and Guidance on Unsecured PHI. The CD-ROM also includes several of the tools from figures in the text and some additional tools.

   Good luck as you implement your information security plan. I hope you'll send me an e-mail at Margret@Margret-A.com to let me know how you're doing!

Margret Amatayakul

ACKNOWLEDGMENTS

It is very gratifying to have worked with so many knowledgeable and encouraging professionals, who, like most in the healthcare field, are deeply engaged in the implementation of information privacy and security.

A deep debt of gratitude is also extended to Ted Cooper, MD, FACMI, an ophthalmologist with a practice in Redwood City, California. Dr Cooper has been chair of the Privacy and Security Committee at Kaiser Permanente Northern California and chair of the Privacy and Security Task Force of the Health Information and Management Systems Society (HIMSS), where he served as the lead content developer of the HIMSS product CPRI TOOLKIT: Managing Information Security in Healthcare.

Special acknowledgment also goes to the co-authors of the first edition of this book, without whom this second edition would not be feasible:

Steven S. Lazarus, PhD, FHIMSS, is president and co-founder of Boundary Information Group (BIG), a consortium of healthcare information and technology consulting firms offering comprehensive solutions to improve healthcare value. He is past chair of the Workgroup for Electronic Data Interchange (WEDI) and former executive responsible for research and information systems activities at the Medical Group Management Association (MGMA). Dr Lazarus earned his doctoral degree from the University of Rochester and received the Extraordinary Achievement Award in 2002 for his contribution to the development and implementation of HIPAA's Administrative Simplification provisions.

Tom Walsh, CISSP, is a nationally recognized speaker and health information security consultant. He is the president of Tom Walsh Consulting, LLC, based in Overland Park, Kansas. The firm focuses on conducting security training, assessments, and remediation activities for healthcare clients. Tom's background also includes more than 20 years of experience working as a contractor with the US Department of Energy helping to secure its nuclear weapons program. Tom is a Certified Information Systems Security Professional (CISSP).

Carolyn Hartley, MLA, CHP, is president and CEO of Physicians EHR, Inc., based in Jacksonville, North Carolina, a company that provides training, education, and consulting to physicians adopting EHRs. She is co-author of several HIPAA training products published by the American Medical Association, including *Field Guide to HIPAA Implementation, HIPAA Policies and Procedures Desk Reference*, and *HIPAA Plain and Simple*. She also supports the privacy and security workgroup with the North Carolina Healthcare Information and Communications Alliance (NCHICA).

Gratitude must also be expressed to Carol Scheele, JD, who meticulously reviewed the draft manuscript, and also to the editorial staff at AMA—Elise Schumacher, Nancy Baker, Michael Ryder, and Meghan Anderson, among many others—for helping to get this book into your hands.

Margret Amatayakul, MBA, RHIA, CHPS, CPEHR, FHIMSS, is president of Margret\A Consulting, LLC, a health information management and systems consulting firm based in Schaumburg, Illinois. The firm focuses on providing synergies between healthcare regulations, such as HIPAA and HITECH, and information technology deployment, including electronic health records, health information exchange, and other clinical infrastructure issues.

Margret "A" contributed to the Institute of Medicine patient record study and, as a result, helped found the Computer-based Patient Record Institute (CPRI), which now resides within the Healthcare Information and Management Systems Society (HIMSS) as the Nicholas E. Davies Award of Excellence. She has a long career history including working for direct care providers, working with the American Health Information Management Association (AHIMA), serving as faculty in health informatics master's programs at the University of Illinois and the College of St. Scholastica, and finding practical solutions to information systems problems for her clients. She has written several books, chapters, articles, and columns on EHRs, HIPAA/HITECH, and workflow and process management for AHIMA, the Medical Group Management Association (MGMA), HCPro, CRC Press, the Healthcare Financial Management Association, the American Academy of Dermatology, and the American Academy of Pediatrics. She holds a master's degree in business administration with concentrations in marketing and finance and maintains current professional credentials as a Registered Health Information Administrator (RHIA), Certified in Healthcare Privacy and Security (CHPS), Certified Professional in Electronic Health Records (CPEHR), and Fellow in the Healthcare Information and Management Systems Society (FHIMSS).

Why Information Security Is Important

If you're like most people, you try to follow commonsense security measures: You know it is important to lock your doors, avoid losing your credit cards, file your important papers in a safe, and comply with the Health Insurance Portability and Accountability Act of 1996 (HIPAA). But have you made security a way of life to fully protect all the information in your office, especially in light of increasing use of electronic health records (EHRs), cloud computing, data aggregation services for new health reform structures, and other uses of information technology (IT)?

The Health Insurance Portability and Accountability Act of 1996 (HIPAA) required physicians and other healthcare providers who conduct any of the HIPAA electronic transactions (eg, claim, eligibility verification) as well as health plans to adopt certain privacy and security measures to safeguard protected health information (PHI). The HIPAA Security Rule was issued in 2003 and has been in effect since 2005. It is often viewed as focusing on confidentiality and limited to PHI in electronic form. It is very important to protect PHI from "prying eyes" and other wrongful disclosures. But the HIPAA Security Rule is more than just confidentiality. It is also about data integrity and availability—making sure data have not been altered and that they are available when needed. Electronic PHI may generally be considered more vulnerable than PHI in paper records. Yet, there is clear indication from the nature of PHI breaches and audit findings that the focus of HIPAA Security Rule enforcement must be on both electronic and paper PHI, with laptops, network breaches, e-mail, portable devices, desktop computers, and paper records theft listed as the most common sources of breaches. In addition to breaches, paper can be stolen or destroyed in a fire, flood, or other natural disaster, and electronic PHI can be rendered unavailable as a result of a power outage, server crash, down Internet Service Provider (ISP), or a hack on a local or remote server.

Today there is heightened attention on the HIPAA Security Rule. There are increased penalties for noncompliance, required reporting of breaches, more audits being performed, and inclusion of security requirements for earning the federal incentives for acquiring and making meaningful use of certified EHR technology. In fact, with the Health Information Technology for Economic and Clinical Health (HITECH) Act of 2009 promoting adoption of EHRs through various incentive programs, significantly more attention to all aspects of information security is needed not only to assure the confidentiality of health information, but to establish contingency plans that assure the information will be available when needed. But information security is important not just for PHI—in any form—but for all important information in the practice, including clinician credentials, health plan care contracts, data in quality programs, credit card information, accounts receivable, and other information about you, your staff, your patients, and your practice. Such information in the wrong hands or simply lost can also greatly impact a physician practice.

HOW TO USE THIS CHAPTER

This chapter builds the business case for heightened scrutiny of your information security practices. It:

■ Emphasizes the importance of the C-I-A of information security
■ Identifies drivers for enhanced security
■ Recognizes the importance of security for other types of information

This chapter helps focus thinking about security from the narrow HIPAA Security Rule compliance perspective to a much broader perspective for which a return on investment can be anticipated—from avoiding the cost of breach notification now required by HIPAA and many states, recovering lost data, and protecting against liability when your patients' health information is not available, as well as addressing noncompliance with HIPAA. Each of the major topics covered in this chapter will then be explored in depth in subsequent chapters in the book.

THE C-I-A OF SECURITY

Confidentiality, integrity, and availability (C-I-A) are the cornerstones of information security—whether for protecting PHI or other types of important information.

Confidentiality

The HIPAA Security Rule defines confidentiality as "the property that data or information is not made available or disclosed to unauthorized persons or processes." Physicians have long practiced confidentiality as part of adherence to the Hippocratic Oath.

With respect to security, confidentiality is a principle that works to ensure that information is not disclosed to unauthorized entities, ie, people or information systems. In the paper environment, locking doors and file cabinets, generally "keeping an eye on" the charts, and requiring authorizations from the patient for disclosures have been the most common form of security. Confidentiality protections in an automated environment add a number of dimensions. Some of these require special training and awareness building.

Although physicians are beginning to use the cloud, many still save data on flash drives, give patients a visit summary on CD, and so on. Device and media controls are considered necessary—though they are not applied as often as they should be given the continuously increasing number of lost and stolen computers. Access controls, audit logging, and authentication mechanisms are designed to protect the confidentiality of data when stored in computer files and accessed by authorized individuals. Encryption is increasingly being applied as data are transmitted out of the practice, but still not to the extent advisable.

Integrity

Data integrity, in lay terms, refers to information being whole or sound. The HIPAA Security Rule defines integrity as "the property that data or information have not been altered or destroyed in an unauthorized manner."

Usually data integrity involves electronic data transmission. However, it may also involve alteration of data by accident or intent—and then it applies equally to paper and electronic forms of information. For example, recording information about one patient on another patient's chart occurs by accident and is not unusual. When it happens, the integrity of the data is altered. To correct this situation, the recommended practice in the paper world is to initial and date it, and out the erroneous entry, then record the information in the correct patient's chart, which may require a brief explanation of why it is out of sequence or was not documented at the time the information was acquired.

Nefarious purposes for altering information, such as to attempt to cover up an error in a health record or skim accounting records, are more troublesome to deal with, in both paper and electronic form.

All potential data integrity issues would benefit from security measures (including measures for confidentiality). Sophisticated data integrity routines that scan or check for alterations are worth considering

Availability

Availability is also referenced explicitly in the Security Rule as "the property that data or information is accessible and useable upon demand by an authorized person."

Availability may seem contradictory to security. Yet, if the information is so secure that it is not available when needed, two things may happen: Often the first is a vow to never use security controls again. The other is that the lack of information can result in poor healthcare outcomes. If the information is not immediately accessible, erroneous assumptions may be made that can be detrimental to the patient.

Many in health care see the word "control" associated with security services and fear lack of availability. Unfortunately, there has been so much emphasis on the "keeping out" rather than the "service" aspect of security that the result often is less than desirable availability. In fact, this has been carried to such an extreme that many health information system vendors still do not build into their products the—albeit more sophisticated—services that would afford both confidentiality and easier availability.

In addition to easier to use but more sophisticated security services, availability also requires that information be backed up and that there be contingency plans for disasters. Many in health care have been involved in disaster drills—but more often focusing on the personal safety aspects and more frequently in hospitals or nursing homes where patients are less able to move out of beds to safety. The Hurricane Katrina disaster perhaps did the most to solidify the general need in health care for disaster planning and highlighted that electronic records made availability easier. More recently, Web-based systems and cloud computing have raised awareness of the need for contingency planning of all types—though thankfully not (yet) as a result of a disaster. "Denial of service" is a term often used to describe the lack of availability in information systems, and even more specifically is used to refer to a form of attack on a computer that causes it to crash. Denial of service, however, is actually any action that prevents a system or its resources (eg, electrical power) from functioning in accordance with its intended purposes.

In summary, then, a good way to think about security is illustrated in Figure 1.1. Security should not be limited to confidentiality, but all aspects of the C-I-A set of principles should be employed to protect from wrongful disclosure, alteration, or denial of service (D-A-D).

FIGURE 1.1

Use C-I-A to Protect D-A-D

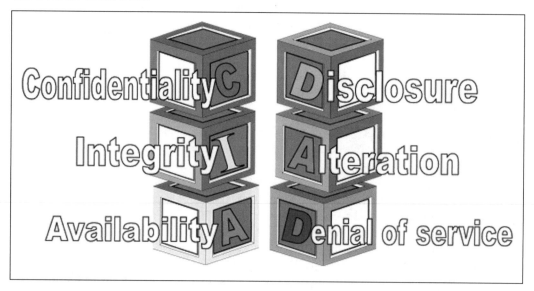

DRIVERS FOR ENHANCED SECURITY

Few would argue that security is not a good thing. However, the extent to which security services are implemented in a physician practice often depends on the amount of risk the practice is willing to assume. Often, however, a true risk analysis, or assessment, is not performed. The Security Rule defines risk analysis as "an accurate and thorough assessment of the potential risks and vulnerabilities to the confidentiality, integrity, and availability of PHI held by the covered entity."

Entities that must comply with HIPAA (health plans, healthcare clearinghouses, and providers who transmit any health information in electronic form in connection with financial and administrative transactions—referred to as "covered entities") have a tendency to focus on the vulnerabilities, or gaps, in security services, and not on the likelihood that a vulnerability would be exploited. Rarely does a practice consider how likely threats in its environment might create vulnerabilities in its information systems—and what impact they might have. A risk analysis has always been required as part of HIPAA Security Rule compliance. It is also now required for earning incentives under the program to promise meaningful use of EHR (see Chapter 5 for detailed information on conducting a risk analysis). Yet even for that, the analysis is more often focused only on gaps; and decisions are made relative only to how much it costs to fix the gap. A true risk analysis that considers factors driving the need for security might actually identify areas of cost savings in an overall security program. These drivers include:

- Patient awareness
- EHRs
- Health information exchange
- Identity theft and medical identity theft
- Reportable breaches
- Compliance enforcement

Patient Awareness

Patient awareness of security needs may seem like an unusual driver, or one that perhaps should be relegated to closer to the bottom of the list. No statistics are available from the US Department of Health and Human Services (HHS) on who files complaints about privacy and security, but there is strong evidence that patients are the most likely to file such complaints, followed closely by staff. Others—such as business associates or the general public—are a distant third. Since the Privacy Rule went into effect in 2003 through the end of 2010 (the last available data at the time of this writing), almost 60,000 complaints had been filed with the HHS Office for Civil Rights (OCR). The most common complaints involve disclosure to persons or entities that the patient believes is inappropriate; lack of (or the perceived lack of) security safeguards to protect health information; failure to provide patients access to their health information; disclosure of more information than necessary when sharing information with another person or entity; and an array of issues associated with distribution of the notice of privacy practices (NPP) that the Privacy Rule requires, training, mitigation of harmful occurrences arising out of Privacy Rule or Security Rule issues, and lack of attention to complaints patients make to the covered entity (see Table 1.1).

TABLE 1.1

Most Frequent Types of Complaints to the OCR (April 13, 2003, to December 31, 2010)

Privacy

- Impermissible uses and disclosures
- Safeguards for confidentiality, integrity, and availability of protected health information. (This abbreviated requirement within the Privacy Rule is considered a "mini-security rule" and illustrates the fact that privacy and security are linked. Security services provide confidentiality controls that support privacy.)
- Access, where a patient's right to access his or her health information was denied
- Minimum necessary, where more information was disclosed than what is believed necessary for the recipient to need
- Notice of privacy practices, training, mitigation, complaints to covered entity

Security

- Information access management, which includes the administrative processes associated with granting permission for access to health information
- Access controls, which are the technical measures used by the information systems to carry out the access permissions
- Awareness and training
- Electronic device and media controls
- Incidents, which are events where a gap in a security process or technology results in wrongful disclosure, alteration of data, or lack of availability of data

---

Source: The Office for Civil Rights. http://www.hhs.gov/ocr/privacy/hipaa/enforcement/highlights/index.html.

Impermissible uses and disclosures can range from an accidentally misdirected fax or well-intended but wrongful sharing of information about a friend, to a huge breach due to loss of a computer, failure to destroy paper properly, or many other things. In fact, these are the very issues patients are most concerned about when asked whether they support health care moving to digital record keeping. While there have been significantly fewer complaints filed about the Security Rule per se than the Privacy Rule, the fact that lack of safeguards is the second most common complaint suggests that many patients are aware of the need for security measures and that they believe these measures are not being applied adequately.

They may not fully be aware of the technical security requirements and often end up translating their concerns into issues about the Privacy Rule. For example, if they see that a practice member has not logged on, they may not report that the practice did not use proper "authentication" and "access controls," but that they fear their privacy is not being fully protected. Even older patients are becoming more aware of computer use and misuse. Even those who do not use a computer themselves may have read about issues in the popular press.

The third most common complaint filed with the OCR is about patient access to protected health information (this slipped from second to third just recently). Complaints about access refer to the fact that patients have been denied access to their health information. Although this is more of a Privacy Rule issue than a Security Rule issue, it is important for practices to understand. This very common complaint occurs more frequently in physician practices than in hospitals (see Table 1.2). (See also Chapter 10 on providing patients access to their health information.) It is well known that patients have a more difficult time gaining access to their health information from physician practices than from hospitals, outpatient departments, health plans, or pharmacies (in order of frequency from most frequent to least frequent). The meaningful use incentive program is changing this to some extent with the requirements to provide patients with summary of care information and, increasingly, direct access to their health record. But greater electronic access could very likely heighten concerns about lack of safeguards if safeguards are not well addressed. The most frequent complaint levied under the Security Rule is, in fact, related to information access.

TABLE 1.2

Most Frequent Sources of Complaints to the OCR (April 13, 2003, to December 31, 2010)

- Private practices
- General hospitals
- Outpatient departments
- Health plans
- Pharmacies

Source: The Office for Civil Rights. http://www.hhs.gov/ocr/privacy/hipaa/enforcement/highlights/index.html.

Observations that patients (or members of the healthcare team) file complaints are not intended to discourage practices from entering the digital age or suggest that an environment of suspicion be created in a practice. But health care is a competitive industry—even when health reform requires shared risk/reward structures and greater sharing of health information for coordination of care. As a result, patients can—and increasingly are encouraged through public reporting to—evaluate the source of their health care and consider where optimal care is provided among a selection of providers. It behooves practices, therefore, to consider information security in the mix of factors that drive patients to or from their doors. At a minimum, proactively communicating privacy and security measures can help significantly.

ELECTRONIC HEALTH RECORD ADOPTION

Virtually every new technology seems to have both good and bad features. EHRs are no exception. Much can be discussed about both the benefits and drawbacks of such systems, but from the perspective of information security, EHRs have the potential both to provide highly effective controls and to be the subject of breaches, exposure to attack, and lack of system availability. The good news is, however, that the outcomes are largely in the hands of the user.

It is no surprise that HIPAA includes privacy and security requirements. As electronic financial and administrative transactions were adopted, the general public wanted assurances that such information exchange would be safeguarded. It is no surprise either that as the HITECH Act of 2009 encouraged adoption of EHRs, more privacy and security protections were included. These provide regulations for breach notification that became effective in September 2009, significant increases in enforcement penalties that became effective in October 2009, authority for state attorneys general to bring civil actions on behalf of state residents for violations of the HIPAA Privacy Rule and Security Rule, and modifications to the Privacy Rule, Security Rule, and Enforcement Rule (proposed in July 2010, and not finalized as of this writing). Regulations providing the criteria for EHR technology, the EHR certification process, and the standards for incentives for meaningful use of EHR technology all require attention to security features.

EHRs can be made more secure than their paper counterparts because they can explicitly incorporate requirements for who may access what information under what circumstances. EHRs can be stored and backed up to one or more remote locations so that their information content can be available virtually anywhere and at any time—excepting a disaster so enormous that backup power supplies fail. If there is no power to the office, the fact that information is located remotely means nothing because lack of power precludes access to the remote data. In fact, if data are stored both locally and remotely, the office could run on battery-powered devices containing the data for some period of time in order to gracefully close down necessary services if there is an extended power outage. EHRs can be and often are designed to alert users to potential security incidents (eg, virus attack) and thwart them before they occur. Data can be encrypted such that it is extremely unlikely that anyone other than an authorized user would be able to read the information. Enveloping structures added to encryption of the data can be used to transmit data securely.

However, a practice can decide the level of security it will apply to its EHRs (and all other information under its control). The risk-based nature of the Security Rule is intended to afford a flexible approach to accommodate different sizes, complexities, and capabilities of covered entities. For example, if a solo practitioner with one nurse and one office staff member has an EHR, a complex system of access controls generally would be considered unnecessary. However, a 500-physician clinic will need access controls that reflect the treatment relationship of each person in the practice to each patient.

With respect to the risk-based nature of the Security Rule, some industry experts believe the rule is weak because its compliance is risk based. It does not identify precisely what must be done in every scenario. Others, however, view the Security Rule as being practical because its compliance is risk based. A one-physician practice is not going to need the level of security of a huge academic medical center. Irrespective of personal views, the Security Rule is risk based, and it is the responsibility of the covered entity applying the rule to determine, within the defined constraints, how it will apply the Security Rule standards. Case Study 1.1 provides an example of a risk-based analysis that is all too commonly incomplete.

This case study represents a practice's focus only on the most obvious of requirements and a lack of attention to many of the nuances of the HIPAA Security Rule and good security practices in general. Unfortunately, it is a very common scenario—especially in small practices. The risks taken are ones that do not appear risky on the surface—potentially not even to the computer maintenance company, which is likely accustomed to working with small businesses on tight budgets. Still, a more comprehensive risk analysis and continued monitoring of the environment could have prevented many, if not all, of these issues.

The second decision related to risk-based compliance is the level of risk any one practice or individual within the practice is willing to assume. This is about whether or not to

CASE STUDY 1.1
Risk-Based Compliance With the HIPAA Security Rule

A practice uses a client/server-based EHR with its servers stored within the office, and the practice has prohibited transmission of PHI outside of the office. The practice has decided to forego encryption of the data in its servers because the servers are locked in a closet. Only practice staff and the computer maintenance company that maintains the servers have access to the room. The staff members have been trained on security, and the computer maintenance company has signed a business associate agreement. Access controls require every user to enter a password to access the system. Encryption of data retained within the covered entity is an addressable standard—and the decision this practice has made is not at all uncommon and generally would not be considered out of compliance with the HIPAA Security Rule.

However, the following series of issues may not have been part of the risk analysis and cause the practice in the case study to be out of compliance: The closet in which the servers are located heats up as a result of the small space and lack of proper ventilation or cooling systems. The heat generated by the servers eventually causes a crash—making the system unavailable to the users. There is no automated backup. The computer maintenance company periodically makes copies of the EHR data on compact disks and takes them to a storage vault at the company. But the computer maintenance person that did the last back up left the company a few weeks ago and the last backup disk is missing.

While these issues may not seem too risky on the surface because paper can always be used in the interim (although time must be spent later to scan or otherwise enter the data into the system), there are actually several concerns. The first is that there is the inability to review patients' information, potentially including recent lab results or medication history. The lab and other sources of information may be contacted, but this is time consuming. If access to needed information is not accommodated on a timely basis, lab work may be unnecessarily repeated, patients may be inconvenienced by being asked to come back for another visit, or care decisions may be made without the applicable information. Another concern is the possible loss of a small amount of data being entered at the instant the servers crashed. There may also be data integrity issues if the server was not on an uninterruptable power supply (UPS) that would allow the server to power down so that there would be no loss or alteration of the data on the server. The degree to which some or all of the data on the server are lost or altered cannot be predicted. Finally, there is the concern of the missing disk. This very likely is a notifiable breach, which the covered entity is required to address within very specific time limitations. Numerous issues can result from such a breach and become quite costly to address.

adopt the security controls recommended through the risk analysis. A practice could consider the risk analysis and take steps to address every single element to the best of their ability. They would very likely be considered in compliance, or at least not out of compliance due to laxity or intent. However, many in health care—not only small practices but very large institutions—are willing to take greater risks. Despite the fact that health care is generally considered a risk-averse industry, many covered entities simply do not want to spend the money, do not want to take the time, and/or assume "it will not happen here." They may not overtly choose to be out of compliance, but they make clear choices that put them out of compliance. In many cases, this also includes permitting (actively or passively) individuals within the practice to choose not to adhere to the compliance requirements adopted by the practice. Case Study 1.2 provides an example that is all too common—especially as EHRs are becoming more commonplace and users who have previously never used a computer are asked to do so with very little training, workflow redesign, or other support.

CASE STUDY 1.2
Assuming Risk Under the HIPAA Security Rule

One or more users in a practice find it time-consuming and distracting to log in and out of the EHR each time a patient is seen (even though they are not using what is generally considered "strong" passwords). They decide to log in once and leave the system accessible all day, possibly every day for a long period of time. When patients do not see a user logging in, they may become aware that security practices are lax. Leaving the computer accessible in this fashion permits access to the EHR and patients' PHI by anyone physically in the office (including patients who are left alone in the examining room to disrobe). In addition to potentially providing access to other patients' PHI, patients could potentially access other services that could result in opening the EHR system to a hack attack. This can cause alteration of data, wrongful disclosure, and/or a system crash.

Unfortunately, while hack attacks have been less common in health care, recent findings suggest this is changing. As big banks and other traditionally targeted institutions have significantly locked down their information systems, hackers are looking for easier marks. It is said that where the street value of a social security number is $1, the street value of a health insurance number is $50!

The scenario described in this case study could be prevented by setting the system to timeout user logins, requiring strong passwords and frequent changes, acquiring services that detect and disable rogue devices attached to systems, and implementing antivirus and other software to reduce the likelihood of hack attacks. More likely than not, however, some or all of these features are not in place, or in other cases, they are available but have been disabled as annoyances.

HEALTH INFORMATION EXCHANGE

Health information exchange (HIE) in the general sense is the ability to share health data seamlessly across information systems, primarily for coordination of care. Most frequently, such HIE begins within an integrated delivery system—where practices can exchange health information with one another, and with hospitals. The incentive program for meaningful use of EHR technology is also encouraging HIE with patients, initially in Stage 1 by providing patients with an electronic summary of their care, and moving to providing patients access to their EHR through a portal (or similar means) in Stage 2 (Centers for Medicare and Mediocaid Services [CMS], Medicare and Medicaid Programs, EHR Incentive Program—Stage 2, August 23, 2012).

Ultimately, the intent of HIE is to be able to share data with other providers, patients' personal health records, health plans, and others authorized to have the data who are using information systems that are not a part of the originating entity's infrastructure. For example, Practice A in New York City can exchange data with Hospital B's emergency department in Rochester, NY, where the patient is on vacation and has fallen ill. The two provider organizations are unrelated, and the exchange of information is aided by a health information exchange organization (HIO) that manages such exchanges. Participants in the HIO sign participation agreements and business associate agreements that establish requirements for privacy and security, connectivity, and other aspects of use—potentially including a fee structure, the ability to aggregate data for the creation of evidence-based knowledge, and information support for coordination of care across providers.

There are several challenges in HIE, not the least of which is interoperability, or the ability to exchange data seamlessly across disparate computer systems. However, privacy and security are also of great concern. If a formal HIO is being used, a number of the security elements will be addressed at the level of the HIO. But individual providers need to understand their responsibility with respect to these security elements. Security for transmission of information by the provider generally must meet the minimum requirements set by the HIO. If data are aggregated by the HIO in order to provide population health analysis as a service to the members, the data should be de-identified according to the HIPAA Privacy Rule requirements for removal of all identifiers from the data. Other uses the HIO is permitted to make of the data must also be understood. Many HIOs only serve as a switch that routes data from one location to another and do not retain any PHI, but where they do retain data (such as for data aggregation services), it should be very clear who is responsible for breach notification.

IDENTITY THEFT AND MEDICAL IDENTITY THEFT

Identity theft is a fast-growing crime in the United States. As a consequence, the Federal Trade Commission highlights the importance of being aware of medical identity theft (http://ftc.gov/bcp/edu/pubs/consumer/idtheft/idt10.shtm). The World Privacy Forum tracks medical identity theft. In testimony to the National Committee on Vital and Health Statistics (NCVHS) in 2005, this organization observed that medical identity theft was on the rise. In 2011, Joy Pritts, JD, of HHS updated the NCVHS with recommendations surrounding the importance of protecting victims of medical identity theft. Note the street value of medical information previously described as one incentive for such theft.

Table 1.3 describes a few examples of the impact of medical identity theft. Both patients and providers alike are impacted by such occurrences. In many of the cases, more thorough due diligence could have spotted a potential medical identity theft issue. However, the balance between the need to do what is right with respect to patient care (eg, delivering a baby) and doing what is right with respect to the potential privacy and security ramifications can literally become an ethical dilemma. Ideally a choice should not have to be made if sufficient controls and processes are in place. For example, the mother in labor would not be turned away from the hospital in any circumstance, but eligibility verification with the health plan would have led to other arrangements for the newborn and mitigated the loss to the hospital.

TABLE 1.3

Examples of the Impact of Medical Identity Theft

- Individual received a $44,000 bill for surgery never performed
- Mother was told her children would be taken away by Department of Children and Family Services because "her" newborn tested positive for meth, but her last baby was born eight years ago
- Innocent person was arrested at pharmacy after clerk noticed ID theft flag
- A hospital incurred a loss of $400,000 when an insurance card was accepted for a 57-year-old woman presenting in labor who delivered a high-risk baby (the daughter had used her mother's card—and both women were nowhere to be found when the police went after them)
- Physician office unaware of identity theft disclosed inaccurate information to another provider, resulting in inappropriate treatment given by the recipient provider
- Physician office that inadvertently incorporated a thief's record into another patient's record was sued by the original patient for reporting HIV-positive status to public health authorities

---

Source: World Health Forum, 2006, and author-compiled data.

Unfortunately, not only does medical identity theft impact patients and providers directly as illustrated in the examples, but providers can unwittingly be the source of medical identity theft. And not all of the theft is a result of automation. More than 30 years ago, this author learned firsthand of a coding clerk in a hospital who was calling an attorney every time a patient's chart revealed an external cause of injury. It was not until the organization received a call from a distraught patient about a call from an over-zealous attorney wanting to sue on her behalf that the hospital was able to identify what had been going on for several years! Subsequently, a number of similar incidents have been reported, the most recent case in a Florida hospital resulting in an arrest (*Modern Healthcare*, September 29, 2012).

Once again, a practice does not want to create an environment of suspicion. But open communications, training, awareness, and planning go a long way toward ensuring that good practices in place are not abused.

BREACHES

A breach is defined in HITECH Breach Notification (August 2009) regulation as "the acquisition, access, use, or disclosure of protected health information in a manner not permitted by the HIPAA Privacy Rule which compromises the security or privacy of the protected health information."

California enacted the first state data breach notification law in 2002. Subsequently 46 states have established some form of data breach statute. (Providers interested in checking on their state's statute may find helpful the Web site of the National Conference of State Legislatures at http://www.ncsl.org/issues-research/telecom/security-breach-notification-laws.aspx.) State laws preempt federal laws when the state law is more stringent.

In 2009, the federal government released guidance on safeguarding PHI, and federal breach notification regulations were adopted. Reporting of large breaches (impacting 500 or more individuals) is required at the time the breach occurs; breaches involving fewer than 500 individuals must be reported by the end of the calendar year in which they occur. As of this writing in August 2012, the total number of large breaches since reporting began in September 2009 is 477, impacting more than 21 million individuals. All large breaches are posted and described on the OCR Web site available at http://www.hhs.gov/ocr/privacy/hipaa/administrative/breachnotificationrule/breachtool.html. A quick review of the list for causes and types of media involved can be insightful, pointing out areas to watch for potential breach issues in one's own practice. Table 1.4 provides a summary of these findings. In addition, it is known that approximately 20% of all large breaches involved business associates. For the same reporting period, there were more than 30,000 small breaches, often involving only one individual.

TABLE 1.4

Causes and Types of Media in Large Breaches

Top Causes of Large Breaches in Order of Frequency

- Theft (54%)
- Unauthorized access (20%)
- Loss (11%)
- Hacking/IT incident (6%)
- Improper disposal (5%)
- Other/unknown (4%)

(*continued*)

T A B L E   1.4 (continued)

Causes and Types of Media in Large Breaches

Types of Media Involved in Large Breaches in Order of Frequency

- Laptops (36%)
- Paper records (28%)
- Desktop computers (18%)
- Portable electronic devices (18%)

Source: The Office for Civil Rights. http://www.hhs.gov/ocr/privacy/hipaa/administrative/breachnotificationrule/breachrept.pdf.

Breaches of any type are costly. For physician practices, a large breach can cost upwards of $50,000 in productivity loss, reputational harm, loss of patient goodwill, loss of revenue, fees for outside consultants and attorneys, lawsuits, and employee morale. However, despite these potential losses, inadequate budget for privacy and security is the number one weakness that can lead to a data breach. The cost of implementing controls is generally less than the cost of a breach. Other factors contributing to the inability to prevent a breach are many of the same issues described in the case studies: insufficient risk assessment, lack of trained staff and end users, lack of enabling technologies, lack of governance and leadership, lack of policies and procedures, and lack of manual controls.

ENFORCEMENT AND AUDITS

In April 2012, a settlement with HHS for $100,000 with a five-provider practice (Phoenix Cardiac Surgery) served as a wake-up call for small providers. This practice was posting clinical and surgical appointments for its patients on an Internet-based calendar that was publicly accessible. Upon further investigation, OCR found that the practice had implemented few policies and procedures to comply with the HIPAA Privacy Rule and Security Rule, and had limited safeguards in place to protect patients' health information.

Requirements under the HITECH Act that increased the civil monetary penalties for noncompliance with the Privacy Rule and Security Rule also included stepped-up audits to assess compliance. To implement this mandate, OCR initiated a pilot audit program in November 2011 with the intent of auditing 115 covered entities. The last 75 covered entities are to be audited by the end of December 2012. Findings from the first of the audits reveal that small covered entities had many more issues than large ones, and that despite provider entities representing only half of those audited, they accounted for 81% of deficiencies identified. Finally, the majority of deficiencies were found to be related to the Security Rule. Table 1.5 lists the major privacy and security results reported in the HIPAA audits to date (steps to take to respond to an audit are discussed in Chapter 10).

T A B L E   1.5

Major Privacy and Security Issues Reported in HIPAA Audits

Privacy issues involved:

- Review processes for denials of patient access to records
- Failure to provide appropriate patient access to records
- Lack of policies and procedures
- Uses and disclosures of decedent information
- Disclosures to personal representatives
- Business associate contracts

(continued)

T A B L E 1.5 (continued)

Major Privacy and Security Issues Reported in HIPAA Audits

Security issues involved:

■ User activity monitoring

■ Contingency planning

■ Media reuse and destruction

■ Risk assessment

■ Granting and modifying user access

Source: Sanchez, L. 2012 HIPAA Privacy and Security Audits. OCR/NIST Conference, Safeguarding Health Information: Building Assurance through HIPAA Security. June 7, 2012. http://www.vorys.com/assets/attachments/day2-2_lsanches_ocr-audit.pdf.

If the reader is seeing a trend in the top complaints, case study findings, causes of breaches, and audit findings discussed in this chapter, there is indeed similarity among all of them—and there are lessons to be learned.

SECURITY FOR IMPORTANT INFORMATION

Although it should be enough to worry about security for PHI, as noted at the start of this chapter information security should extend beyond PHI to any other information that the practice considers confidential, that constitutes intellectual property, or the loss of which would be detrimental to the practice in some way. Sometimes the protection of such other information is referred to as data stewardship. In business, data stewardship is the management of a corporation's data assets in order to improve their reusability, accessibility, and quality.

In health care, the American Medical Informatics Association (AMIA) defines health data stewardship as "the responsibilities and accountabilities associated with managing, collecting, viewing, storing, sharing, disclosing, or otherwise making use of personal health information."[1]

Note that the corporate definition of data stewardship refers to data as assets and that the AMIA definition of health data stewardship refers to these assets as *personal* health information—extending the responsibilities and accountabilities to all health information, whether protected under HIPAA or not. Considering all information in a practice as assets to be managed is an excellent approach to affording the right level of privacy and security in support of confidentiality, integrity, and availability.

The AMIA definition of health data stewardship also incorporates "sharing, disclosing, or otherwise making use of" personal health information. While a culture of privacy exists in health care, the HIPAA Privacy Rule and Security Rule also seem to have created a culture of fear of sharing any health information, as well as a focus on health information to the exclusion of other valuable information assets. Further, as evidenced by the consistent issues associated with denial of access to patient information, HIPAA is being used as an excuse to not share information with patients. But as the incentive program for meaningful use of EHR technology pushes ever further toward engaging the patient through much more sharing of information, a culture of transparency is also needed. Much could be said about the need for transparency in health care in general, but with respect to assuring the

---

1. Bloomrosen, M & Detmer, DE. Advancing the Framework: Use of Health Data—A report of a working conference of the American Medical Informatics Association. *Journal of the American Medical Informatics Association*. 2008; (15): 715–722.

confidentiality, integrity, and availability of information, practices would be wise to take advantage of their patients' ability to help assess the accuracy of their information and to share more consciously in its protection.

MAKE INFORMATION SECURITY A WAY OF LIFE

Information security, not just "compliance" with federal rules and regulations, should be a way of life for healthcare organizations. Often as a result of focusing solely on compliance, the minimum necessary to comply becomes the focus, rather than what medical practices really need to assure that their patients' records are held confidential, safe from alteration, and readily available when needed. When information security is put in the context of harm and the likelihood of harm to patients and practices, the reality of practicing good data stewardship—for all information—should make compliance with the HIPAA Security Rule, its subsequent enhancements, and general best practices of information security management more important.

CHECK YOUR UNDERSTANDING*

Characterize each of the following as a security concern relating to confidentiality (C), data integrity (I), or availability (A):

1. Data transmited through the Internet are altered by an attacker.

2. A large amount of paper health records was being taken by a shredding service to its office when the truck was involved in an accident resulting in the records being strewn all over the highway.

3. Your servers and software are hosted by a vendor. Your Internet connection just went down, and you have no other way to connect to the vendor.

4. You receive an encrypted e-mail from a referring provider, but you cannot verify the authenticity of the sender.

5. A hacker has been eavesdropping on your cell phone communications with a patient.

Identify the five most common security complaints to the Office for Civil Rights:

6. _____

7. _____

8. _____

9. _____

10. _____

List the top three causes of large breaches of PHI:

11. _____

12. _____

13. _____

List the top two types of media most commonly involved in large breaches of PHI:

14. _____

15. _____

_____

*For answers, refer to the Answer Key at the end of the book.

chapter 2

Overview of HIPAA and HITECH

The Health Insurance Portability and Accountability Act of 1996 (HIPAA) requires physicians and other healthcare providers who conduct electronic transactions, as well as payers and healthcare clearinghouses, to adopt certain security measures to safeguard protected health information (PHI) in electronic form. The Security Rule complements the HIPAA Privacy Rule and Transactions and Code Sets Standards. The HIPAA Security Rule affords safeguards for the confidentiality, integrity, and availability of the PHI in a practice. The Health Information Technology for Economic and Clinical Health (HITECH) Act of 2009 recognizes the importance of information privacy and security as heightened use of EHRs is encouraged under HITECH's meaningful use incentive program. HITECH requires notification of breaches of PHI, for which guidance and regulations have been issued (and which is discussed in depth in Chapter 10), and makes certain modifications to the HIPAA Privacy Rule (for which regulations have not been issued as of the writing of this book, but which are described in this chapter to the extent they are discussed in the HITECH legislation, pending regulation). Other laws and regulations may also impact a medical practice, and these are identified and discussed as applicable in subsequent chapters.

In order to assure confidentiality, integrity, and availability of information, the HIPAA Security Rule includes the following safeguards:

- Administrative safeguards address your operations. They include assigning responsibility to someone for security and having policies and procedures in place to direct your security efforts.
- Physical safeguards include locks and keys, where computers are located, disposal of electronic media, and generally how to make the environment safe.
- Technical safeguards are controls directly applied to information systems. They identify who may have access to information systems, provide access to sets of data and specific functions in systems, audit persons who have used systems, and protect systems from malicious acts.

A key premise of the HIPAA Security Rule is to determine what safeguards are appropriate for the size and type of physician practice you have. HIPAA requires you to perform a risk analysis to create a blueprint for decision making for what is right for your practice. These decisions should be documented in policies and procedures and apply the controls that you have determined are right for your practice.

HOW TO USE THIS CHAPTER

This chapter gives you an overview of security in general. It:

- Reviews the context in which the Security Rule exists within HIPAA
- Reminds you about the "mini-security rule" within the Privacy Rule

■ Describes the principles on which the Security Rule is based

■ Defines some unique security terms and concepts

■ Defines numerous Privacy Rule concepts

■ Introduces you to how the Security Rule is structured

Compliance with the HIPAA Security Rule was required by April 2005. Many practices reviewed the basic requirements of HIPAA and implemented various security services as applicable at the time. However, much has changed since 2005. Practices have become more automated in general and specifically are upgrading or acquiring practice management systems, adding EHRs and other applications, and increasingly exchanging health and other data (such as payments) electronically. The HIPAA Security Rule has been enhanced with federal guidance documents, required reporting of breaches, stepped-up penalties and enforcement, and proactive auditing. In addition, there are increasing risks to providers as a struggling economy shifts the threat of identity theft to what are generally considered more vulnerable targets. Not only does the meaningful use incentive program require a (renewed) risk analysis, but common sense suggests it is time to upgrade information security measures (and possibly personal safety measures). Complaints leading to investigations and proactive auditing also require more formal documentation of your security measures.

HIPAA ADMINISTRATIVE SIMPLIFICATION

HIPAA was signed into law on August 21, 1996. The law includes several provisions, among which are the Administrative Simplification provisions. The purpose of Administrative Simplification is to "improve . . . the efficiency and effectiveness of the health care system, by encouraging the development of a health information system through the establishment of standards and requirements for the electronic transmission of certain health information" (Public Law 104-191, Subtitle F, Sec. 261). The Security Rule is one of four major rules that contribute to a health information system. The four rules provide standards for:

■ Transactions and Code Sets

■ Identifiers

■ Privacy

■ Security

Other publications provide in-depth explanations of the first three rules. Following is a brief overview that describes how they are related to the Security Rule and how they also are being updated and enhanced.

Transactions and Code Sets Standards

HIPAA required all payers, including Medicare, Medicaid, and private insurers, as well as providers who perform any electronic transactions, to adopt new standards for electronic financial and administrative transactions and code sets. In 2002 the Administrative Simplification Compliance Act (ASCA) expanded the requirements for all but the smallest providers who participate in Medicare to file claims electronically with Medicare. As a result, almost all providers are covered entities. Compliance with updated versions of the transaction standards was required by January 1, 2012. Now the Affordable Care Act (ACA) of 2010 requires Medicare to make payments to providers using electronic funds transfer (EFT) by January 1, 2014. Standards for electronic eligibility verification, claim status, remittance advice, and precertification/referral authorization were also adopted under HIPAA. These electronic processes are used variably by providers, with some making more use of them than others. However, these transactions as well as claim attachment transactions will soon become easier and more beneficial to use. ACA is requiring the development of operating rules that should improve the uniformity and consistency with which the transaction standards are applied by health plans.

Physician offices that adopt electronic standards can find that staff members spend less time on the phone, eligibility verification is easy enough to perform for all patient visits, claims are being processed faster, denials are diminished as a result of better understanding the status of claims, and manual posting to accounts receivable can virtually disappear with electronic remittance advices that link directly to EFT payments. To achieve these benefits, your practice management or billing system must be upgraded. For some, this may only require time to install, test, and manage an upgrade; for others, it may afford an opportunity to create a strategy for a full cycle of business process and revenue cycle management improvements.

Identifier Standards

HIPAA called for standard identifiers to be used in financial and administrative transactions. Table 2.1 identifies these standards.

TABLE 2.1

HIPAA Identifier Standards

Standard Unique Identifier For . . .	Status	Comments
Employer	Compliance by July 30, 2004	This is the federal Employer Identification Number (EIN) issued by the Internal Revenue Service. The HIPAA transactions currently used by providers for billing require this identifier.
Provider	Compliance by May 23, 2007	The National Provider Identifier (NPI) is a 10-digit, intelligence-free number assigned by the Centers for Medicare and Medicaid Services (CMS) through the National Plan and Provider Enumeration System (NPPES) and is required on all claims (not just Medicare or Medicaid).
Health Plan	Final rule was issued on September 5, 2012	A Health Plan Identifier (HPID) is similar in structure to the NPI but includes a form for health plans and a form for other entities (the Other Entity Identifier [OEID]) that are related to the billing process.
Individuals	On hold	Congress precludes any federal expenditure on a unique health identifier for individuals until such time that a federal privacy law is enacted. (The HIPAA Privacy Rule is regulation only and does not address the universality desired in a federal privacy law.)

Privacy Standards

HIPAA's Administrative Simplification requirements were intended to promote adoption of information technology. Technology improves productivity, supports patient safety, and promotes clinical quality. However, the US Department of Health and Human Services (HHS) believed consumers would demand privacy standards that protect their health information in the move to an electronic environment. Increasingly, patients are interested in communicating with their physician offices via electronic means and gaining access to health information. They want to make appointments online, reduce redundancy in filling out health questionnaires, have prescriptions filled more conveniently, and better understand and manage their care. In addition, physicians are pressed for time and also need better communication tools. Managers of information exchange want these tools to be easy to use and readily available, but they also need to assure that the privacy of the information is maintained and that security measures are in place to afford confidentiality, integrity, and availability of the information as it is used, stored, exchanged, and potentially disposed of electronically.

PURPOSE OF THE PRIVACY RULE

The HIPAA Privacy Rule is designed to protect confidentiality and provide individuals rights as they relate to individual health information. The Privacy Rule introduced the concept of PHI (patient identity and health information).

Privacy Rights

The Privacy Rule describes how patients may:

- Have access to their health information
- Offer an amendment to correct an inaccuracy or add information (within reason)
- Request restrictions on uses and disclosures (if you are able to accommodate these)
- Receive confidential communications, such as having an appointment reminder or billing statement sent to an alternative address or holding a conversation in a different location
- Obtain an accounting of disclosures (that you have made other than for treatment, payment, and operations and when the patients have authorized disclosure)

Your policies and procedures with respect to patient rights concerning their health information should also be reflected in your notice of privacy practices (NPP). Patients' right to access their health information has been a troublesome standard for practices—and a frequent topic of complaint to the OCR. The federal incentive program for making meaningful use of EHR technology promotes electronic access by patients to their health information.

Protected Health Information

Protected health information is defined in the HIPAA Privacy Rule as "individually identifiable health information . . . that is transmitted by electronic media, maintained in any medium described in the definition of electronic media . . . or transmitted or maintained in any other form or medium."

Individually identifiable health information is defined as ". . . health information, including demographic information, collected from an individual, and . . . created or received by a healthcare provider . . . and relates to the past, present, or future physical or mental health or condition of an individual; the provision of health care to an individual; or the past, present, or future payment for the provision of health care to an individual; and that identifies the individual . . ."

Notice of Privacy Practices

The Privacy Rule requires that you give your patients a NPP and have them acknowledge receipt. Any time your privacy policies and procedures change you must reissue the NPP. The NPP is not an authorization. It explains how the practice uses patients' PHI and to whom the practice may make disclosures for treatment, payment, operations and when required by law. It also provides information on how patients may file complaints within your office and to the OCR.

Uses and Disclosures, Authorizations, and Consents

The Privacy Rule provides a number of standards that explain how and under what circumstances PHI may be used and disclosed—with and without authorization. When an authorization is required under the Privacy Rule for specified disclosures, the rule specifies a number of elements that must be included. The elements required in an authorization are a description of the PHI to be used and disclosed, the person authorized to make the use or disclosure, the person to whom the covered entity may make the disclosure, an expiration date, and, in some cases, the purpose for which the information may be used or disclosed. With limited exceptions, covered entities may not condition treatment or coverage on the individual's providing an authorization. Although the Privacy Rule is silent on the medium required for authorization, it is generally held under the Electronic Signatures in Global and National Commerce (ESIGN) Act of 2000 that when law is silent with respect to medium, a document may be executed as an electronic document.

The Privacy Rule also permits, but does not require, consent for disclosure. Consent in the context of the Privacy Rule does not require a specified process. Where an authorization requires elements to be documented on a form with a patient signature, consent could be verbal agreement, an opt-in or opt-out request, or a form similar to or even more extensive than an authorization as required by HIPAA. Some states and many health information exchange organizations (HIOs) require consent (see State Preemption below). Covered entities have complete discretion to design a consent process that best suits their needs. However, the Privacy Rule states that such consent is not effective to permit a use or disclosure when an authorization is required or other condition must be met.

State Preemption

HIPAA's privacy standards establish a "level playing field" of protections. Where state law is more protective of individually identifiable health information or affords greater rights to individuals in their health information, state law prevails. Make sure your policies and procedures address any state laws applicable to the state in which you practice that are more stringent.

Documentation of Policies and Procedures

HIPAA requires that you document your privacy policies and procedures, including how your practice uses and discloses health information. These policies and procedures should describe when an authorization from the patient is required for a use or disclosure, when an authorization is not required, and when and how to verify the identity and authority of an individual requesting PHI. There should be guidance on how to receive requests from patients exercising their privacy rights, how you will respond, and what due process should be afforded if you must deny a patient's request to access or amend PHI in your designated record set.

Training

Processes to train staff, trainees, volunteers, and others who are members of your work-force on your privacy policies and procedures should be in place. Documentary evidence of such training should be retained for the period of time that HIPAA requires all such documentation (including authorizations, policies and procedures, training materials, activity/event logs, designations, etc) to be retained, which is six years from the date of creation or the date when it last was in effect, whichever is later.

Ongoing Monitoring and Compliance Assurance

HIPAA is not a one-time event. Mechanisms need to be in place to monitor your compliance with the law and follow what you said you would do in your NPP.

Business Associate Agreements

Because HIPAA only covers physicians and other providers, health plans, and healthcare clearinghouses that process financial and administrative transactions, you must establish a contractual obligation of confidentiality with those you do business with that have access to PHI.

Proposed Modifications to the HIPAA Privacy Rule

The HITECH Act of 2009, which brought a huge infusion of funds into the industry for workforce training, best practices for use of health information technology, and the incentives for meaningful use of EHR technology also required enhancements to the HIPAA Privacy Rule. A proposed modification to the HIPAA Privacy Rule was published on July 14, 2010, but as of this writing the rule has not been finalized. The proposed modification would:

- Extend applicability of certain requirements of the Privacy Rule and Security Rule to business associates
- Establish new limitations on use and disclosure of PHI for marketing and fundraising
- Prohibit the sale of PHI without patient authorization
- Require consideration of a limited data set as the minimum necessary amount of information
- Expand individuals' rights to access and receive an accounting of disclosures of their PHI and obtain restrictions on certain disclosures of PHI to health plans (where individuals pay cash in full)

Security Standards

The final Security Rule notes that security and privacy are inextricably linked. Protecting the privacy of information depends in large part on the existence of security measures. The final Security Rule provides standards for administrative, physical, and technical safeguards for electronic protected health information (ePHI). The Privacy Rule, however, does not distinguish paper from electronic PHI, and includes a standard entitled "Safeguards" that many have dubbed a "mini-security" rule that imposes essentially the same requirements as the Security Rule in a more general way.

"MINI-SECURITY" RULE IN THE PRIVACY RULE

The Privacy Rule's standard on safeguards requires "appropriate administrative, technical, and physical safeguards to protect the privacy of protected health information."

All Forms of PHI

The safeguards standard in the Privacy Rule provides the basis for securing all forms of PHI, not just ePHI. (In fact, with the combination of this "mini-security" rule and the HITECH Breach Notification Rule requiring reporting of any paper or electronic breaches, the notion of "ePHI" has essentially been dropped from our collective vocabulary.) The Privacy Rule safeguards standard, therefore, protects PHI that is verbally expressed, written solely on paper, copied via a standard copy machine, sent through a paper-to-paper fax, discussed in a person-to-person telephone call or video teleconference, or left as a message on a voice-mail system.

Safeguards

Safeguarding PHI in nonelectronic form requires attention to your operations. Offices vary significantly in the safeguards that are required. Some suggestions for safeguarding paper-based PHI include:

- Hold conversations in private areas. Move into an office or empty examining room to discuss PHI about a specific patient. Avoid discussing patient care-related matters in public areas away from the office. Even if you never mention the patient's name, those who overhear such a conversation may believe you are violating someone's privacy.

- Safeguard paper documents, whether they are created by hand or through a computer. Evaluate where your charts are stored. If they are in public view, your patients' heightened awareness of privacy could suggest that these documents are not as protected as possible. Determine if encounter forms and other chart documents are kept at the registration desk, in an office, or in any other location where patients may be able to see PHI.

- Avoid misuse of copy machines. If copy machines need to be located near publicly accessible areas, place them where a staff member can monitor them for inappropriate use. If your office is serviced by a cleaning service at night, make sure that all charts are in locked file cabinets or in a locked room that is not accessible to the cleaning crew or, at a minimum, make sure that the copy machine requires an access code.

- Take precautions when faxing. Always use a cover sheet that includes your name, fax number, and telephone number; the number of pages being faxed; and a confidentiality statement that includes a request that the recipient of a misdirected fax destroy the information and contact you immediately. Even if you are using an electronic fax covered by the Security Rule, always make sure a cover sheet is sent through your system. Do not assume that just because you sent the fax electronically it will be received electronically. Misdirected faxes account for many small breaches. For standard faxing, take the following steps:
  - Verify the number you have dialed before pressing the send button.
  - Program frequently used fax numbers into your machine to avoid errors in dialing. (Use an address book for your electronic faxes.)

- Review the transmission report to ensure that the intended machine received it. If you suspect a fax went to the wrong place, check the internal log and send a separate fax to request that the recipient destroy the information. (Do the same for any faxes you receive in error.)

- Avoid faxing especially sensitive information. If you must fax such information, call ahead to ask the intended recipient to stand by the fax and either send a fax confirmation back to you or call you to let you know that the fax has been received.

- If you are receiving faxes with PHI after office hours, set your fax machine to store these faxes in memory until you can print them in a secure manner when you return.

- Verify caller identity and authority. When you are handling telephone calls, make certain you know to whom you are speaking. The Privacy Rule permits you to disclose information to all those involved in the patients' care, but only when you give the patients the opportunity to agree or object. For example, if a daughter frequently accompanies her father to your office and the father has agreed that disclosures can be made to her, you may speak with the daughter about her father's care on subsequent occasions. If you are uncertain with whom you are speaking, ask for positive identification. For example, the daughter should be able to supply her father's insurance information, account number, the date of his last visit, and/or legal documentation that identifies her. The Privacy Rule also permits you to share information about a patient for treatment purposes. If a hospital or other office calls and you cannot identify the person as a regular caller, place a callback to verify the caller's identity and authority. If you have any suspicions about whether there is a treatment relationship, ask for more information about the patient or ask for a patient authorization.

- Be careful when leaving messages. When leaving a message on voice mail or with someone who answers a phone, make sure you are following all directions your patients may have given for confidential communications. Even when following your patients' directions, never leave more information than the minimum necessary.

- Consider use of secure messaging. A secure Web portal in which you establish secure access for your patients and then notify them when they have mail waiting is an excellent way to ensure privacy. A secure Web portal can also be used to access hospital documents, instead of relying on a fax. Not only is this process more secure, it is also less time consuming.

Incidental Uses and Disclosures

The Privacy Rule's safeguards standard further requires a covered entity to "reasonably safeguard PHI from any intentional or unintentional use or disclosure that is in violation of the standards" and "to limit incidental uses or disclosures . . ."

What Is an Incidental Use or Disclosure?

Incidental use or disclosure is defined in the HIPAA Privacy Rule as "a use or disclosure made pursuant to an otherwise permitted or required use or disclosure."

Use with respect to health information means "the sharing, employment, application, utilization, examination, or analysis of such information within an entity that maintains such information."

Disclosure means "the release, transfer, provision of access to, or divulging in any manner of information outside the entity holding the information."

In summary, an incidental use or disclosure is one that is not normally permitted by HIPAA but occurs as an unavoidable part of the daily routine related to treatment, payment, and operations. Take steps to avoid such incidental uses and disclosures to the extent reasonable and practical. If such steps have been taken, an incidental use or disclosure may not be considered a violation of HIPAA.

Finding Solutions to Manage Incidental Disclosures

Put yourself in your patient's shoes. Periodically conduct a walk-through of your office as if you were a patient. Some offices even use a checklist to document this walk-through as a good practice for documentation of compliance. What do you see or hear that could be of concern to your patients? If you don't use a checklist, make a list of these potential concerns.

Once you have identified your concerns, decide what kinds of safeguards can be put into place to reduce their occurrence or minimize their impact. Your list of safeguards will likely include a range of solutions, from those that are behavioral changes to those that are technical or physical in nature. In all likelihood, the behavioral changes will be the most difficult to implement but the least expensive. Some will reinforce existing policies, and in other cases new policies may need to be implemented. Engage all in the office to think about such solutions and encourage their input. Such engagement encourages their buy-in for the change. Technical or physical changes may be the easiest to implement but more expensive. You will then need to decide what is most reasonable and practical for you.

CASE STUDY 2.1
Incidental Disclosures

During a walk-through or even possibly from complaints from patients who have been to the office, you find that it is possible to overhear conversations from another examining room. While this is not a violation of HIPAA per se, it could be construed as a violation, and could cause concerns for your patients. Some possible solutions include:

- Lower your voices. This is a behavior that will likely take a long time to acquire and is not always feasible, especially with older or hearing-impaired patients.

- Build soundproof rooms. This is costly and often impractical.

- Install tranquility fountains in areas where conversations can be overheard, such as a waiting room near an examining room, or even in examining rooms that are physically next to each other. The fountains can provide just enough white noise and distraction that patients cannot discern what is being said in conversations in other rooms. They also add a nice touch that most patients enjoy.

- Reposition furniture, put up wall hangings, pipe in music, or turn a radio or TV on low. Any or all of these are relatively low-cost solutions. An inappropriate solution, however, would be to not identify a patient by name. Although this may technically eliminate PHI from the conversation, the practice may be perceived as cold and impersonal, and it creates a patient safety issue.

Perceptions vs Reality

Individuals have different thresholds for what they feel violates their personal privacy. For one patient, having another patient know about an allergy may be meaningless with respect to privacy, but to another, it may be much more of a concern. It is impossible to implement safeguards that address every conceivable perception of a privacy problem. The HIPAA Privacy Rule recognizes this and makes provisions for incidental uses and disclosures. However, this provision is tightly linked to safeguards. Reasonable and practical steps should be taken to provide safeguards, especially if the majority of your patients would have some type of concern. For example, a family practice physician would want to be especially careful to not leave HIV test results on a desk where someone else could see them. A psychiatrist would not have patients sign in on a public sign-in sheet.

Patient Privacy Quotient

An important step to take in determining what privacy practices are right for your office is to heighten your awareness of patient privacy issues. You can do the following to gauge your "patient privacy quotient":

- Evaluate patient responses to your NPP. If your patients seem anxious and ask many questions about the NPP, they may be reflecting heightened concern. If you have not issued NPPs for some time except to new patients but find an increasing number of complaints or body language that suggests privacy concerns, reissuing the NPPs as patients arrive may be a way to both diffuse concerns and gauge reactions. There is nothing in the Privacy Rule that precludes more frequent distribution of the NPP.

- Consider others' experiences. A recent incident in your community may increase overall attention to privacy. An office in a technology corridor may experience an increase in hacks or identity thefts. An office in an urban area may experience an increase in drug or computer thefts. Both situations have the potential for a breach of confidentiality.

- Evaluate patient complaints. Encourage patients to file complaints with the designated information privacy official (IPO) in your office. Handle all complaints seriously, but with a customer service attitude. Be cautious about what you say. Acknowledge the importance of the complaint and tell the patient that your office values privacy and security, but do not accept that a breach of confidentiality or a security incident took place until you have a chance to investigate. You may want to consider writing some scripts to respond to complaints or even find a local seminar on customer relations to give your staff some pointers.

IIIPAA is a complex set of regulations. The industry and even the government are still in the process of interpreting the regulations, often adding Frequently Asked Questions to the OCR Web site (http://www.hhs.gov/hipaafaq) under various circumstances. As always, proceed cautiously—but also do not go overboard. Many practices refuse various requests for information as being against HIPAA regulations, when they actually are not. It is very important to apply safeguards where possible rather than to continue a practice that is open to misinterpretation. However, safeguards must be balanced with what is good for patient care, including disclosing PHI to others you know are involved in the patient's treatment. HIPAA stresses the use of professional judgment in complying with the standards. When in doubt, evaluate the situation from both the privacy and patient care aspects and document decisions in a log if necessary. If the OCR receives a complaint, you will be required to demonstrate compliance or submit a corrective action plan. Be sure you have the documentation to substantiate your compliance and describe the steps you are taking to achieve ongoing compliance.

Privacy Complaints

Details about how privacy complaints may be filed with the HHS OCR may be found at http://www.hhs.gov/ocr/privacy/hipaa/complaints/index.html, by calling 1-800-368-1019, or by contacting an OCR regional office. Complaints may be mailed or faxed to the applicable OCR regional office or sent via e-mail to OCRComplaint@hhs.gov. OCR asks that you encourage patients to file a complaint with your office first.

SECURITY RULE PRINCIPLES

The Security Rule is based on three principles: comprehensiveness, scalability, and technology neutrality.

1. Comprehensiveness refers to the fact that the Security Rule addresses all aspects of security. This means that security measures address confidentiality, data integrity, and availability.
2. Scalability assures that the Security Rule can be effectively implemented by covered entities of all types and sizes.
3. Technology neutrality means the Security Rule does not define specific technology requirements, thereby allowing covered entities to make use of future technology advancements.

Comprehensive

The Privacy Rule is pervasive and impacts virtually every aspect of your operations. The Security Rule is even more pervasive than you might think. Do not delegate security to "the information technology person" and think you have security solved; people make security happen. Security must be understood and practiced by every person in the office.

Privacy and security are tightly linked. Table 2.2 shows you similarities between privacy and security standards.

T A B L E 2.2

How Privacy and Security Are Linked

Privacy Standard	Complementary Security Standards/ Implementation Specifications
Minimum Necessary	Use Information Access Management
	Access Controls
Verification of Identity and Authority	Person or Entity Authentication
Sanction Policy	Sanction Policy
Training	Training
Business Associate Contracts	Business Associate Contracts
Policies and Procedures	Policies and Procedures
Privacy Official	Security Official
Uses and Disclosures Consistent With Complaints to the Covered Entity	NPP Information System Activity Review
Evaluation	Incident Procedures
Safeguards	Facility Access Control
	Workstation Security
	Device and Media Controls

Security is not just about technical controls; it is about people doing what they are supposed to do. The standards require human actions to implement and maintain. The Security Rule is focused on PHI when it is maintained in your computer systems and as it is transmitted throughout an internal or external network or in any other electronic media. The Security Rule standards safeguard PHI from unauthorized access, alteration, and deletion. *Electronic media* means electronic storage media including memory devices in computers (hard drives) and any removable/transportable digital memory medium, such as magnetic tape or disk, optical disk, or digital memory card; or transmission media used to exchange information already in electronic storage media. Transmission media include, for example, the Internet (wide-open), extranet (using Internet technology to link a business with information accessible only to collaborating parties), leased lines, dial-up lines, private networks, and the physical movement of removable/transportable electronic storage media.

The preamble to the Security Rule also clarifies that certain transmissions, including of paper, via facsimile, and of voice, via telephone, are not considered to be transmissions via electronic media. However, telephone voice response and faxback (that is, a request for information from a computer made via voice or telephone keypad input with the requested information returned as a fax) systems fall under the Security Rule because they are used as input and output for computers.

Scalable

You should be able to fit the Security Rule to your needs—whether you have a small office or a large clinic. The Security Rule emphasizes being reasonable and appropriate.

What Is Reasonable and Appropriate?

In deciding which security measures to use, focus on scalability. The Security Rule specifically provides factors to be taken into account when deciding which security measures to use. These factors cause the Security Rule to be risk based and include considerations for:

■ Size, complexity, and capabilities
■ Technical infrastructure, hardware, and software security capabilities
■ Costs of security measures
■ Probability and criticality of potential risks to PHI

However, the Security Rule cautions that cost is not meant to free covered entities from the responsibility to maintain adequate security measures.

Risk Analysis and Risk Management

The Security Rule specifies that you must conduct an accurate and thorough assessment of the potential risks and vulnerabilities to the confidentiality, integrity, and availability of PHI your practice holds and implement security measures that are reasonable and appropriate to reduce risks and vulnerabilities to an acceptable level. The probability and criticality of potential risks to PHI must be determined.

Technology Neutrality

The concept of technology neutrality is based on the fact that information technology changes very rapidly. A technology-neutral standard allows the Security Rule to be stable, yet flexible enough to take advantage of state-of-the-art technology.

OVERVIEW OF THE SECURITY STANDARDS

The chapters in this book walk you through the specifics of the Security Rule. The Security Rule standards are listed within each category in the order in which you should address them, which is the order in which they are explained in this book. Table 2.3 lists all of the standards and their implementation specifications. Some standards do not have specific implementation specifications.

TABLE 2.3

Security Rule Requirements

Security Standards	Code of Federal Regulations Sections	Security Implementation Specifications (R) = Required, (A) = Addressable
Administrative Safeguards		
Security Management Functions	§164.308(a)(1)	Risk Analysis (R) Risk Management (R) Sanction Policy (R) Information System Activity Review (R)
Assigned Security Responsibility	§164.308(a)(2)	(R)
Workforce Security	§164.308(a)(3)	Authorization and/or Supervision (A) Workforce Clearance Procedure (A) Termination Procedures (A)
Information Access Management	§164.308(a)(4)	Isolating Healthcare Clearinghouse Function (R) Access Authorization (A) Access Establishment and Modification (A)
Security Awareness and Training	§164.308(a)(5)	Security Reminders (A) Protection From Malicious Software (A) Login Monitoring (A) Password Management (A)
Security Incident Procedures	§164.308(a)(6)	Response and Reporting (R)
Contingency Plan	§164.308(a)(7)	Data Backup Plan (R) Disaster Recovery Plan (R) Emergency Mode Operation Plan (R) Testing and Revision Procedure (A) Applications and Data Criticality Analysis (A)
Evaluation	§164.308(a)(8)	(R)

(*continued*)

T A B L E   2.3 (continued)

Security Rule Requirements

Security Standards	Code of Federal Regulations Sections	Security Implementation Specifications (R) = Required, (A) = Addressable
Business Associate Contracts and Other Arrangements	§164.308(b)(1)	(R)
Physical Safeguards		
Facility Access Controls	§164.310(a)(1)	Contingency Operations (A)
		Facility Security Plan (A)
		Access Control and Validation Procedures (A)
		Maintenance Records (A)
Workstation Use	§164.310(b)	(R)
Workstation Security	§164.310(c)	(R)
Device and Media Controls	§164.310(d)(1)	Disposal (R)
		Media Reuse (R)
		Accountability (A)
		Data Backup and Storage (A)
Technical Safeguards		
Access Control	§164.312(a)	Unique User Identification (R)
		Emergency Access Procedure (R)
		Automatic Logoff (A)
		Encryption and Decryption (A)
Audit Controls	§164.312(b)	(R)
Integrity	§164.312(c)(1)	Mechanism to Authenticate PHI (A)
Person or Entity Authentication	§164.312(d)	(R)
Transmission Security	§164.312(e)(1)	Integrity Controls (A)
		Encryption (A)

Each federal regulation is included in the Code of Federal Regulations (CFR), which is indexed for ease in finding any regulation. HIPAA Administrative Simplification regulations are added to subchapter C of title 45 of the CFR, as parts 160, 162, and 164. The Security Rule sections are in part 164. (A copy of the HIPAA Security Rule is included in the appendix of this book. Refer to it frequently.) One difference between the Security Rule and the Privacy Rule is that although there are standards and implementation specifications within both, the implementation specifications in the Security Rule are labeled *Required* or *Addressable*. You must comply with every standard. You must also comply with every implementation specification that is labeled *Required*. However, implementation specifications that are marked *Addressable* mean you must make a choice on how you will address them. They are not optional.

Required vs Addressable

Every standard in the HIPAA Security Rule must be implemented. Security implementation specifications are either:

- Required—You must implement this specification as stated.
- Addressable—You may:
    - Implement the specification as stated.
    - Implement an alternative that you believe suits your office better.
    - Address the standard in another way because the implementation specification is not applicable to your situation.

Regardless of how you approach the addressable implementation specifications, you must document why you chose the approach you did to implement the specification or address the standard.

Always remember, every standard is required. Just because a standard contains only addressable implementation specifications does not mean you can ignore it. Addressable does not mean not required nor does it mean optional. It means you must address the specification in some way or address the standard itself in some way. The purpose of this feature of the Security Rule is to ensure that it is comprehensive, scalable, and technology neutral.

UNDERSTANDING THE RULES

You are now prepared to begin your journey through the HIPAA Security Rule. Chapter 3 provides a step-by-step approach to reviewing and upgrading your security measures and creating a culture of privacy and security awareness. Chapter 4 helps you review your organization and its relationships in order to meet requirements of both your internal organizational needs as well as those of others with whom you exchange information. It also describes needed policies and procedures, and helps you with documentation. Chapter 5 is devoted to risk analysis—a critical step in determining how you will apply the Security Rule in your office. Chapters 6, 7, 8, and 9 review for you each standard and the related implementation specifications. Chapter 10 concludes with practical tips for applying security controls, responding to an OCR complaint or audit request, and essentially prepares you to fully enter Health 2.0.

CHECK YOUR UNDERSTANDING*

Match the following terms with their definitions:

1. Notice of Privacy Practices _____

2. Authorization _____

3. Consent _____

4. Use _____

5. Disclosure _____
    a. Document that describes how you will use and disclose PHI
    b. Permission for specified disclosures that meet the requirements of HIPAA
    c. Sharing of PHI within a covered entity
    d. Transferring of PHI outside of a covered entity
    e. Permission for using or disclosing PHI (which a state or covered entity may require)

Indicate which of the following are most likely incidental disclosures (I) rather than wrongful disclosures (W):

6. Patient overhears nurse state a patient's weight by scale _____

7. Nurse checks neighbor's health record to see if lab results show improved health condition _____

8. Physician asks barista at coffee shop how she is feeling after returning from maternity leave _____

9. Receptionist asks patient who has presented to the office to go to the lab for a tuberculosis test _____

10. Lab technician asks patient to roll up sleeve to draw blood _____

*For answers, refer to the Answer Key at the end of the book.

chapter 3

Your Approach to Security

Irrespective of how you previously approached Health Insurance Portability and Accountability Act of 1996 (HIPAA) Security Rule compliance, it is very appropriate to take a fresh look at your approach. Much has changed since 2005 when compliance was first required.

First, creating a culture of privacy and security awareness is as important as security technology. Embracing security as a way to ensure confidentiality, integrity, and availability of information—of any type. This focus should reduce the emphasis on the controlling aspects of security and focus instead on the service aspect.

From there, your approach should begin with ensuring a solid understanding of the HIPAA Security Rule. Assigning/affirming responsibility for security, conducting/updating a risk analysis, and developing/maintaining an information security plan are steps that prepare the practice for identifying and implementing needed information security services. A vendor selection may be conducted to determine the best security services for your needs—whether or not you end up acquiring security services from your incumbent vendor or the vendor of other information systems applications you are in the process of acquiring. This is a good time to ensure the existence of and/or update business associate contracts/agreements.

Implementation of security services entails developing/reviewing security policies; installing/enhancing administrative, physical, and technical services; evaluating and redesigning current workflows and processes that may be impacted by new security services; and developing, delivering, and reinforcing security training and awareness—for all in the practice as well as patients. Ideally at each step you should document what you are doing. Documentation is often relegated to the end of a project, which often means it does not get done. However, the saying that "if it wasn't documented, it wasn't done" is just as true for information security as it is in health care itself. Many have failed compliance reviews or audits due to lack of documentation alone. You may have best practices in place, but unless the documentation is available to prove these practices have been performed, the office is out of compliance.

In addition to periodic review and upgrading of security services, information security management needs to be an ongoing program. Documentation helps focus continual monitoring and planning for future enhancements. Because of the implications of being out of compliance with HIPAA regulations, incorporating information security into your overall compliance program assures attention to information security on an ongoing basis and integrates security with privacy, requirements for use of EHRs, and other applicable compliance activities.

HOW TO USE THIS CHAPTER

This chapter walks through the series of steps in an information security management program. It provides an overview of each of the steps in such a program, which are further explained in subsequent chapters in this book:

1. Create a culture of privacy and security awareness.
2. Ensure a solid understanding of the Security Rule.
3. Assign/affirm responsibility for information security.
4. Conduct/update a risk analysis.
5. Develop/maintain an information security plan.
6. Select applicable vendors for security services.
7. Implement security policies, procedures, and services.
8. Document information security compliance.
9. Develop/manage ongoing security monitoring.
10. Incorporate security compliance into overall compliance program.

STEP 1: CREATE A CULTURE OF PRIVACY AND SECURITY AWARENESS

Health care has always had a culture of privacy, but security tends to be viewed as more controlling, limiting, and bothersome. Unfortunately, many security measures fit that description well, but they don't have to! It is incumbent upon the practice to find the right measures and apply them consistently.

A key measure of security is developing a culture of security. There are a number of steps that can be taken to integrate security into the fabric of your privacy culture and your overall management. Perhaps the first is to take a look at the overall culture of the practice's management. Consider Case Study 3.1 as an example of a management culture that turned itself around.

CASE STUDY 3.1
Turning Around a Management Culture

A three-physician practice was busy—but not so busy that physicians could not still take an occasional afternoon off for golf or that the office manager could not sometimes come in late or leave early. Yet, the office constantly seemed in a topsy-turvy state of affairs, with a "revolving door" for staff, patients often spending a long time in the waiting room, phones ringing off the hook, and paperwork seemingly everywhere. The practice was considering acquiring an EHR system and invited another physician already using an EHR system to visit the practice and talk about the buying process, provide tips on implementation, and describe how to overcome reduced productivity.

One of the things the EHR physician brought to the practice was an article by Dr Ken Adler that appeared in *Family Practice Management* a few years ago.[1] This article highlighted the importance of the "three T's"—team, tactics, and technology. In discussing that "everyone in your practice will play some role in the success or failure of your EHR implementation," Adler observes two key success factors for EHR implementation. First, people are key to success, and leadership is one of the most important keys. Second, he noted that "if your practice is broken, you need to fix it before you try to bring an EHR on board. Dysfunctional organizations are likely to have dysfunctional implementations. Excellent communication, clear lines of authority, and an explicit decision-making process promote success." After recommending this article to the practice, the EHR physician asked the practice: Who will be your EHR champion, and how will you assure that your practice is running at its best before you start the EHR journey?

The practice was somewhat taken aback by these questions. Upon probing, the EHR physician talked about observations made upon entering the office. The EHR physician empathized with the practice, describing the trials and tribulations of dealing with the same issues, but observing that

---

1. Adler, KG. How to successfully navigate your EHR implementation. *Fam Pract Manag*. February 2007. Available at http://www.aafp.org/fpm/2007/0200/p33.html.

recognizing the problem was 90% of the solution. As a result of this conversation, the practice closed for a day and conducted a retreat away from the office for the physicians and manager in the morning and staff in the afternoon. A facilitator was used to help everyone get issues "off their chest" and to structure positive activities the practice could take immediately, to fix not only management issues but workflow and process issues, and then to start carrying those activities over to their EHR project. Each person in the practice came away from the retreat with both a list of things to do and a sense of accomplishment that the issues could even be verbalized in a non-threatening environment. One of the activities on everyone's list was a biweekly 10-minute huddle to review progress—initially on overall organization issues, then later to discuss the EHR. Each huddle acknowledged special contributions and updated action lists.

Most people intellectually understand the importance of accessibility and communications, education and awareness, monitoring goal achievement, and celebrating success. Unfortunately, these things are not always top of mind during the routine activities of work. Sometimes it is necessary to take a time-out, regroup, and consciously take steps to make a difference. While it is not essential to close the practice for a day and hire a facilitator, such an investment is actually minor in comparison to the hours spent hiring and training new staff, reworking errors, and implementing major technology improvements. There may well be setbacks and days that are particularly trying, but doing the right thing is the task at hand for everyone. Figure 3.1 lists some specific tactics that can aid an office turnaround and build a strong organizational culture that will be a start toward ensuring a culture of both privacy and security.

F I G U R E 3.1

Tactics for Changing an Organization's Culture

1. Recognize the need for a "culture boost" by taking time to assess:

    a. Are you generally happy? Or do you dread going to the office and are you anxious to leave? With respect to information security, do you resent access controls and often share your password by handing off data entry in an EHR to a staff member?

    b. Are others with whom you work generally happy? Or do they complain, take a lot of time off, injure themselves on the job, snap at their fellow workers and patients? These individuals may be most likely to file complaints about the privacy and security of the practice.

    c. Do your customers ie, patients) appear happy? Or do they seem unpleasant when approaching you, complain, appear not to follow directions? Such patients may also be likely to file privacy and security complaints with the Office for Civil Rights.

2. Take a time-out to discuss what is working and what is not working. Assure that there is a mix of clinical, financial, and administrative issues discussed. Always focusing only on one area of the practice is a disservice to other issues that will only fester and get bigger. When possible, integrate privacy and security into the discussion—not only as an issue but as part of a solution. The amount of time needed to discuss issues should be determined by the size of the issue. Don't beat yourself up; take some time to celebrate the positive, but be realistic about what is happening and address it head on. Agree to take positive steps, including writing specific, measurable, achievable, realistic, and time-based (S.M.A.R.T.) goals that each person is involved in developing and monitoring for himself or herself. Goals should be focused on all aspects of the practice's business of providing health care—from patient follow-up to helping patients access their health information from your portal.

(continued)

FIGURE 3.1 (continued)

Tactics for Changing an Organization's Culture

3. Set a specific time each day, week, or other convenient period to check that the goals for the period are being met. If things are going well, let everyone know: say thank you, post to a report card, provide cookies, or do whatever is applicable for the action. If things are behind, correct course: If one person needs help, seek the person out in private to ask what issues are being faced and how you can help. If more than one person is involved, call for a quick huddle and ask what isn't working and for ideas to solve the problem. Act on those ideas. Periodically walk around the office and observe what is going on as if you were a patient. Would you feel your privacy was being violated if you overhead much of a conversation between the physician and another patient? (White noise can help.) Do you see printouts of health records left unattended? (Determine the root cause of why there are printouts to begin with. Reduce printing and get shredder boxes for necessary printouts.) Ask patients how their visit went and if there is anything you can do to help make their visit easier; thank them for using your practice. If patients seem uneasy, explore further their concerns. Don't use HIPAA as an excuse for not engaging patients in accessing their health information and learning more about their care.

4. Communicate key messages regularly. Weave together a message that integrates caring for fellow staff members, patients, quality of care, correct coding, privacy, security, and any other "hot buttons" for the office: "We got a request for an on-site audit of our coding. Let's make sure we let everyone know, have our charts ready, and use a guest password." In all walks of life communication is the lynchpin for keeping everything together. Do not underestimate the power of a few kind words, a smile, and a "thank you."

5. Never give up. Managing the office, the accounts receivables, patients' care plans, privacy and security—all are ongoing programs, not short-term projects. And because they are ongoing programs, they periodically need to be refreshed. One office adopted the theme of "Get Caught! Doing the Right Thing." Despite how well this worked initially, it eventually lost its luster. (They next tried "Anyone leaving without logging off buys donuts for breakfast," and quickly got hungry!) Many physician practices believe such activities may not be very professional. But everyone has a lighter side and needs to be acknowledged for his or her efforts. Remember, we all need a dose of laughter, for it truly is the best medicine.

STEP 2: ENSURE A SOLID UNDERSTANDING OF THE SECURITY RULE

Part of creating a culture of privacy and security is to ensure that everyone understands the rules as they apply to him or her. For example, everyone in the office benefits from understanding that it is a requirement to back up the computer systems on a regular schedule. For some, knowing that the office is performing backups may be a sufficient amount of information to instill trust that the office is in compliance with this requirement and that the information entered into electronic systems will be available when needed. For others, more information may be needed or simply desirable. Obviously, for the person responsible for the backup process, full details are essential. It also very important, however, to ensure that any detailed information about the process is accessible to at least one other person. Ensuring information is accessible and that a backup person at least knows who to call if necessary is very much a part of backing up any process. (Refer to Table 2.3 for a list of all Security Rule requirements and their implementation specifications.)

STEP 3: ASSIGN/AFFIRM RESPONSIBILITY FOR INFORMATION SECURITY

Make sure that one person in your office is assigned the responsibility for managing the Security Rule compliance and that there is an information security official (ISO), who should be knowledgeable about technical security services and does not have to be a staff member. While everyone should be involved in compliance, having one person whose job it is to manage the overall security program is essential. This person does not have to be the ISO. See Chapter 4 for more information on organizing responsibility for security in your office.

STEP 4: CONDUCT/UPDATE A SECURITY RISK ANALYSIS

The risk analysis is the key to determining what information security services are needed for your office. After you've read Chapter 5, you'll have a better understanding of how to perform and document the risk analysis required in the Security Rule.

The most important thing to bear in mind with respect to the risk analysis, however, is that risk refers to the probability, or likelihood, that a threat will take advantage of a vulnerability and the degree of impact that will have. A threat is an indication that something wrong or harmful could happen. A vulnerability is a weakness.

We know it is human nature to be curious. Leaving a computer on in an examining room when the patent is alone is a vulnerability. But how likely is it that the curious 85-year-old with cataracts will actually be able to navigate the computer? (In fact, the greater threat is probably that the patient bumps into the computer and causes physical harm to self and/or the computer—but this is not as a result of leaving the computer on and there is no harm to the information in the computer system unless it is a stand-alone system.) Compare this to the patient who is a college student in the same environment, and both the likelihood that curiosity is exercised and the impact of a wrongful disclosure are known to increase.

Because office environments change, it is necessary to periodically update the security risk analysis. In fact, the Security Rule includes an "Evaluation" standard that requires performance of "a periodic technical and nontechnical evaluation, based initially on the standards implemented under this Rule and subsequently, in response to environmental or operational changes affecting the security of electronic PHI that establishes the extent to which an entity's security policies and procedures meet the requirements." This requirement is the primary reason that a security risk analysis is required for earning the incentives in the meaningful use of EHR technology program. More recently, the privacy and security audits that the OCR is conducting are revealing that 65% of all audit findings relate to security, where only 26% relate to privacy and 9% relate to the breach notification rule. Small practices were especially lacking in both security and privacy compliance.[1] The audit protocol, available at http://www.hhs.gov/ocr/privacy/hipaa/enforcement/audit/protocol.html, will be further discussed in Chapter 10.

Many other things have changed since the Security Rule became effective in 2005. Use the list of common changes in Figure 3.2 as your own checklist to determine how likely it is that your risk analysis will reveal new threats and/or vulnerabilities.

---

1. Sanches, L. OCR Senior Advisory, Health Information Privacy, Lead, HIPAA Compliance Audits, 2012 HIPAA Privacy and Security Audits. US Department of Health and Human Services, Office for Civil Rights. Available at http://csrc.nist.gov/news_events/hiipaa_june2012/day2/day2-2_lsanches_ocr-audit.pdf.

Examples of Common Environmental or Operational Changes Impacting Security Risk

- Breach Notification Rule
- Incentives for meaningful use of EHR technology
- Proposed modifications to the Privacy Rule
- Use of mobile devices, such as cell phones and tablets
- Use of mobile storage media, such as flash drives and CDs
- Use of social media
- Interest in using personally owned devices
- Upgrades to the practice management system
- Adoption of operating rules for HIPAA transactions and code sets
- Requirements for Medicare providers to accept electronic funds transfer (EFT) payments
- Cloud computing
- Patient portal
- Support for personal health records
- Health information exchange and the Nationwide Health Information Network
- "Big data" analytics where your data are aggregated with others' data to support evidence-based medicine
- Health reform risk/reward sharing (eg, patient-centered medical home, accountable care organizations, bundled payments)

STEP 5: DEVELOP/MAINTAIN AN INFORMATION SECURITY PLAN

Your next step is to develop an information security plan. This involves the steps addressed here. As you read the rest of this book, modify the checklist for an information security plan in Table 3.1 to suit your needs.

Pace yourself in completing the timeline, but be aware of external factors necessitating certain enhancements. These might include the risk analysis required for earning incentives for meaningful use of EHR technology or directly using the HIPAA electronic transactions that are being made easier to use with the operating rules being adopted by federal regulation.

Identify when a budget will need to be created so that you have adequate time to plan your next budget cycle. Also, be sure adequate resources are allocated to the process so that implementation does not impact cash flow.

STEP 6: SELECT APPLICABLE VENDORS FOR SECURITY SERVICES

While some security services may well be supplied by the vendors for the information systems you already have in the office or are contemplating acquiring, you may find that some of these services are not as sophisticated or easy to use as you would like them to be. As you identify from your risk analysis that new or enhanced security services are needed, it is a good practice to evaluate what the marketplace has to offer. Even if you end up acquiring the service from the vendor supplying the underlying information systems application, it can be useful to evaluate what is available in the marketplace. This may give you leverage to acquire better services from the information systems vendor.

T A B L E   3.1

Checklist of Tasks, Timeline, and Resources

Tasks/Subtasks	Timeline	Resources		
		Who	**What**	**Budget**
1. Create a culture of privacy and security awareness		Board and management	*Handbook*, Chapters 1–3	
2. Ensure understanding of the Privacy Rule and Security Rule				
a. Review the regulations		Board and management	*Handbook*, Chapter 2	
b. Learn about security controls			*Handbook*, Chapters 6, 8, 9	
3. Assign/affirm responsibility for security				
a. Appoint information security official (ISO)		Board and management	*Handbook*, Chapter 4	
b. Organize staff to participate in risk analysis and remediation efforts			*Handbook*, Chapter 4	
c. Determine need for external resources			*Handbook*, Chapter 4	
4. Conduct/update a risk analysis				
a. On list of security standards, identify if you have policy and procedure for each standard, and match the security features in your information systems to the standards		ISO	*Handbook*, Chapter 5	
b. Assess vulnerabilities and threats and record on list of security standards		ISO or consultant	*Handbook*, Chapter 5	
c. Prioritize risks based on probability of a threat occurring and criticality of impact		ISO, office manager, chief medical officer (CMO)	*Handbook*, Chapter 5	
d. Identify potential security measures to reduce risks and budget for these		ISO, vendor, CMO	*Handbook*, Chapters 6–9	
5. Develop/maintain an information security plan				
a. Make a list of PHI and other confidential information maintained in or transmitted through information systems		ISO and information privacy official (IPO)	*Handbook*, Chapters 3, 6, 7, 9	
b. Document how you intend to address every HIPAA security standard in policy		ISO	*Handbook*, Chapter 3	
c. Review the security features included in your information systems		ISO, information systems vendor	*Handbook*, Chapter 3	

(*continued*)

T A B L E   3.1 (continued)

Checklist of Tasks, Timeline, and Resources

Tasks/Subtasks	Timeline	Resources		
		Who	**What**	**Budget**
d. Use this checklist or other method to identify the tasks, timeline, and resources you need to become compliant with HIPAA security		ISO, office manager	*Handbook* Chapter 4	
6. Select applicable vendors for security services				
a. Identify your requirements, scan the marketplace, and perform due diligence		ISO, office manager, CMO	*Handbook,* Chapter 3	
b. Negotiate contract		Office manager	*Handbook,* Chapter 3	
7. Implement administrative, physical, and technical security services				
a. Plan a detailed implementation timeline, including installation, testing, and potential certification for all new or upgraded services		ISO, office manager	*Handbook,* Chapter 10	
b. Document procedures; develop forms and tools to accompany new controls		Office manager	*Handbook,* Chapters 2, 8	
c. Identify who needs what training; deliver and document training		ISO	*Handbook,* Chapter 6	
d. Use ongoing reminders to build awareness			*Handbook,* Chapter 6	
8. Document information security compliance				
a. Maintain policies and procedures		ISO	*Handbook* Chapter 3	
b. Maintain record of all training performed and materials		ISO, office manager	*Handbook* Chapter 6	
c. Document all security incidents and other actions, activities, and assessments		ISO	*Handbook,* Chapter 6	
d. Manage all security breaches		ISO, IPO, board	*Handbook,* Chapter 6	
9. Develop/manage ongoing security monitoring processes				
a. Integrate privacy complaints and security incidents as applicable		ISO, IPO	*Handbook,* Chapter 6	
b. Develop an auditing program for ongoing review of compliance		ISO, consultant	*Handbook,* Chapters 6, 10	
c. Monitor regulation changes and additions		ISO, IPO	*Handbook,* Chapters 6, 10	
10. Incorporate security compliance into overall compliance program		IPO, ISO, compliance officer, board	*Handbook* Chapters 4, 10	

Task list reprinted with permission from Margret\A Consulting, LLC.

The following are important steps to take in selecting vendors to supply your security services for you:

1. Identify the security service that best meets the needs identified in the risk analysis.
2. Conduct a formal vendor selection process:
   a. Identify your office's specific information security requirements based on your risk analysis.
   b. Scan the marketplace for the most likely vendors to fit your needs, including your incumbent vendor(s) or those from whom you are planning to acquire information systems applications.
   c. Issue to a select group of vendors a request for proposal (RFP) for a major service, such as disaster recovery services for a large practice, or a request for bid (RFB) for a small appliance or other service for a small practice. If you are currently in the process of selecting an EHR or other major information systems application, include your office's specific information security requirements in the RFPs or RFBs that go to those vendors as well as any stand-alone security service vendors you are considering.
   d. Evaluate each product offering to determine whether it meets your office's specific information security requirements. Get a demonstration of how it works, and check references.
3. Review the vendor contract, negotiating any aspects that put the office at risk. There are several potential risk concerns. Many of them are standard contractual issues your attorney will identify. One of the growing areas of concern, however, may not even be spelled out in a contract. Some vendors underwrite part of the cost of their services by using your data for other purposes. Some of these uses may benefit you directly, but others may not. If any vendors will have access to your data, especially in a storage or backup capacity, make sure there are explicit descriptions in the contract with respect to your ownership of the data and any uses you permit them to make of the data. The fact that they de-identify and use your data does not absolve them of the need to tell you about this and for you to explicitly permit or disallow the use. What uses you permit of your data should be spelled out in your business associate contract/agreement. If you are acquiring new technology from an incumbent vendor, it is also a good practice to review the business associate contract to make sure it is up to date.

STEP 7: IMPLEMENT SECURITY POLICIES, PROCEDURES, AND SERVICES

Once the risk analysis has helped you determine what security measures will best help you thwart threats and address vulnerabilities so that you may select the most appropriate vendor for your needs, you will enter the implementation phase. Implementation encompasses many substeps.

Identifying the policies associated with each security measure you have or acquire is a helpful strategy for ensuring that the implementation of the services or their ongoing maintenance meets your needs. Policies are the overall directives, or objectives, that the security measures will accomplish. For example, if you decide to implement daily computer backups, your policy should state that you expect backups to be performed every day and that you will be able to recover all data entered into the information system up to the time of the backup the day before. As you implement this service, check the actual implementation against the policy.

It is helpful to consider that auditors gauge compliance with the risk-based Security Rule from a three-step perspective. First they look at your risk analysis to determine if it is comprehensive and that a fair assessment has been made of both threats and vulnerabilities. Second they look at your policies to determine that they accurately reflect your risk-based decisions. Finally they look at the security services you have implemented, including ongoing monitoring of their effectiveness, to make sure you are following what you identified as your needs and how you were going to address those needs. Figure 3.3 illustrates the feedback mechanism in this approach.

Information security policies should be written in a manner such that they are applicable and understandable to all in the office and even to patients. Policies, however, are not the same as procedures. Information security procedures should be retained as confidential documents as these are highly detailed specifications of how security services are implemented and could give away the "keys to the kingdom" if made available to anyone who does not have a need to know.

The most obvious step of implementation involves installing, configuring, adjusting workflows and processes, testing, and training to implement your new controls.

For administrative measures, this step involves identifying an ISO, writing/reviewing sanctions policies to address information security accountabilities, establishing information access privileges, making sure those in the practice who terminate their relationship have returned office-owned items and access has been removed, security incident management, contingency planning, and training and awareness building.

For physical controls, this step may involve ensuring the presence of specific services relative to physically controlling access to information. For example, installing ventilation in a server closet or a chiller in a data center of a large practice aids server maintenance. Where and how workstations are used fall under security controls. Some physical security controls are the same as personal safety controls, such as locks on doors or camera monitoring of the office's physical environment if warranted. Physical security controls address devices and media, including both contingency operations for electronic systems and man-

FIGURE 3.3

Security Auditing Perspectives

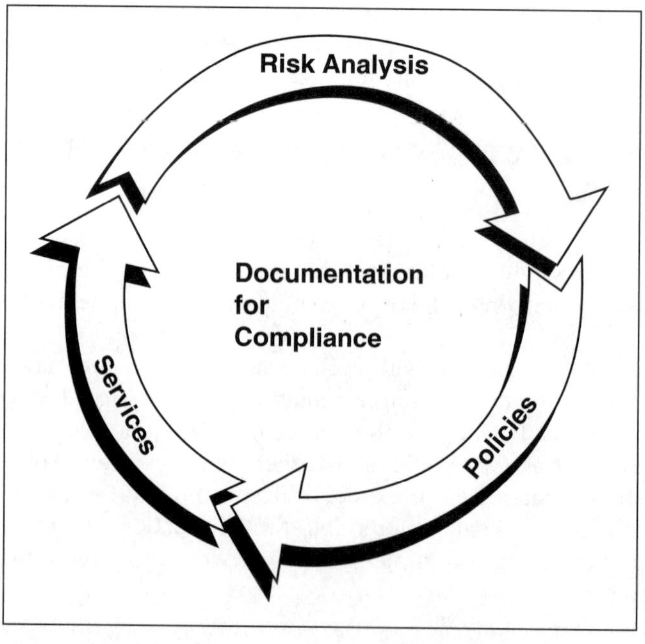

agement of paper containing confidential information (PHI and other). Mishandled paper is a leading cause of breaches posted to the HHS Web site.[2]

For technical controls, you may be installing new authentication services, such as tokens that are required for using e-prescribing for controlled substances. Some needs for technical security controls may not initially seem obvious or may seem to fit other categories of controls. For example, using a personally owned device, such as a Mac when the office uses PCs, may not seem to be a technical security concern. However, there are at least two major issues with this practice. First, the user is very likely to take the device home and may not apply the same level of physical security controls over who uses the device or where it is stored as would be required in the office. Hence it is subject to unauthorized access, theft, or destruction. Second, however, are technical security issues of maintaining many different devices. It is important to remember that it is no longer just about PC vs Mac, but all the various cell phone/tablet devices with many more operating systems. Knowing the inner workings of each device places a great burden on what typically is a very small IT staff. As a result, for example, security patches may not be as well managed and data stores residing on a local partition of the drive may not be known and properly secured. Another major cause of breaches is loss or theft of devices that contain unencrypted PHI. Users of such devices may be very well-intentioned. They want to keep up with their workload, or they want to study the implications of different treatment modalities on patients with a specific disease. Many of these risks can occur on office-owned devices as well, but the risk tends to increase on personally owned devices for the reasons discussed here and others.

As controls are implemented, managing their installation and configuration is an important element that assures they will work in your environment. Whether acquired from your primary vendor or a third party, every security service needs to be adapted to your specific technical infrastructure.

Reviewing and redesigning workflows and processes so that the security services mesh with your practices and so that you are taking advantage of new opportunities for process improvement is also an important part of implementation and one that is often overlooked. Something as simple as suggesting to users that they always state out loud that they are logging on to the patient's record gives the user "air time" with the patient and is reassuring. Many new users of EHRs in particular find that they seem too focused on the computer and not on the patient. Communications such as this help fill the gaps and let the patient know that what you are doing relates to their care process.

Developing, delivering, and reinforcing security training and awareness is an essential element of implementation. Training may entail specific instructions on how to use the new security service or the underlying technology that has been impacted by the service. Training should also include a review of policies and applicable procedures and new workflows and processes adopted. Some offices require a competency evaluation. Awareness building impacts all users and patients. Consider using posters, brochures, or simply short, well-timed references to new security services.

STEP 8: DOCUMENT INFORMATION SECURITY COMPLIANCE

Documenting your security practices and services is truly your best protection. All unique configurations and other changes to information systems, product/service instruction manuals, policies and procedures, logs, reports of events, records of actions, training manuals, training logs, awareness posters, risk analysis findings, and more are forms of documentation

---

2. US Department of Health and Human Services, Office for Civil Rights. *Annual Report to Congress on Breaches of Unsecured Protected Health Information for Calendar Years 2009 and 2010.* Available at http://www.hhs.gov/ocr/privacy/hipaa/administrative/breachnotificationrule/breachrept.pdf.

you should create and retain for six years from the date of their creation or the date when they were last in effect, whichever is later.

As part of getting your documentation in order, it would be a good idea to consider whether your documentation will be easy to retrieve in the event of an audit and whether it will stand up to scrutiny. For example, many IT staff keep e-mails about changes made, but such e-mails may get deleted on a faster turnaround schedule than other information. They may also be difficult to locate or assemble as a complete document. Where e-mails can serve as a record of a request or other form of communication about something, they rarely serve as an ongoing monitoring or logging tool. For example, an invitation to a training program on security does not verify actual attendance.

STEP 9: DEVELOP/MANAGE ONGOING SECURITY MONITORING

Security is an ongoing process. You will need to develop a process to make sure your security measures continue to work effectively and efficiently. HIPAA's standard on risk analysis also requires risk management. As previously noted, an Evaluation standard requires attention to security services when there are changes in the environment or organization. In addition, HIPAA includes standards on information system activity review and incident procedures designed to pinpoint when additional security scrutiny is needed.

The status of security services can change rapidly. Many new tools are constantly being developed as new threats are identified. In addition, physician practices are rapidly moving from a closed environment where data are only compiled, used, and stored in the office to increasingly sharing information with patients and other providers, using a health information exchange organization (HIO), or even the Nationwide Health Information Network. For example, physicians practices may be able to participate in the Centers for Medicare and Medicaid Services (CMS) pilot program using the Nationwide Health Information Network for submitting documentation in support of a claim audit through Medicare's Electronic Submission of Medical Documentation (esMD) program (see https://www.cms.gov/Research-Statistics-Data-and-Systems/Computer-Data-and-Systems/ESMD/index.html?redirect=/ESMD/).

The federal government's audit findings and enforcement procedures may also generate additional guidance or requirements in the form of FAQs, formal guidance documents, contractual requirements for participating in Medicare and/or using the Nationwide Health Information Network, or even modified or new regulations.

STEP 10: INCORPORATE SECURITY COMPLIANCE INTO OVERALL COMPLIANCE PROGRAM

It has been noted that privacy and security must work hand in hand with one another. But there are other privacy/security laws, regulations, guidance, and requirements with which a practice may need to comply. Most notably would be certain federal privacy and security laws and regulations (discussed below), as well as state statutes that may preempt the HIPAA Privacy Rule. In addition, there are laws and regulations that require compliance with treatment billing and coding practices, address practice ethics, prohibit kickbacks in referrals, and require credentialing. These will not be discussed in this book, except to note that an overall compliance strategy benefits all required compliance activities. Any one compliance officer may not be able to address the technical nuances of every compliance requirement, but can provide consistency in application of requirements so that the office is not jeopardized.

With respect to complementary privacy and security requirements, already alluded to is the Breach Notification regulation under which notifications of breaches—large immediately and small annually that must be made to HHS and those potentially harmed. Information on the Breach Notification Rule is covered in more depth in Chapter 10.

Not directly applicable to HIPAA covered entities but important to be aware of is that there is also a Federal Trade Commission (FTC) Health Breach Notification Rule (http://www.ftc.gov/os/2009/08/R911002hbn.pdf) that was issued the same day as the HHS Breach Notification Rule. The language and requirements in these two regulations are virtually the same, except the FTC Health Breach Notification applies to vendors who offer (sell or otherwise make available) personal health records (PHRs) directly to individuals. The FTC was chosen to protect the information in such PHRs under its consumer protection mission. Where a PHR vendor violates its privacy policy with respect to PHR data, the FTC can impose applicable penalties. Providers who recommend that their patients use PHRs or even direct them to a specific PHR may want to further understand the implications surrounding this practice.

Other federal privacy and security compliance requirements arise out of the following:

- The Privacy Act of 1974 establishes a Code of Fair Information Practice that governs the collection, maintenance, use, and dissemination of personally identifiable information about individuals that is maintained in systems of records *by federal agencies.* While this act is not applicable to private practice physicians, it can be helpful to be aware of this law with respect to patients familiar with it, who perhaps serve in the military, have records in the Indian Health Service, etc. An overview of this act is available at http://www.justice.gov/opcl/1974privacyact.pdf.

- Confidentiality of Alcohol and Drug Abuse Patient Records regulations (42 CFR Part 2) were enacted in 1975 and impact records of individuals in federally funded substance abuse treatment programs. A useful comparison between these regulations and the HIPAA Privacy Rule compiled by the Department of Justice is available at http://www.samhsa.gov/healthprivacy/docs/samhsapart2-hipaacomparison2004.pdf.

- The Family Educational Rights and Privacy Act (FERPA) of 1974 protects the privacy of student education records, including health information that may be included therein. Joint Guidance from the Department of Education and HHS issued in 2008 is available at http://www2.ed.gov/policy/gen/guid/fpco/doc/ferpa-hipaa-guidance.pdf.

- The Genetic Information Nondiscrimination Act (GINA) of 2008 prohibits use of genetic information in health insurance and employment. Further information is available at http://www.gpo.gov/fdsys/pkg/PLAW-110publ233/pdf/PLAW-110publ233.pdf.

- The Confidentiality section of Title X of the Public Health Service Act is part of the Title X Family Planning program enacted in 1970. The program is designed to provide access to contraceptive services, supplies, and information. The Confidentiality section requires individual consent for disclosure. To review the provisions, see http://ecfr.gpoaccess.gov/cgi/t/text/text-idx?c=ecfr&sid=973ca5ad9a106c9ebe32151f16121e8a&rgn=div8&view=text&node=42:1.0.1.4.43.1.19.11&idno=42.

- The Patient Safety and Quality Improvement Act (PSQIA) of 2005, with regulations at 42 CFR Part 3, became effective in 2009 and establishes a voluntary reporting system to enhance the data available to assess and resolve patient safety and healthcare quality issues. To encourage the reporting and analysis of medical errors, PSQIA provides federal privilege and confidentiality protections for patient safety information called *patient safety work product.* Further information is available at http://www.gpo.gov/fdsys/pkg/FR-2008-11-21/pdf/E8-27475.pdf.

TAKE A POSITIVE APPROACH FOR POSITIVE RESULTS

This chapter has described a tried-and-true approach to ensuring your practice complies with the HIPAA Security Rule, as well as best practices for securing all confidential information in the practice. Any task that first appears daunting can be made easier if a structured approach is laid out and one step is undertaken at a time.

CHECK YOUR UNDERSTANDING*

1. Which of the following might help your office become more aware of information security?
   a. Avoid discussing security incidents or controls that make people nervous
   b. Base pay raises on information security training test scores
   c. Post a set of policies and procedures to your Intranet for anyone to review if they wish
   d. Set goals for information security with each person and have each person monitor his or her achievement

2. What does "addressable" mean in relationship to the HIPAA Security Rule?
   a. Implement an alternative
   b. Optional
   c. Required
   d. Situational

3. A risk analysis should be performed:
   a. Annually
   b. Every three years
   c. Once when first complying with HIPAA
   d. Whenever there are significant changes impacting risk

4. Which of the following is true about security services?
   a. Some services will be add-ons to information system applications
   b. They are embedded in your use of the Internet
   c. They will be supplied by your information systems vendors
   d. You will have to acquire all security services yourself

5. Which of the following is an example of the need to monitor the ongoing status of your security policies?
   a. Breach of PHI occurred in your office
   b. Patient filed a privacy complaint with your office
   c. Staff are increasingly using social media
   d. All of the above

Characterize each of the following as a threat (T) or vulnerability (V):

6. Bad weather

7. Security service on network not updated

8. Leaving a computer on in an exam room without logging off

9. Human curiosity

10. Management inattentive to security

*For answers, refer to the Answer Key at the end of the book.

Organizing for HIPAA

What you know about your organizational environment can help you perform your HIPAA security compliance activities, such as conducting the required risk analysis, developing appropriate policies and procedures, selecting and documenting the controls that best fit your needs, and exchanging data with other providers and patients.

The HIPAA Privacy Rule establishes a number of different organizational structures in which physician offices may be included. The HIPAA Security Rule uses these same organizational structures to describe applicability to its standards. Although each covered entity is responsible for its own compliance with HIPAA, it is important to understand how these various organizational structures impact your security risk and what safeguards are necessary.

Although not addressed in either the Privacy Rule or the Security Rule, if you participate in a health information exchange organization (HIO); are using the Nationwide Health Information Network—perhaps with Centers for Medicare and Medicaid Services (CMS) contractors to submit additional information for claims audits; have joined an accountable care organization, patient-centered medical home, or other type of health structure that broadens the scope of coordination of care beyond your practice; and/or are supporting use of personal health records for your patients, new forms of agreements are often involved. Many of these new relationships are just now forming, and most err on the side of extra protections. Be sure to document these relationships and consider how they may impact your security plans.

HOW TO USE THIS CHAPTER

This chapter establishes the context in which your office will manage its HIPAA security compliance. It describes:

- Organizational relationships
- Documentation for compliance
- Assignment of security responsibility

This chapter describes organizational relationships among covered entities and with non-covered entities. Because you are reading this book, it is assumed that you either are a covered entity under HIPAA or believe security is important to your office and your relationships with your patients and others with whom you share data. Hopefully it is both. If you are unsure if you are a covered entity, this chapter provides a quick tool for you to use to double-check your status.

No physician practice exists in isolation. Physicians are credentialed members of the medical staff at one or more hospitals. Your practice may be part of a larger covered entity or hybrid entity. You have relationships with other businesses with which PHI may be shared, whether in electronic format or not. Each relationship contributes a level of security risk to your office that should be on your radar screen as you plan your security efforts.

As you gather information about the organizational relationships in which you participate, you will need to establish a way to document your findings and your decisions. Such documentation may be recorded in policies, organization charts, statements of ownership, various agreements with other parties, etc. If you believe you are not a covered provider under HIPAA, it would be a good practice to write out your answers to the covered entity analysis tool ("Are You a Covered Entity?") in this chapter as evidence of the consideration you have given this. Also, if you have been given an exception by CMS for filing Medicare claims electronically, you should keep that as well. However, the principles of good security still apply.

Although breaches in confidentiality or a security incident may occur at any time, documentation of your ongoing efforts to implement appropriate safeguards will prove invaluable if you are required to supply evidence of your efforts. Documentation can be used to determine who is responsible for what security controls and can be used to ensure that all parties have carried out their responsibilities.

Finally, a key organizing factor for compliance with the HIPAA Security Rule is assigning responsibility for security management and security practices.

COVERED ENTITY STATUS

A covered entity is a person or organization that must comply with the HIPAA regulations. Expanded clarification of covered entities is discussed in the following paragraphs.

Health plans including Medicare, Medicaid, other government programs such as the Veterans Health Care Program and Indian Health Service, Blue Cross and Blue Shield plans, health maintenance organizations, commercial insurers, many employee welfare benefit plans, and any other individual or group plan that provides or pays for the cost of medical care are covered entities. (If your practice has a group health plan, it is covered under HIPAA as a health plan unless it has fewer than 50 participants and is self-administered.) That health plans are covered entities under HIPAA is the good news with respect to HIPAA. In general and with respect to the financial and administrative transactions and code sets requirements in particular, every health plan must comply with HIPAA regulations as do covered providers.

Healthcare clearinghouses are companies that convert the HIPAA financial and administrative transactions (eg, claims, eligibility inquiry, remittance advice) from nonstandard format to standard format or standard format back into nonstandard format. These include billing services, repricing companies, community health management information systems, value-added networks, and switches that direct the transmission of the transactions. However, not all billing services and other such companies are covered entities. Only those that perform conversion between the HIPAA financial and administrative standard and nonstandard transactions are covered clearinghouses. Clearinghouses can also be business associates when they perform not only the conversion process but also other services for your practice. This is important to recognize when identifying your business associates and understanding your security risk relative to the PHI included in transmission of financial and administrative transactions. For instance, e-prescribing networks, such as Surescripts, perform similar functions as healthcare clearinghouses, but are not covered entities. The HI-TECH Act (which provides incentives for meaningful use of EHR technology) clarifies that they are business associates.

Providers who transmit any health information in electronic form in connection with a HIPAA financial and administrative transaction are covered entities. Providers are individuals or entities that provide medical or health services or that furnish, bill, or are paid for health care in the normal course of business. Electronic form includes any of the following:

- Direct transmission of HIPAA (ASC X12N) standard transactions to a payer
- Direct data entry of transactions via a dedicated computer (eg, using a dumb terminal and dial-up connection) or Web browser
- Mailing transactions (whether in HIPAA standard format or not) via any electronic media such as floppy disk or CD to a clearinghouse to be transmitted on to the payer in electronic form
- Sending information on paper to a billing service or clearinghouse to be converted into a claim transaction or other designated HIPAA standards

Because the Administrative Simplification Compliance Act of 2001 (ASCA) required all but very small providers to file claims electronically with Medicare by October 16, 2003, virtually all physician offices are covered providers. Exceptions to the Medicare rule are made for providers with fewer than 10 full-time equivalent staff (including physicians), for suppliers with fewer than 25 full-time equivalent staff, or where a waiver is obtained from the secretary of HHS. Other health plans, such as some state Medicaid programs and a few commercial payers, also mandate or contractually require use of electronic transactions.

Are You a Covered Entity?

In summary, if you answer "yes" to either of the following questions, you are a covered entity under HIPAA:

1. Do you transmit or does someone on your behalf transmit electronic claims or use any form of direct data entry or other electronic form to check eligibility, obtain precertification or referral authorization, make claim status inquiries, and/or receive electronic remittances?
2. Do you employ 10 or more full-time equivalent staff (including physicians) and participate in Medicare?

Why Is Covered Entity Status Important to Security?

First, if you are a covered entity under HIPAA, you were required to start complying with the Security Rule by April 20, 2005. As well, there are requirements for ongoing activities to maintain your security practices consistent with changes in your environment.

Second, if you exchange PHI with a noncovered entity, permit access to PHI by a non-covered entity, or have a noncovered entity create PHI for you on your behalf, such a non-covered entity may be a business associate, in which case you must have a business associate contract in place between you and the business associate. You may also need a business associate contract with other covered entities if they perform services for you in a capacity other than as a member of your workforce. For example, if you have contracted with the hospital where you serve on the medical staff to perform professional billing services for you, the hospital is a business associate with respect to that purpose.

The Privacy Rule and Security Rule define business associates in the same manner, although each provides specifics in relationship to the standards being addressed. For example, under the Privacy Rule, business associate contracts must assure that the business associate is be able to make PHI available for access to the individual as applicable, provide information for the covered entity to account for disclosures, etc. Under the Security Rule, the business associate contract must require the business associate to report to the covered entity any security incident of which it becomes aware.

HITECH brings additional requirements with respect to the business associate. The business associate must notify the covered entity of a breach. The business associate contract, therefore, must include specifics on timeliness of reporting breaches, what information must be supplied, and how the breach notification will be handled (see Chapter 10). The relationship of business associates to the HIPAA Privacy Rule and Security Rule is also changing under HITECH. Although as of this writing specific regulations have not been promulgated, HITECH requires business associates to be directly accountable to certain aspects of the HIPAA Privacy Rule and Security Rule, and to be subject not only to contractual requirements established by their covered entity clients but also to enforcement directly by HHS. (More details on business associates and contracts required by the Security Rule are provided in Chapter 7.)

Business Associate Defined

A business associate is ". . . a person who on behalf of . . . a covered entity or of an organized healthcare arrangement in which the covered entity participates, but other than in the capacity of a member of the workforce . . . performs . . . a function involving use or disclosure of individually identifiable health information . . . or provides services . . . where the provision of the service involves the disclosure of individually identifiable health information . . . to the person" (§160.103).

Workforce Defined

Workforce is defined in HIPAA as "employees, volunteers, trainees, and other persons whose conduct, in the performance of work for a covered entity, is under the direct control of such entity, whether or not they are paid by the covered entity" (§160.103).

ORGANIZATIONAL RELATIONSHIPS

In addition to having relationships with business associates, you may be a part of one or more HIPAA-defined organizational relationships. These relationships describe how you may relate to other covered or noncovered entities.

Types of Covered Entity Relationships

The organizational relationships in which you are likely to participate are described in the following paragraphs.

Affiliated covered entities (ACE) are "legally separate covered entities that may designate themselves (including any healthcare component of such covered entity) as a single affiliated covered entity for purposes of [compliance with the Privacy Rule and Security Rule], if all of the covered entities designated are under common ownership or control" (§164.105[b]). Common ownership exists if an entity possesses an ownership or equity interest of 5% or more in another entity.

Common control exists if an entity has the power, directly or indirectly, to significantly influence or direct the actions or policies of another entity. Integrated delivery networks frequently have common ownership and control over multiple, legally separate covered entities. They generally are interested in designating these entities as ACEs in order to achieve economies of scale in compliance with HIPAA.

A formal, written designation is required for the creation of ACE status. If you have not entered into such a designation with another covered entity that has at least partial ownership or control of your practice, you may want to investigate this.

The advantages of the ACE designation are primarily economies of scale, in which you may share the same notice of privacy practices (NPP), privacy and security policies and procedures, business associate contracting, and other HIPAA activities. Members of an ACE can have access to one another's health information for operational purposes, such as quality assurance. Although some lessening of autonomy may seem like a disadvantage under ACE status, there would not necessarily be more or less control than what common ownership or common control already permits.

Another way in which you may be in an ACE status (especially if you have a mid-to-large-sized practice) is if you have a self-insured employee health plan. Unless this health plan is self-administered and has fewer than 50 participants, it is a covered entity (and the third-party administrator is a business associate of the health plan). Not only must the health plan comply with all requirements of HIPAA, including the ability to send and receive the HIPAA standard transactions and code sets, but it can also be desig-nated with you as an ACE. You should be aware that there are special Privacy Rule pro-visions for group health plans, including some differences in how the NPP is provided as well as some exceptions to administrative requirements. The Privacy Rule also forbids you to use information from the group health plan to make employment-related deci-sions about individuals.

An organized healthcare arrangement (OHCA) is another organizational relationship that HIPAA defines. An OHCA may exist because there is "a clinically integrated care setting in which individuals typically receive health care from more than one healthcare provider, an organized system of health care in which more than one covered entity participates and in which the participating covered entities hold themselves out to the public as participating in a joint arrangement and participating in joint activities that include at least . . . utilization review . . . quality assessment and improvement . . . or payment activities . . ." (§160.103). It also provides for HIPAA economies of scale but does not require common ownership or common control.

This is a looser relationship than exists in the ACE status, but there is no sharing of risk relative to compliance because there is no sharing of ownership or control. HIPAA does not require formal designation of an OHCA, although most covered entities do document the relationship, and all members of an OHCA must be stated in any common NPP. Members of a hospital's medical staff, for example, may be considered a part of an OHCA with the hospital. If you are a member of the medical staff of a hospital that is treating itself as an OHCA, you do not need a separate NPP for your practice at the hospital, and you will be required to comply with the hospital's privacy practices when practicing there. Generally, formal action by a vote of the medical staff is taken to con-firm this. Again, if you are a member of the medical staff at one or more hospitals and have not been notified of such a relationship, you may want to determine whether such a structure exists and what it may do for you relative to HIPAA.

A hybrid entity is a "single legal entity that is a covered entity whose business activities include both covered functions and noncovered functions, and that designates healthcare components as covered components" (§164.103). The most frequent examples of hybrid entities are universities that have medical school faculty who are healthcare providers, gov-ernments (state, county, local, tribal) that provide healthcare services such as in a public health department, and other businesses that include provider or health plan functions, such as a company-run clinic or self-insured health plan. If you fall into this category, you should understand the requirements for designation of healthcare components under HIPAA (§164.105).

Other Relationships

For completeness and comparison purposes, there are two other relationships that exist within HIPAA—the limited data set recipient and the trading partner. These are described in the following paragraphs.

A limited data set recipient is an individual or entity that has received from a covered entity, in accordance with a data use agreement, a set of PHI that has had most, but not all, identifiers removed.

HIPAA's Privacy Rule requires the removal of 18 different identifiers to de-identify data. Increasingly, there are issues surrounding how business associates who process data on behalf of covered entities are using the data, including whether they are fully de-identifying the data when such a practice is agreed to in the business associate contract. Use Figure 4.1 as a checklist.

FIGURE 4.1

Identifiers Required to Be Removed to De-identify Data

The following identifiers of the individual or of relatives, employers, or household members of the individual must be removed:

- Patient's name
- Address, except state and the initial three digits of the zip code in geographic units containing more than 20,000 people
- All elements of dates (except year) of birth, admission, discharge, death; and all ages over 89 and all elements of dates (including year) indicative of such age, except that such ages and elements may be aggregated into a single category of age 90 or older
- Telephone numbers
- Fax numbers
- E-mail addresses
- Social security numbers
- Health plan beneficiary numbers
- Medical record numbers
- Account numbers
- Certificate/license numbers
- Vehicle identifiers and serial numbers, including license plate numbers
- Device identifiers and serial numbers
- Web universal resource locators (URLs)
- Internet protocol (IP) address numbers
- Biometric identifiers, including fingerprints and voice prints
- Full-face photographic images and comparable images
- Any other unique identifying number, characteristic, or code, except as permitted in this list; and for which the covered entity does not have actual knowledge that the information could be used alone or in combination with other information to identify an individual who is a subject of the information

---

Once de-identified, the information is no longer considered protected and may be used and disclosed without patient authorization or other agreement. However, this information may be proprietary business information that you will want to keep confidential aside from HIPAA reasons.

A limited data set is similar to de-identified information because most identifiers are removed. However, it retains the patient's city, state, and zip code information as well as all dates. This set of data is still considered PHI. It may only be disclosed for the purpose of research, public health, and operations and only when a data use agreement has been signed by the recipient of the data set.

Physician offices increasingly need to be assured either that de-identification is occurring correctly or that a limited data set is used under the proper agreement. No longer are de-identified data used only by physicians involved in clinical trials or other research, but they are often used in ways of which providers may not be aware. For example, participation in many of the new health reform structures will necessitate aggregation of data and analysis that helps providers understand their patient population and coordinate their healthcare needs, but will create a store of data subject to potential other uses.

In 2012, the Food and Drug Administration (FDA) proposed adoption of the unique device identifier (UDI) system that would improve evaluation of medical devices and support recalls. It included in the proposed regulation that no PHI would be used; however, an EHR vendor or surgery information system (SIS) vendor may collect these data on behalf of a provider for submission to the FDA, and, in turn, use the data directly or sell the data to others. EHR vendors have a huge amount of access to PHI. Even in a client/server environment where PHI is maintained in your own practice-housed server, a vendor needs to have access to your systems to help support them, troubleshoot system problems, and supply upgrades. EHR products are increasingly being offered through an application service provider (ASP) where the EHR is delivered over the Web or through software as a service (SaaS), where the software is built on a Web-services architecture and is maintained in the cloud. In addition, many EHR vendors offer discounts to providers who agree to contribute their data for population analytics.

In fact, "big data analytics" is a new term that has been created to describe analysis of large volumes of data to provide feedback in the form of evidence-based medicine in near real time. Some EHR vendors even have direct sales built into their products, so that as data are entered by the provider, ads for certain drugs, devices, or other services may be offered specific to the needs of that patient. Not only must the vendor analyze the data as being entered to supply the applicable ad, but it may also use click-stream analysis to further contact you—or your patient—to sell directly. It is not that these services are illegal or not in compliance with HIPAA—so long as the provisions in the business associate contract are very clear and specific as to what you choose to permit within the constraints afforded by the Privacy Rule and Security Rule.

A trading partner is a person or entity who is a party to an exchange of electronic transactions with another person or entity. If your office connects directly with a payer to send electronic claims, you and the payer are trading partners.

Frequently, a trading partner agreement will be used to specify the duties and responsibilities of each party in the exchange of the transactions. This may describe the telecommunications requirements, establish security requirements, and provide for other contractual obligations between the parties to the agreement. As part of your Security Rule compliance activities, review any trading partner agreements you have now or will receive in the future and ensure that they address appropriate security controls.

HIPAA does not require a trading partner agreement, although it does specify that participants in electronic transactions may not have a trading partner agreement that changes the HIPAA transaction standards.

What Is the Difference Between a Business Associate and a Trading Partner?

A business associate is anyone outside of your workforce who has access to PHI in the course of assisting you with your operations, including obtaining payment. This may be a contract transcriptionist, an information system vendor with remote access, or your malpractice insurance carrier. HIPAA requires you to have a contract with all business associates so they will safeguard PHI. A trading partner is usually a health plan or healthcare clearinghouse/billing service with whom you electronically exchange financial and administrative transactions. HIPAA does not require an agreement with a trading partner, but it is a good idea. A trading partner agreement describes technical aspects, including security measures, of how the transactions will be transmitted.

Table 4.1 provides a summary of the key attributes of each type of HIPAA relationship that may exist between a physician office and another person or organization.

TABLE 4.1

Summary of HIPAA Relationships

	Business Associate	Affiliated Covered Entity	Organized Healthcare Arrange-ment	Hybrid Entity	Limited Data Set Recipient	Trading Partner
Applicable rule(s)	Privacy, Security	Privacy, Security	Privacy, Security	Privacy, Security	Privacy	Transactions and Code Sets
Required?	Yes	No	No	Yes	Yes	No
Purpose of relation-ship	Establish protections for PHI	Economies of scale	Economies of scale	Establish separa-tion	Protect limited data set	Engage in electronic commerce
Documen-tation	Business associate contract and other agreements	Designa-tion	None required, strongly rec-ommended	Designa-tion	Data use agreement	Trading part-ner agreement (optional)
Documen-tation origi-nated by	Covered entity	Covered entity	Covered entity	Hybrid entity	Covered entity	Trading partner
With whom	Business associate	Owned/ controlled covered entity	Nonowned/ controlled covered entity	Covered compo-nents	Researcher, public health, covered entity, or business associate for opera-tions	Covered entity

Reprinted with permission from Margret\A Consulting, LLC.

SAFEGUARD REQUIREMENTS

Your organizational relationships will determine your overall responsibility for implementing security safeguards. For example, if you are part of an accountable care organization, consider whether it is an ACE or an OCHA (see definitions in the previous section of this chapter), or has no relationship with respect to HIPAA—in which case you need to safeguard PHI in the same manner as you would when you share PHI with any other provider for treatment purposes today. Although HIPAA permits such sharing without patient authorization, many providers are seeking patient authorization—either to be "on the safe side" or to be more transparent with their patients.

The following describes the extent to which your security requirements may be impacted by your relationships.

No Relationships

If you have no organizational relationships, your risk of other entities' accessing your information is minimal. However, the compliance burden is totally on your shoulders. Most physicians have at least business associate relationships, increasingly have trading partner relationships, and even more recently find themselves sharing PHI with other providers and patients more directly than ever before. These relationships do not reduce your compliance requirements, but should receive extra attention and may extend compliance requirements to noncovered entities.

Hybrid Entity Relationship

If you are in a hybrid entity situation, you may have significant risk from noncovered components potentially accessing your information, but the risk is not yours alone. The risk is borne by the organization as a whole. You have an employee–employer obligation to point out needed security measures and to help ensure compliance.

ACE or OHCA Relationship

As previously noted, if you are in an ACE, your security decisions may be made, to a degree, based on the nature of your information systems and the extent of common ownership and control of your office. If your information systems are currently integrated within the structure that constitutes the ACE, you may already be relying on the organization's overall security program for many technical controls and possibly some administrative and physical controls. However, be aware that your office must still review its administrative and physical security practices and determine if the technical controls offered by the larger organization meet what is believed to be prudent for your office. You may decide to participate in an overall security-planning program for the ACE. Whether you do so or not, document the controls that are provided by the larger organization. Then check off the controls you believe meet your risk requirements and those you will either work on with the larger organization to seek improvements in or manage yourself.

If you are in an OHCA, your security efforts may still rely to some extent on whether or not your information systems are integrated within those of the larger organization. However, since the OHCA is a relationship of convenience, not a risk-sharing relationship, you are solely responsible for fully complying with the HIPAA security requirements, whether you share information systems or not. You must comply either by ensuring that the organization from which you purchase information systems services is providing the security you need or by providing the security on your own. Document whether you purchase or provide your own information services and how the security requirements are addressed.

If you believe the existing security measures do not meet your needs, you must take one of the following actions:

- Work with the organization to improve security measures
- Acquire information systems services from another organization that provides stronger security measures
- Bring the information systems in house and manage the security yourself

DOCUMENTATION

In describing organizational relationships and your responsibility for safeguarding your PHI, you must document all findings and decisions. Some physicians may be concerned that such documentation can be a risk factor in itself. There are important considerations related to this documentation discussed in the following paragraphs.

Managing Your Documentation

Generally speaking, "documentation defends its friends." Good documentation generally supports any situation in which an action is called into question. In health care, the mantra is "if it's not documented, it wasn't done." This is also true in security.

No documentation or poor documentation does not mean that you do not have a security risk. In fact, the better the documentation, the more likely it is for an external investigator to believe that an undocumented risk did not previously exist. Your diligence in documenting risks and your decisions relative to them can demonstrate that you made the effort to identify as many risks as reasonable and practical. If one is overlooked, you are much less likely to be faulted than if your documentation is poor or nonexistent and you attempt to claim the risk was not previously present.

A documented risk must be addressed; otherwise, you could be in violation of the compliance requirements. Addressing a risk does not mean that you must institute the most expensive solution available. In fact, HIPAA states that the purpose of identifying risks is to decide the appropriate level of controls. Not identifying a security risk because you do not want to address it is no excuse!

Documentation Requirements

Both the Privacy Rule and the Security Rule require documentation of policies and procedures, as well as of actions, activities, assessments, or designations.

The Privacy Rule and Security Rule include standards on policies and procedures (§164.530[i] and §164.316[a], respectively). The standards indicate that the policies and procedures should be designed taking into account the size of the covered entity and the types of activities related to PHI that are undertaken by the covered entity. This clearly reflects that organizations have different work flows, technical capabilities, and needs. Although the Privacy Rule requires that any changes in policies and procedures be reflected in the organization's NPPs, the Security Rule permits changes at any time, provided they are documented and made in accordance with the rule.

Policies

HIPAA does not define the term *policy*, nor does it specify the content of policies. Rather, it relies on standard business practices for policy development. Policies, however, are not necessarily easy to write. The following guidance is offered to ensure that your policies are developed in as effective and efficient a manner as possible.

The purpose of a policy is to:

- Guide members of the workforce in taking action that is consistent with legal, ethical, and organizational requirements
- Conform to applicable laws and the requirements of licensing and accrediting agencies
- Reflect the mission and culture of the organization

Well-written policies:

- Establish measurable objectives and expectations for everyone within the organization
- Assign responsibility for decision making and a frame of reference for action
- Define enforcement and consequences for violations

Procedures

HIPAA does not define the term *procedure*. Procedures are understood to be explicit, step-by-step instructions that implement the organization's policies. Procedures may be modified within organizational units or departments. However, this variation must not change the intent of the overall policy for which the procedures are providing direction.

Procedures, with respect to an action, explain:

- What is to be done
- When it is to be done
- Where it is to be done
- Who is to do it
- Exactly how it is to be done

Policies and procedures may be written and maintained as a single document, or they may be two separate documents. In general, it is a good idea to include policy statements with procedures because procedures are intended to carry out policies. However, it may not be advisable to add procedures to some privacy and security policy documents. Some security procedures need to be very specific, including identifying IP addresses for ports to keep open or the day of the week that the backup vendor picks up backup tapes. This information should be considered highly sensitive information that not everyone in the practice needs to know and that people who do not need to know it could be put at risk for knowing. A sample policy and procedure on developing security policies and procedures is provided in Figure 4.2.

F I G U R E   4.2

Sample Policy and Procedure

Title: Documentation of Security Policies and Procedures	Number:
Date Effective:	Approved by:
Date(s) Reviewed/Revised/Retired:	By:

POLICY

A. Policy: This office will establish and maintain policies and procedures as applicable to direct the establishment and use of reasonable security measures to safeguard the confidentiality, integrity, and availability of all protected health information (PHI) in accordance with the Health Insurance Portability and Accountability Act of 1996 (HIPAA) Security Rule, other state and federal regulations, and other applicable governing bodies.

B. Definitions:

Policy: A statement that guides action consistent with legal, ethical, and organizational requirements.

Procedure: Instructions for carrying out the intent of policy.

PHI: Individually identifiable health information.

PROCEDURE

The information security officer will:

1. Obtain and review reference material to understand regulatory and other requirements with respect to the security of PHI and other confidential or sensitive information.

2. Conduct, document, and periodically review, in association with the office's governance body, a security risk analysis to determine the office's vulnerabilities and threats with respect to security requirements.

3. Develop and maintain an information security plan that identifies solutions for how these risk factors will be reduced. Working with the office's information systems vendors, solutions take into account:

   a. Size, complexity, and capabilities of the office

   b. Technical infrastructure, hardware, and software security capabilities

(continued)

FIGURE 4.2 (continued)

Sample Policy and Procedure

> c. Costs of security measures
>
> d. Probability and criticality of potential risks to PHI and other confidential and sensitive information
>
> 4. For each security requirement, create or revise an existing policy and procedure that documents actions and instructions for implementing the security solution.
>
> 5. Retire any existing policy and procedure that is contradictory to a newly created policy and procedure.
>
> 6. Test the policy to ensure that it can be understood by all and fits the office's environment.
>
> 7. Obtain approval for the new or revised policy from the office's governance body.
>
> 8. Train all members of the workforce on the new policy and all applicable members of the workforce on the new procedure.
>
> 9. Retain documentation of the policy and procedure for six years from the date when it last was in effect.
>
> 10. Review the security policies and procedures as any changes occur in the office's information systems, as new technology becomes available, when there are new or modified regulations, or otherwise biannually.

Reprinted with permission from Margret\A Consulting, LLC.

Retention of Policies and Procedures

HIPAA requires documentation to be retained for six years from the date of its creation or the date when it last was in effect, whichever is later. Many organizations prefer to keep their policies for the duration of the organization's existence and their procedures for the six years required by HIPAA or state law. They keep policies for a longer period of time because actions taken by long-term members of the workforce may need to be tracked back to the policy that was in effect at the time the action was taken. State laws on business records in general, statutes of limitations, and professional licensure, as well as requirements imposed by malpractice insurance carriers and others, are also useful in determining the applicable retention period for documentation. The HIPAA six-year period should be considered the minimum retention period for documents associated with its regulations. HIPAA documentation does not have to be retained in paper form. It may be created and maintained permanently in electronic form, providing the date of creation and any modifications can be identified.

Tracking Policies and Procedures

If policies and procedures applicable to security are included in policies and procedures that are broader than security (perhaps privacy and security, all of compliance, or employment), it is a good idea to track the policies and procedures in which each security standard is addressed. A document management tool, such as the one shown in Table 4.2, can be used to identify what policies and procedures are needed for each HIPAA security requirement and then to track them over time. A security requirement may be addressed by more than one policy; this can easily be reflected in the documentation management tool. If an investigation requires evidence of policies and procedures relating to specific standards, this tool can also be used.

For example, although a physician's office may have a separate policy on sanctions, frequently the office will have an employee handbook or other general policy on employment practices that addresses sanctions. The office may also have bylaws for the medical staff that address sanctions. In addition, the Privacy Rule has a standard on sanctions, so whatever sanction policy is created to meet the Security Rule requirements should also meet the Privacy Rule requirements.

TABLE 4.2

Documentation Management Tool

Security Standard	Existing Policy, Procedure Form	Create? Revise? Retire?	New Document(s)	Responsible	Date Completed	Date Approved
1. Security management process—Risk analysis	None	Create	Security Risk Analysis	Information security official (ISO)		
2. Security management process—Risk management	None	Create	Security Risk Management Policy	ISO		
3. Security management process—Sanction policy	Employee handbook, medical staff bylaws	Revise		Office manager, chief medical officer (CMO)		
4. Security management process—Information system activity review	Internal audit	Retire	Information system activity review procedure and checklist	Information technology (IT) staff member		
6. Workforce security—Authorization and/or supervision	(Practice only)	Create	Workforce security policy and procedure	Office manager		

Reprinted with permission from Margret\A Consulting, LLC.

Actions, Activities, Designations, or Assessments

In addition to policies and procedures, HIPAA's Privacy Rule and Security Rule require that actions, activities, designations (privacy), or assessments (security) be documented and retained for six years. Actions and activities refer to anything that has been performed and must be documented according to HIPAA regulations. For example, the Security Rule requires that security incidents and their outcomes be documented. The Privacy Rule requires that denial of requests for amendment be in writing to the individual. Designations are those documents used to identify affiliated covered entities and other organizational relationships. Assessments refer to the identification of your potential risks and vulnerabilities to the confidentiality, integrity, and availability of electronic PHI. Case Study 4.1 illustrates a scenario in which such documentation was lacking and significantly impacted an emergency department physician group.

CASE STUDY 4.1
Documentation Defends Its Friends

A man was brought by his wife to the emergency department with chest pain. A physician assessed the patient's condition and after initial stabilization, including some respiratory therapy, determined that the patient was fit to go home. The physician dictated a summary of the visit, and the respiratory therapist handwrote comments on the therapy. Unfortunately, the man died that evening, and his wife sued the hospital, the independent physician group, and the physician. During discovery, the defendant's attorney reviewed the patient's emergency department record, in which there was inconsistency in information between the physician and therapist, with apparent inconsistencies in the date/time of the dictation and transcription. In pursuing how such inconsistencies occurred, the hospital claimed that the dictation information system crashed at the time the physician was dictating and that the physician was requested to re-dictate the summary when it was discovered that part of the dictation was missing. However, there was no record of a system crash and no documented request for re-dictation. In the meantime, findings from an expert medical witness suggested that there was no mismanagement of the care of the patient. The settlement, however, was significantly more than what might have been had documentation surrounding the dictation not suggested an attempt to cover up something.

Assigned Security Responsibility

The HIPAA Security Rule requires assignment of a security official to be responsible for the development and implementation of the policies and procedures required in the rule (§164.308[a][2]). This individual is frequently referred to as an information security official (ISO) to distinguish from protective services personnel who aid personal safety and security.

The question often arises as to who should be the ISO and what the ISO's responsibilities are, which then leads to consideration about reporting relationships. The ISO should be knowledgeable about information security practices. In addition, the individual should be someone who is a good communicator and trainer, with the ability to be aware and create awareness concerning potential information security issues. The ISO's primary responsibilities are to develop, implement, and maintain the security policies and procedures. But this is more than just documentation. It is making the actual determination of what controls and services are needed, implementing them, training users, and maintaining documentation. Figure 4.3 identifies the general responsibilities of the ISO and may be used for compiling a job description.

The ISO may be a staff member or contracted support. If there are not sufficient skills within the office to staff this position directly, the person designated for this responsibility should have contract support or the office might want to outsource the ISO function entirely. Whoever is designated, the ISO should not be the same person who is your primary information technology (IT) staff member (or the chief information officer in a large practice). The ISO should report directly to the CEO or compliance officer. The ISO needs to be unbiased. An ISO that reports to IT may feel pressure to overlook certain things that IT has difficulty implementing or to not report inappropriate actions relative to how security is handled in IT. Many small practices do well with designating the office manager or com-

FIGURE 4.3

Responsibilities of the Information Security Official

The information security official (ISO) should be able to:

- Develop and manage administrative processes, including policies and procedures
- Understand and work with technical staff, vendors, and consultants to develop and maintain security technology
- Understand and work with staff responsible for physical security, including security consultants and vendors
- Maintain records documenting the organization's rationale for its security policies and procedures, the policies and procedures themselves, and related forms and records
- Coordinate policy and procedure development, internal complaint processing, and enforcement with the information privacy official (IPO)
- Collaborate with the IPO regarding the analysis and resolution of joint security and privacy issues that arise
- Communicate with all members of the workforce including providing training, selecting controls, and describing the risk analysis to practice leadership

pliance officer as the ISO and then also using a contractor who is a security expert and who can also provide an unbiased perspective. Figure 4.4 illustrates a common organizational structure, which would need to be adjusted based on the size of the organization.

The amount of external assistance you need depends on the sophistication of your information technology infrastructure and staff available to support it. Your ISO should not be providing day-to-day security measures for the same reason the ISO should not report to IT. Your information systems vendor(s) should assure that your needs are met based on your risk analysis. You may also find that some external assistance in conducting the risk analysis provides an unbiased view, the ability to share lessons learned from other similar organizations, and pointers to the most appropriate tools. Security risk analysis can be performed without such assistance, but using external assistance is a best practice. On an ongoing basis, you may want independent assessments to validate your ongoing compliance.

Others in the office also must be involved in information security management. It is strongly recommended that the information privacy official (IPO) not be the same individual as the ISO. The knowledge and skills required are quite different, as the IPO role is much less technical and more focused on working with people, privacy protections, and privacy rights. However, as previously noted, privacy and security are inextricably linked. The IPO and ISO should coordinate their activities. One area of great importance is with respect to privacy breaches and security incidents. Security incidents can often cause privacy breaches. Likewise, there is a direct relationship between the Privacy Rule's minimum necessary requirement and access controls in the Security Rule. In general information security theory, this is called "need to know," and who may access what information is based on the need to know.

Your chief medical officer (CMO), board of directors, and partners also have key roles. This is especially true when you are defining your level of risk tolerance and approving security policies and associated controls for which they are paying. Physicians are also the primary users of the information that needs to be protected, and their attention to privacy and security sets the tone for the entire office.

Last but not least, every individual in the office has a responsibility for personally managing how he or she uses information security services.

FIGURE 4.4

Organizational Structure Illustrating ISO and IPO Relationships

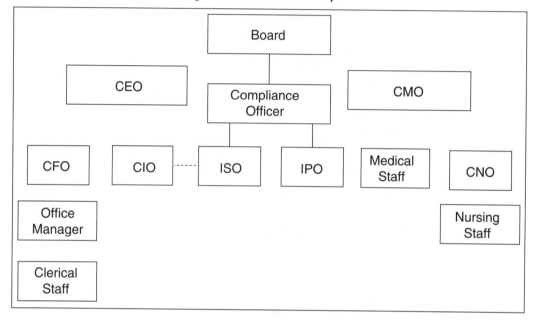

RISK-BASED DECISION MAKING

You are now ready to learn how to conduct a security risk analysis. Remember, although your information security policies should be readily accessible to members of your workforce, information about your risks and their mitigation procedures should be treated with the utmost confidentiality and their identification aided by a knowledgeable ISO. Not everyone in your office should have access to security services documentation.

CHECK YOUR UNDERSTANDING*

1. Which of the following is *not* a HIPAA covered entity?
   a. Commercial lab
   b. Health insurance company
   c. Hospital
   d. Information systems vendor

2. An example of a hybrid entity under HIPAA is:
   a. Grocery store with retail clinic
   b. Hospital with reference lab
   c. Physician office with co-located pharmacy
   d. Nursing home with hospice services

3. What is a policy?
   a. Agreement to abide by specified terms
   b. Guidance on decision making
   c. Instructions on what is to be done
   d. Record of action

4. Documentation associated with HIPAA must be retained for at least:
    a. 6 years
    b. 20 years
    c. State statute of limitations
    d. As long as practice is in existence

5. Which of the following should be shared with all of your employees?
    a. Incident tracking and response
    b. Results of network analysis
    c. Security policies
    d. Security procedures

Match each entity or documentation type to its definition:

6. Business associate agreement ___

7. Trading partner ___

8. Healthcare clearinghouse ___

9. Affiliated covered entities ___

10. Organized healthcare arrangement ___

    a. Legally separate covered entities that may designate themselves as a single covered
       entity for purposes of HIPAA compliance
    b. Clinically integrated care where providers hold themselves out to the public as
       participating in a joint arrangement; provides HIPAA economies of scale without
       common ownership or control
    c. Any party (covered entity or noncovered entity) to an exchange of (any) electronic
       transactions
    d. A HIPAA covered entity that converts financial and administrative transactions from
       nonstandard format to standard format or standard format back into nonstandard
       format for the convenience of health plans and/or providers
    e. An alternative term used by the federal government to establish a relationship
       between a covered entity and a noncovered entity for purposes of assuring
       compliance with the HIPAA Privacy Rule and Security Rule

*For answers, refer to the Answer Key at the end of the book.

chapter 5

Security Risk Analysis

The very first standard in the HIPAA Security Rule is the Security Management Process. Performing such a process sets the stage for determining how you will become compliant with the Security Rule and its standards. The implementation specifications of risk analysis and management are the keys to identifying and selecting the services you will use to manage your security risk.

HOW TO USE THIS CHAPTER

This chapter:

- Defines security risk analysis and its relationship to security risk management
- Describes how to conduct a risk analysis
- Offers tools to assist you in performing and documenting your risk analysis and risk management
- Emphasizes the importance of keeping the security risk analysis up-to-date

Review this chapter before you go on to the remainder of this book. As you read the subsequent chapters, which contain specific information about the Security Rule standards, consider what risks exist in your environment and either document them or return to this chapter to study risk analysis in more depth and then document your analysis.

RISK ANALYSIS AND RISK MANAGEMENT REQUIREMENTS

Risk analysis and risk management are complementary functions. Risk analysis is performed to determine your current security risks, and risk management is the ongoing process of ensuring that these security risks are kept under control. You cannot eliminate all security risk, but you can understand the level of risk you have through risk analysis and keep the risk at an acceptable level through risk management.

Implementation Specifications

Risk analysis is a required implementation specification (§164.308[1][ii][A]) within the HIPAA Security Management Process standard. It requires you to "conduct an accurate and thorough assessment of the potential risks and vulnerabilities to the confidentiality, integrity, and availability of electronic protected health information (ePHI) held by the covered entity."

The Risk Management implementation specification (§164.308[1][ii][B]) is complementary to risk analysis and is also required by HIPAA. It calls for you to "implement security measures sufficient to reduce risks and vulnerabilities to a reasonable and appropriate level to comply with [the general requirements of the Security Rule]."

Although risk analysis and risk management are required standards for HIPAA compliance, other federal regulations also either imply the need for or explicitly require a security risk analysis. The Health Information Technology for Economic and Clinical Health (HITECH) Act requires breach notification that implies the need for a risk analysis and management process. HITECH also mandated modifications to the HIPAA Privacy Rule and Security Rule, adoption of which will require a review of the security risk analysis. As of the writing of this book, the modifications have not been issued as final regulations. However, in some cases the proposed modifications clarify current Privacy Rule requirements, and in other cases they strengthen requirements. HITECH's meaningful use incentive program explicitly requires risk analysis as one of the measures that must be performed to earn the incentives. In addition, the risk analysis process is a basic security function performed in much the same way in all segments of our society to assure the confidentiality, integrity, and availability of confidential or sensitive information.

Flexible Approach

The risk analysis and risk management standards of HIPAA have introduced a new concept for health care with respect to complying with regulations. Typically, physicians look to government regulations to be very specific, and their response to regulations typically has been: "Tell me exactly what I have to do and I'll (try to) do it." HIPAA is different. Even where the Privacy Rule is relatively proscriptive, it calls for reasonable measures to be taken with respect to the standards.

The Security Rule is even less proscriptive than the Privacy Rule. In fact, you decide what your potential risks and vulnerabilities are, and then you decide how to apply safeguards within the framework of the Security Rule. In explaining the concept of risk analysis and risk management in the preamble to the rule, the government notes: "This [Security Management Process] and its component implementation specifications form the foundation upon which an entity's necessary security activities are built" (Preamble to Security Standards; Final Rule, Federal Register, Vol. 68, No. 34, February 20, 2003, p. 8446).

To enforce the rule, the government looks for a documented risk analysis and evidence of risk management. The risk analysis must be periodically reassessed and updated to keep security measures current. For example, software applications change, computer hardware is upgraded, new security (hardware and software) tools become available, and your environment changes in other ways. As an example, there is increasing risk of medical identity theft. Your practice needs to be aware of this and take appropriate measures both to avoid being a victim of a stolen identity acquired somewhere else and being a source of theft for a stolen identity to be used elsewhere. As there is an increasing electronic exchange of health information with other providers, health plans, patients, public health departments, and others, transmission security becomes increasingly important. You will need to determine the impact these and other changes have on your security and take necessary steps to update security processes and services.

RISK ANALYSIS AND RISK MANAGEMENT PROCESS

A risk analysis involves identifying risks and vulnerabilities. The risk management process then requires that you implement security measures sufficient to reduce these risks and vulnerabilities to a reasonable and appropriate level. This level must comply with the general requirements of the Security Rule, including the safeguard requirements in the Privacy Rule.

HIPAA General Security Requirements (§164.306[a])

Covered entities must do the following:

1. Ensure the confidentiality, integrity, and availability of all PHI the covered entity creates, receives, maintains, or transmits.
2. Protect against any reasonably anticipated threats or hazards to the security or integrity of such information.
3. Protect against any reasonably anticipated uses or disclosures of PHI that are not permitted or required under [the Privacy Rule].
4. Ensure compliance with [the Security Rule] by its workforce.

HIPAA references the National Institute of Standards and Technology (NIST; part of the US Department of Commerce) publication "Risk Management Guide for Information Technology Systems" (Special Publication 800-30) as a source of guidance for conducting a risk analysis. The process included in the NIST document is very comprehensive and fairly technical. The basic principles are adapted in this book for physician practices.

The NIST guidelines and the HIPAA implementation specifications are based on the premise that threats can target vulnerabilities to cause harm. The objective is to reduce your risk of that happening. The Security Rule indicates that "covered entities may use any security measures that allow [them] to reasonably and appropriately implement the standards and implementation specifications as specified [in the Security Rule]" (§164.306[b][1]). It further specifies that

> a covered entity must take into account the following factors:
>
> ■ Size, complexity, and capabilities of the covered entity
> ■ Covered entity's technical infrastructure, hardware, and software security capabilities
> ■ Costs of security measures
> ■ Probability and criticality of potential risks to PHI (§164.306(b)[2])

Prepare to Conduct a Risk Analysis

Because it is so important to document your risk analysis for any compliance review purposes—whether for internal review or external audit—it can be helpful to maintain a security risk analysis documentation program. This can be a simple spreadsheet, as illustrated in Figure 5.1.

In using the spreadsheet illustrated in Figure 5.1, your office may wish to post only high-level summary information, keeping more detailed documentation in associated files. Using a spreadsheet, however, enables you to also use it as a project plan when the risk analysis findings suggest the need for updated policies, procedures, practices, or technical controls. The following steps are recommended for undertaking an initial risk analysis. Once a baseline analysis is performed, each element can then be easily reviewed.

Security Risk Defined

Risk is a function of the probability of a threat attacking a vulnerability and resulting in critical impact on your practice.

Reprinted with permission from Margret\A Consulting, LLC.

FIGURE 5.1

Risk Analysis and Management Form

Security Rule Requirement	Vulnerability	Potential Threat	Probability	Criticality	Risk Score	Control (Date Implemented)
Security Awareness and Training—Reminders (§164.308[a][5])	Specific training on security has not been provided, and no reminders are posted	Workers not accountable for selecting weak passwords, which were compromised by terminated employee and used to gain access to confidential information	Medium	High	6	Annual training; immediate termination of all worker access privileges (January 2005)
Workstation Use (§164.310[b])	No policy exists on workstation use, and everyone has Internet access	Workers could think it is acceptable to download executable software that launches a denial of service attack	Low	Medium	2	Workstation use policy; Internet access for select workstations only (July 2004)

Reprinted with permission from Margret\A Consulting, LLC.

Take the following steps to conduct your risk analysis:

1. Understand your information security management practices, including information flow, information processing, information system functions, and security policies and procedures.
2. Identify threats in your environment.
3. Identify vulnerabilities in your environment that threats could attack.
4. Determine the probability that a threat could attack a vulnerable asset, analyze the criticality of the impact, and summarize your risk.
5. Implement applicable security measures.
6. Document your analysis process and results.

Understand Your Information Security Management Practices

A first step in conducting or updating a risk analysis is to identify the information you want to protect and how it flows through your office as it is processed.

Information to be protected will obviously include PHI. You may decide, however, to also include other confidential or sensitive information. The controls put on the different types of information do not have to be exactly the same, although the functions you will consider will be the same. For example, HIPAA requires that there be access controls for PHI. But you may decide that certain other information that is not particularly confidential but troublesome to recreate should it be destroyed would not require access controls but only backup. A record of the security training your staff has taken would not be confidential, but its loss could put you at risk if your security practices were audited and you could not produce documentation of training. Alternatively, your payroll information is not PHI, but would be confidential information you would want secured with access controls.

In order to keep the risk analysis process relatively simple and straightforward, it is recommended that you identify not more than two or three general types of information (these might for example include "PHI," "Other confidential," and "Other secured"). Security practices for PHI must meet or exceed the Security Rule requirements. For other confidential information, you may decide to apply the same practices as for PHI, or even enhance them. Keep a list of what you consider confidential information. For other information that needs to be secured but is not confidential, also keep a list. You may select only certain security practices for these. Determining what to secure, and how to secure it, should be decided by the practice's board in consultation with the information security official (ISO).

After you have identified and categorized the types of information you want to secure, evaluate how the information flows as it is processed in the office and beyond. This is as important for PHI as for other information. Most PHI follows the patient during an office visit, but before and after the visit there are many internal processes and external transmissions that are often not considered during a risk analysis. To ensure a complete understanding of information flow it can be helpful to ask each person in the practice, including all physicians and other providers, to capture this information on a checklist, such as in

FIGURE 5.2

Information Flow Checklist

Please check all of the information you use:

❏ Patient information during visit
❏ Patient information prior to visit
  ○ Registration
  ○ Eligibility verification
  ○ Schedule
  ○ Chart review
  ○ Other (please identify): _____
❏ Patient information after visit
  ○ Coding and/or billing
  ○ Patient accounts
  ○ Quality
  ○ Patient care follow-up
  ○ Submission of data to a registry (eg, immunization, HEDIS, etc)
  ○ Coordination of care with other providers
  ○ Summary for patient or other as directed by patient
  ○ Clinical trials or other research uses
  ○ Other (please identify):_____

(*continued*)

FIGURE 5.2 (continued)

Information Flow Checklist

❐   Other information
     ○   Human resources information
     ○   Payroll
     ○   Provider compensation
     ○   General ledger/accounts payable
     ○   Credentialing information
     ○   Office policies and procedures
     ○   Patient education materials
     ○   Information privacy and security documentation
     ○   Contracts and agreements for vendor services
     ○   Office correspondence
     ○   Other (please identify): _____

Figure 5.2. Obtaining this information serves two main purposes. First, it documents that you have performed an analysis of information flow for purposes of HIPAA compliance. Second, it helps you identify where there may be too much or too little access to certain information and where there may be risks associated with information uses. For instance, if you were unaware that certain persons were compiling a database of PHI, you could investigate the security of that information use.

Another investigative process to undertake is to log what technology is used to capture, retain, or transmit what information. This requires an understanding of your information systems. If you don't already have an information systems inventory, use Figure 5.3. List all individual types of hardware and software (eg, for network devices, list servers, routers, hubs, etc; for workstations, list desktop computers, laptops, tablets, smart phones, modems, electronic fax capability, etc; for storage, include tape drives, CD burners, USB devices, etc). Be sure to include all devices in all locations, whether they connect to your network or not.

FIGURE 5.3

Hardware/Software Inventory

	Date Acquired	Location	Vendor	Maintenance	Version	License	Function	Users
Hardware								
Network devices								
Workstations								
Printers								
Scanners								
Storage devices								
Software and Other								
Scheduling								
Registration software								

(continued)

F I G U R E 5.3 (continued)

Hardware/Software Inventory

	Date Acquired	Location	Vendor	Maintenance	Version	License	Function	Users
Billing								
Practice management								
Scanning								
Coding								
Dictation								
Transcription								
EHR software								
Registry software								
Databases								
Spreadsheets								
Interfaces								
Other *(insert any other information systems)*								

Reprinted with permission from Margret\A Consulting, LLC.

In addition to the hardware and software inventory, make sure you have a network diagram that illustrates how your information system network is configured. The individual who constructed and maintains your network should be able to supply you with this if you don't have one already.

Another useful tool is a facility layout that shows the location of all information systems equipment, power sources, telephone jacks and other telecommunications equipment, wireless access points, fire and burglary equipment, and locations of hazardous materials. If you have a formal data center or, at the least, a special room where you house your servers, create a separate and more detailed layout of this area.

The next step is to identify the various security controls that are in place and the policies and procedures that support them. Typically this is compiled by application (see Figure 5.4); use one copy of the figure for each application. As an alternative, you can expand the spreadsheet in Figure 5.4 to make a column for each security control and describe the features of the controls for each software application. You may want to complete this inventory after you review Chapters 6, 7, and especially 9.

FIGURE 5.4

Information System Security Controls

Security Control	Exists? (Y/N)	Describe Features of Controls	Policy and Procedure in Which Documented
Application:			
Unique user identification			
Access controls			
Emergency access			
Automatic logoff			
Authentication			
Data integrity			
Encryption			
Backup			
Emergency operation plan			
Disaster recovery plan			

Reprinted with permission from Margret\A Consulting, LLC.

Identify Threats

After you document your information flows, information system functions and their security controls, and policies and procedures, you next want to identify the threats and vulnerabilities in your environment.

A threat is an indication or warning of trouble. In security, a threat takes advantage of a vulnerability to cause harm to information.

A vulnerability is an existing condition that could be taken advantage of to cause harm. In reference to PHI, these are gaps in administrative, physical, or technical safeguards.

There are three components to a threat:

- Target
- Agent
- Event

You may have considered some or all of these as you implemented the information systems and general security controls for your office. Unfortunately, threats are becoming much more prevalent and unpredictable and need to be reassessed periodically. By scanning your environment and identifying potential threats, you will be able to comply with the risk analysis standard of HIPAA, which could save your practice from productivity problems, embarrassment, breaches, lawsuits, enforcement actions, and even harm to members of your workforce and to your patients.

Threat Targets

Targets are the objects of a threat. Targets are identified in the Security Rule as confidentiality, integrity, and availability. A threat agent attacks a target using a vulnerability. For example, an unauthorized person (threat agent) breaches confidentiality (target) via an open network port (vulnerability).

Security C-I-A (§164.304)

Confidentiality: The property that data or information are not made available or disclosed to unauthorized persons or processes.

Integrity: The property that data or information have not been altered or destroyed in an unauthorized manner.

Availability: The property that data or information are accessible and usable on demand by an authorized person.

Threat Agents

Threat agents are the motivation and resources for carrying out the threat. Motivation may stem from a variety of human factors. Motivation is typically viewed as intent to harm or otherwise gain personal satisfaction or advantage. A range of such motivation includes curiosity, thrill seeking, rebellion, revenge, competitive advantage, blackmail, or monetary gain. Spotting these can be difficult, which is why one of the Security Rule Administrative Safeguards is Workforce Security and, in particular, an implementation specification of workforce clearance procedures (ie, background checks). These safeguards are applicable to members of your workforce and business associates. Even this safeguard will not necessarily identify the motivations of all persons who pose a potential threat. There are many outside of your workforce who could be motivated to threaten your systems. For example, a practice located across the street from a vocational-technical training institute may be threatened by a student trying a wireless sniffer to attempt to access your wireless network.

There are also unintentional and accidental motivators. These include poor training, lack of policy, weak edit checks, unchanged default settings or unused controls, limited supervision, or even the belief that "it won't happen here." As a result of unintentional motivators, data entry errors occur, programming errors are made, or individuals forget to perform tasks.

Other agents of threats are not related to the human factor. These include natural and environmental threats. Figure 5.5 lists common threat agents.

FIGURE 5.5

Common Sources of Threats

Natural Threats

- Earthquakes, landslides
- Storm damage (eg, snow, ice, and floods)
- Tornadoes, hurricanes

Environmental Threats

- Fire and smoke contaminants
- Building collapse or explosion
- Power (blackouts, brownouts, spikes, surges, noise)
- Utility problems (heating, ventilation, air conditioning)
- Broken or leaking water lines, sewer pipes, natural gas lines

(continued)

FIGURE 5.5 (continued)
Common Sources of Threats

- Toxic materials release
- Contagious disease epidemic

Human Threats

- Accidental acts
  - Input errors and omissions
  - Faulty application programming or processing procedures
  - Phone or network cable broken during construction
  - Chemical spill or contamination
- Inappropriate activities
  - Inappropriate content
  - Waste of corporate resources
  - Harassment
  - Abuse of privileges or rights
  - Workplace violence
- Illegal operations and intentional attacks
  - Eavesdropping
  - Snooping
  - Fraud
  - Theft
  - Vandalism
  - Sabotage
  - Extortion
  - Blackmail
  - External attacks, such as malicious cracking, scanning, demon dialing, and virus introduction
- Other acts
  - War
  - Labor strikes

Reprinted with permission from Margret\A Consulting, LLC.

Threat Events

Events are the result of a threat. In general, there are four types of events:

- Unauthorized access to PHI (relates to the confidentiality target)
- Modification of PHI (causing a data integrity problem),
- Denial of service (making PHI unavailable)
- Repudiation (the inability to identify the source and hold someone accountable for an action)

How to Identify Threats

A significant level of emphasis has been placed on identifying threats because the practice of identifying threats in information systems is somewhat foreign to health care. So, just as you use sterile technique to avoid the threat of an infection, you should apply safeguards to mitigate potential threats to information systems. However, safeguards should not create an environment of suspicion. Instead, create an environment of awareness and accountability. Your staff should have the authority and responsibility to take appropriate security actions. As you institute policies that comply with HIPAA, demonstrate to your staff that the policies are important and that you support diligence in complying with them. Hold people accountable for their actions but also help them take necessary actions through appropriate resources.

Normal business processes, such as upgrading a computer application, can unintentionally expose a security risk if appropriate controls and audits are not in place. Even the nature of your practice may be a risk factor. If you are known for treating high-profile patients, your risk of a security incident could be high. If you treat pediatric patients and have workstations in examining rooms, you have probably already considered childproofing these workstations against sticky fingers and spills. Just as we take clinical precautions to prevent exposures, we must take security precautions to prevent incidents.

Finally, don't forget your contractors and outsourced services. If you outsource your information technology services, be sure you understand what security controls your vendors are using. Remember, you are the covered entity under HIPAA and responsible for compliance. A business associate contract with a vendor does not get you off the hook for your own security. Security is not just an information technology issue. Many needed controls relate to how you use the systems, your policies and procedures, and your daily operations.

Documenting Threats

Use one or both of the following methods to document your threats.

1. Use Figure 5.5 to identify the threats that are likely in your environment. You can categorize these as high, medium, or low, or you can describe the actual nature of the threats in your environment. For example, if you know your office is located on a flood plain, list that. If your office building includes businesses that are not related to health care, assess whether they heighten or lessen your risk.
2. Pair threats with vulnerabilities. This form of documentation is explained in the next section.

Identify Vulnerabilities

A vulnerability is a flaw or weakness in security policies and procedures, design, implementation, or controls that could be accidentally triggered or intentionally exploited, resulting in one or more of the threat events described above. Figure 5.6 illustrates some pairs of vulnerabilities and threats.

FIGURE 5.6

Vulnerability/Threat Pair Examples

Vulnerability	Threat Target	Threat Agent	Threat Event
Terminated employee's access privilege not removed	Integrity Confidentiality	Access by former employee dialing into office's network	Modification of lab results data Disclosure of PHI
Server in area with water sprinklers and no tarpaulins to protect equipment from water damage	Availability	Motivation lacking to correct the vulnerability, lack of fire drills	Denial of service through water damage Electrocution

Reprinted with permission from Margret\A Consulting, LLC.

How to Identify Vulnerabilities

There is a variety of ways to identify your vulnerabilities. Start by making a list of the HIPAA Security Rule standards and implementation specifications as your baseline set of security requirements. Then for each HIPAA requirement, determine if there are any weaknesses or gaps (ie, vulnerabilities). To identify these gaps:

■ Review any audits you may have had performed. This might include an accountant's audit report, a state licensure review, or a previously performed HIPAA risk analysis that was needed to start your Security Rule compliance activities.

■ Visit your hardware and software vendors' Web sites to see if they have any advisories posted. There may be patches or service packs (including those for your computers' operating systems) to be added to your systems.

■ Review any complaints your patients made to you directly or in a patient satisfaction survey. Look at your risk management reports for any privacy issues and any documented security incidents. Although complaints or incidents often address multiple issues, determine if any are the result of a security issue.

■ Conduct a walk-through of your office to identify security weaknesses. With your security auditor's "hat" on, you will begin to see things differently!

■ Consider acquiring an automated vulnerability scanning tool, either for use by your information technology staff or from a vendor. This is an automated system that identifies holes in your network. (A hole might be a flaw in network design, lack of a current patch, or other ways for viruses and other malicious software to be introduced into your network.) Be aware that these will not identify all technical vulnerabilities, may result in false positives, and will not identify weaknesses in administrative or physical controls.

■ Consider conducting a penetration test. This entails an actual attempt to penetrate your information systems. You can download freeware or shareware or buy software to perform such tests yourself. Make sure you understand how to use the software so you don't inadvertently create holes. It is also advisable to use software from more than one vendor as a type of check-and-balance system. If an outside vendor performs this test, make sure you use a reputable company, always make a system backup, and make sure the vendor signs a business associate contract prior to conducting the test. If the penetration test may expose other non-PHI information, add language to the business associate contract that includes all confidential information or require a separate confidentiality agreement to be signed in addition to the business associate contract.

■ Consider having an expert perform a security assessment. In addition to applying vulnerability scanning tools and conducting a penetration test, an overall security assessment will incorporate review of administrative and physical controls as well.

Documenting Vulnerabilities

Figure 5.7 can be used to document your security vulnerabilities and threats. The advantage of this template is that it lists the Security Rule standard and implementation specification, then describes in lay terms the vulnerabilities and threats. The disadvantage of using such a form is that there may be a single vulnerability or threat that targets multiple standards; or there may be different vulnerabilities and threats for different applications with respect to the same standard. For instance, the threat described for Security Awareness and Training—Reminders combines issues associated with Authentication (ie, weak passwords) and Workforce Security (ie, access privileges not turned off after terminating a member of the workforce). Still, for a small physician office, this format is probably the easiest and most practical method of documenting vulnerabilities and threats.

F I G U R E 5.7

Vulnerability and Threat Assessment Results Template and Examples

Security Rule Requirement	Vulnerability	Potential Threat
Security Awareness and Training–Reminders (§164.308[a][5])	Specific training on security has not been provided, and no reminders are posted	Workers not accountable for selecting weak passwords, which were compromised by a terminated employee and used to gain access to confidential information
Workstation Use (§164.310[b])	No policy exists on workstation use, and everyone has Internet access	Workers could think it is acceptable to download executable software that launches a denial of service attack

Reprinted with permission from Margret\A Consulting, LLC.

Determine Probability and Criticality of Risks

Once you identify your vulnerabilities and threats, decide how likely it is for the threats to occur and the magnitude of harm that would result. Although highly quantitative measures could be applied to this analysis, a scale of high-medium-low for both probability and criticality is adequate. Tables 5.1 and 5.2 supply some definitions for these ratings.

TABLE 5.1

Probability Rating Definitions

Probability Level	Definition
High	■ You or another provider like you or near you have experienced one or more successful occurrences of the threat ■ Controls to eliminate the vulnerability are not very effective
Medium	■ You or another similar entity near you have previously been alerted to the threat and could take steps to prevent its occurrence or minimize harmful effects ■ Controls are in place that may impede successful exercise of the vulnerability
Low	■ Neither you nor anyone in your community have experienced the threat ■ Controls are in place that will significantly impede or even prevent success of a threat

Reprinted with permission from Margret\A Consulting, LLC.

TABLE 5.2

Criticality Rating Definitions

Criticality Level	Examples of a Threat Exploiting Vulnerability
High	■ Human death or serious injury ■ Sentinel patient care event ■ High cost of recovery ■ Inability to recover critical and/or sensitive data ■ Major lawsuit ■ Loss of licensure or accreditation
Medium	■ Human injury/harm ■ Complaint to federal or state government ■ Significant cost of recovery ■ Loss of tangible assets ■ Minor lawsuit ■ Public relations issue
Low	■ Loss of some tangible assets ■ Complaint to your office ■ Loss of productivity ■ Nuisance ■ Embarrassment

Reprinted with permission from Margret\A Consulting, LLC.

Add these ratings to your Vulnerability and Threat Assessment Results Template (see Figure 5.7) to create your risk analysis (see Figure 5.8). Note that the example in Figure 5.8 contains sample ratings. You must judge for yourself the probability and criticality of any vulnerability and threat.

FIGURE 5.8

Risk Analysis

Security Rule Requirement	Vulnerability	Potential Threat	Probability	Criticality	Risk Score
Security Awareness and Training—Reminders (§164.308[a][5])	Specific training on security has not been provided, and no reminders are posted	Workers not accountable for selecting weak passwords, which were compromised by a terminated employee and used to gain access to confidential information	Medium	High	6
Workstation Use (§164.310[b])	No policy exists on workstation use, and everyone has Internet access	Workers could think it is acceptable to download executable software that launches a denial of service attack	Low	Medium	2

Reprinted with permission from Margret\A Consulting, LLC.

In addition to describing probability and criticality, assign a numeric score that summarizes the overall risk in each security requirement. Use Table 5.3 to identify the score for each combination of probability and criticality.

TABLE 5.3

Risk Score

Probability	Criticality		
High	3	6	9
Medium	2	4	6
Low	1	2	3
	Low	Medium	High

Reprinted with permission from Boundary Information Group.

Use the overall score for each security requirement to prioritize which requirements need immediate attention. As you implement and test controls, add these to your preliminary risk analysis to create a risk management tool that demonstrates the effectiveness of the controls.

Applicable Measures

Each HIPAA Security Rule standard and its implementation specifications are defined in the remaining chapters. You will not necessarily use all the measures described to meet each standard. Your risk analysis will guide you in selecting the measures that are most suitable for you. Some will be obvious. For example, instituting a security training program should address the vulnerability in training and at least partially address the associated threat that a terminated worker could claim that appropriate training was lacking. Other measures will be less obvious; there may be more options, or there may be a combination of controls required to address the threat to a vulnerability. One measure may even be to purchase insurance to cover an existing risk for which there is not a cost-effective control.

Ongoing Risk Management

After you have completed your risk analysis and identified security controls, you will have a document that substantiates your risk analysis and supports your risk management. The HIPAA Security Rule requires risk management.

The risk management standard (§164.308[a][1][ii][B]) states, "Implement security measures sufficient to reduce risks and vulnerabilities to a reasonable and appropriate level to comply with §164.306(a)." Section 164.306(a) lists the general security requirements of ensuring the confidentiality, integrity, and availability of PHI, protecting against reasonably anticipated threats or uses/disclosures of PHI not permitted or as required under the Privacy Rule, and complying with the Security Rule.

To document your risk management, add a Control column to Figure 5.8 to create a risk management tool (refer back to Figure 5.1). Use the Control column to document controls you use or are planning to use to comply with each Security Rule standard. You may even want to add additional columns for the date by which you expect to implement new/updated controls and when you have completed their implementation. Some offices use this tool to keep their risk analysis current by adding another column to specify the date for the next review.

RISK SUMMARY

Now that you have an understanding of the purpose and process of risk analysis and management, you are ready to review the specific security controls required by the HIPAA Security Rule. Return to this chapter to document your vulnerabilities, threats, level of risk, and controls you plan to put into place. After your initial implementation of the controls, return to this documentation periodically to keep it up to date.

CHECK YOUR UNDERSTANDING*

List the six steps in performing a risk analysis:

1. _____

2. _____

3. _____

4. _____

5. _____

6. _____

Characterize the following scenarios as most likely having high (H), medium (M), or low (L) information security risk:

7. You are located in a small town, the weather is mild, and your staff has been with the practice for many years.

8. You have an obstetrics practice in a newly renovated, trendy neighborhood.

9. You are a plastic surgeon located in the state's capital.

10. You are a primary care provider in an inner city with a large inventory of drug samples.

*For answers, refer to the Answer Key at the end of the book.

chapter 6

HIPAA Security Administrative Safeguards

Information security is often thought to be about user IDs and passwords, audit trails, backups, and other physical and technical controls. But in fact, information security is much more about people, policy, and process. Physical and technical controls are important, but people can thwart those controls. Without policies on handling workarounds or lax practices performed by people and without establishing information security processes that make sense to people, the physical and technical controls will not serve their purpose well. In addition, decisions must be made about the specific controls you need. You need to implement and enforce these controls. You need to be sure your controls are working. HIPAA's Administrative Safeguards answer these questions and more. In particular, administrative safeguards establish the policies and procedures for using various information security controls. The Administrative Safeguards standards relate to security management processes, assigning responsibility for security, authorizing access to PHI, and planning the policies and procedures needed to implement physical and technical security controls.

HOW TO USE THIS CHAPTER

The HIPAA Security Rule includes nine Administrative Safeguard standards and their respective implementation specifications (see Table 6.1). With the exception of the risk analysis and risk management specifications in the first standard, covered in Chapter 5, assigned security responsibility, covered in Chapter 4, and business associate contracts, covered in Chapter 7, the Administrative Safeguard standards are described here in the same order in which they are listed in the Security Rule. This sequence also represents the order in which you should implement them in your office with the exception of assigning security responsibility, which should be your first step.

With each description of the standards and any associated implementation specifications, consider your level of associated risk. Document any current vulnerabilities and threats you believe exist with respect to each standard. Use the risk analysis form in Chapter 5 or another method to record this information. If you determine that you have no current vulnerabilities with respect to a specific standard, document the measures you have already taken to mitigate any previously identified risk or to protect yourself from future risks. Be sure you date your analysis. As the environment changes over time, you will need to return to the risk analysis documentation and update it periodically. This documentation is also evidence that you conducted a risk analysis and describes the controls you currently have in place.

As noted in Chapter 1, you must comply with every standard in some way. An implementation specification labeled *Required* means you must comply with the specification. If the implementation specification is labeled *Addressable*, you need to do one of these:

- Implement the specification as stated.
- Implement an alternative that you believe better suits your office.
- Address the standard in another way because the implementation specification is not applicable to your situation.

Also as previously noted, *Addressable* does not mean optional. If the federal government intended such implementation specifications to be optional they would have used the term *optional*. Perhaps a better way to think about such addressable specifications is "situational." You must address these specifications, but you may do so according to your own situation.

Table 6.1 lists the Administrative Safeguard standards and references the section numbers in the Security Rule. (Note: Not all standards have implementation specifications.)

TABLE 6.1

Administrative Safeguard Standards and Implementation Specifications

Security Standards	Code of Federal Regulations Sections	Security Implementation Specifications (R) = Required, (A) = Addressable
Administrative Safeguards		
Security Management Process	§164.308(a)(1)	Risk Analysis (R) Risk Management (R) Sanction Policy (R) Information System Activity Review (R)
Assigned Security Responsibility	§164.308(a)(2)	(R)
Workforce Security	§164.308(a)(3)	Authorization and/or Supervision (A) Workforce Clearance Procedure (A) Termination Procedures (A)
Information Access Management	§164.308(a)(4)	Isolating Healthcare Clearinghouse Function (R) Access Authorization (A) Access Establishment and Modification (A)
Security Awareness and Training	§164.308(a)(5)	Security Reminders (A) Protection From Malicious Software (A) Login Monitoring (A) Password Management (A)
Security Incident Procedures	§164.308(a)(6)	Response and Reporting (R)
Contingency Plan	§164.308(a)(7)	Data Backup Plan (R) Disaster Recovery Plan (R) Emergency Mode Operation Plan (R) Testing and Revision Procedure (A) Applications and Data Criticality Analysis (A)
Evaluation	§164.308(a)(8)	(R)
Business Associate Contracts and Other Arrangements	§164.308(b)(1)	(R)

SECURITY MANAGEMENT PROCESS STANDARD

The Security Management Process standard requires you to "implement policies and procedures to prevent, detect, contain, and correct security violations" (§164.308[a][1][B]).

Your responsibility for administrative safeguards begins with the required risk analysis and risk management processes described in Chapter 5. Under the Security Management Process standard, you are also responsible for applying a consistent sanction policy and continually conducting an information system activity review.

Sanction Policy

HIPAA requires covered entities to "apply appropriate sanctions against workforce members who fail to comply with the security policies and procedures of the covered entity" (§164.308[a][1][B]). Employees often sign a statement in an employee handbook or a confidentiality form when they start work. A confidentiality statement says the employee acknowledges that violations of office policies may lead to disciplinary action up to and including termination. In many cases, such statements do not provide the guidance needed to ensure that sanctions are applied consistently to all members of the workforce. A sanction policy is also required for compliance with the Privacy Rule. You most likely have a general sanction policy with respect to compliance with office policies in general. These may all be integrated into one policy. However, to ensure you have an effective sanction policy that provides guidance, use Figure 6.1 to review and enhance your current sanction policy as necessary.

FIGURE 6.1

Sanction Policy Checklist

Components of a Sanction Policy	Included? (Y/N)	Rationale
1. Identifies disciplinary actions for all employees, trainees, contractors, volunteers, and other members of the workforce as defined by HIPAA.		
2. Lists examples of violations, such as failure to wear identification badge or knowingly using someone else's password.		
3. For categories of violations relative to their severity, identifies nature of disciplinary action, such as verbal warning, written warning, removal of system privileges, or termination of employment or contract penalties.		
4. Includes notice that civil or criminal penalties may arise for misuse or misappropriation of PHI.		
5. Makes members of the workforce aware that violations may result in notification to law enforcement officials and regulatory, accreditation, and licensure organizations.		

Reprinted with permission from Margret\A Consulting, LLC.

Be sure to apply the sanction policy to all members of the workforce consistently, which includes trainees, contractors, volunteers, and others who are under your control in addition to employees. Physicians and other providers often have a sanction policy as part of their medical staff bylaws, partnership papers, or other documents associated with their relationship to the practice. With respect to privacy and security, such sanction terms should be equivalent to those in the workforce sanction policy and applied consistently.

Information System Activity Review

The Information System Activity Review implementation specification requires covered entities to "implement procedures to regularly review records of information system activity, such as audit logs, access reports, and security incident tracking reports" (§164.308[a][1][D]).

This requirement is not meant to be a formal audit process. Rather, its purpose is twofold. First, to review records of information system activity you must retain such records. Second, simply documenting information system activity will not address potential problems that a review may reveal. Reviewing records of information system activity promotes continual awareness of information system activities that could suggest a security issue. For example, if an audit trail generated by your information system shows that a member of your workforce who is not expected to need access to PHI outside of normal working hours has been accessing information on evenings and weekends, this situation should be investigated as a potential security incident. There may be a logical explanation, or you may find a breach of confidentiality. Another example would be to monitor network traffic to determine if you have sufficient bandwidth so that PHI is available to you when you need it. Document the results as evidence of an information system activity review.

You should have a policy that establishes what must be documented and what reviews will be conducted. A procedure should delineate the manner in which information system activities must be documented, for how long the documentation will be retained, how frequently reviews will be performed, who performs the reviews, and how issues will be escalated and resolved.

HIPAA specifies that information system activities to be documented include items "such as" audit logs, access reports, and security incidents. "Such as" means that there may be other information system activities that may need to be documented. For instance, an audit log might be construed only as the system-generated log of individuals who log into the system. But an audit log should also document attempted logins. In addition, various other logs help you audit other types of system activity. The example provided above suggests that monitoring of system resource availability is important to alert you when you may need more bandwidth, when processing speed is being degraded, and when other indicators that ensure availability require attention. All available security patches, anti-malware updates, and enhancements made to the security of your systems should be documented.

All changes made to software and hardware should be documented. This is frequently referred to as "configuration management" or "change control." Because changes to the configuration of your systems are broader than only security controls, HIPAA did not include a specific, separate requirement for this. However, there is discussion in the preamble to the Security Rule that configuration management as it applies to security is subsumed within the information system activity review function.

Note that if you contract for services that host your hardware and/or software, you should be sure that the company providing such services adheres to these requirements and will be able to produce documentation of such activities as well as regular review of the activities in the event that it is needed to demonstrate your compliance with the Security Rule.

What is considered a "log" is something that should be defined in your policies and procedures. Logs of information system activity are constantly produced by your system. However, such logs can become immense and require extra storage as well as significant effort to review. HIPAA is silent on what it means by "log" in this context. While some organizations do keep all such log data, others believe it is satisfactory to apply a regular review to the logs and then only keep documentation of the review. If you follow the later practice, be sure that the period of time in which you conduct the review is sufficient to identify patterns or trends. A weekly review may not pick up on an employee occasionally accessing information inappropriately or spikes in system usage only once a month. Yet these are the precise things you want to look for in conducting a review.

Identify the logs that are performed by your information systems. Determine how they are generated, whether they retain only activities outside of a normal range, and what software or people support is needed to review the logs, then decide how long to keep the logs. Different systems may have different types of logs and review functions. You may have system review functions that run continuously in your computer's background. This system may generate only a printed report when your computer alerts you to a special situation or when you want to investigate certain activities. Other systems may require special software or someone to manually review for patterns. For example, EHR systems check user names against patient names in order to restrict access to family members. This is relatively easy to program into a computer. However, it may require a manual review to identify that a given user is regularly accessing a record of someone without the same last name but does not regularly need such access. Regardless of how your computer systems work and how you use their activity review functions, document your review process.

WORKFORCE SECURITY STANDARD

The Workforce Security standard requires that you "implement policies and procedures to ensure that all members of [your] workforce have appropriate access to ePHI, as provided under [the Information Access Management standard], and to prevent those workforce members who do not have access under [the Information Access Management standard] from obtaining access to ePHI" (§164.308[a][3]).

There are three addressable implementation specifications within this standard:

- Authorization and/or Supervision
- Workforce Clearance
- Termination Procedures

Authorization and/or Supervision

The Authorization and/or Supervision implementation specification addresses "procedures for the authorization and/or supervision of workforce members who work with PHI or in locations where it might be accessed" (§164.308[a][3][ii][A]).

As you assign duties to members of your workforce, develop job descriptions that include what access the person holding a position has to PHI and the extent to which the access must be supervised.

For example, you may assign a receptionist the ability to "read and write information to update patient demographic information." This means the receptionist may access and view demographic information and change the patient's name, address, and other demographic information in accordance with edit checks built into the information system. However, under this level of access, the receptionist would not be able to view diagnosis and procedure codes or any other clinical information, or print any information. If a supervisor notices that the receptionist's screen is displaying lab results, the supervisor should investigate. The receptionist may be using the login of another member of the workforce, for which both parties would be subject to sanctions.

However, you should carefully consider what access is actually appropriate for each individual in the practice. Too limited access may not be appropriate and could result in the receptionist either not being able to perform duties assigned or having to resort to using someone else's login. It is also important to remember that access to the system is not the only form of access people have.

Here's another example. A billing clerk's job description may indicate the clerk can "read, write, and print patient statements." If the clerk is observed printing out extra copies of certain statements, a potential security incident could exist and should be investigated by the supervisor.

This last scenario highlights the need for security monitoring, while not creating an environment of suspicion. The best way to achieve such a balance is through creating a culture

---

CASE STUDY 6.1
Access Levels for the Receptionist

Many offices need to have the receptionist ask a patient the reason for a requested appointment in order to schedule the appropriate amount of time. This may only be stated as a "follow-up," or the patient may elaborate. You cannot control what the patient is telling the receptionist, but if the receptionist is not supposed to have access to any clinical information, such a conversation would be in violation of at least the Privacy Rule. It may also be a desired practice for the office to request that a patient have lab work performed before certain visits. The receptionist does not necessarily need to know what lab work, although there really would be no harm in this, so long as the receptionist is trained in appropriate uses and disclosure techniques. Certainly if a patient called the receptionist for results of lab work, the receptionist should be trained from a clinical perspective not to disclose this information and how to handle such a request. Some information systems are able to support very granular access controls, such as the ability to view the type of lab work to be performed but no ability to view lab results. Other information systems, however, are lacking in this level of detail, in which case appropriate training is even more important.

CASE STUDY 6.2
Verification of Identity

A computer service technician you do not know arrives from the company you called to service your computer. How do you verify who this person is? A possible solution is when you request the service, ask for the name of the individual who will be sent to your office. When the person arrives, ask to see the person's company badge and driver's license. If the individual cannot present satisfactory credentials, call the company and verify that the person meeting the description is the company's employee. Also have the contractor sign a log that includes the name of the person and company, purpose, date and time of arrival, and date and time of departure. If direct supervision is not practical, ensure that a member of your staff is at least aware of the person's presence in your office and that someone is at least in the "line of sight" of the contractor or is able to periodically check on the person. When the work is completed, the technician should demonstrate to you that your system works as expected. (You will want to check the system to verify work performed; checking applicable system activity logs, such as which patients were accessed and for how long, may also be appropriate.) If the technician will have access to PHI in the course of the work, you must have a business associate contract with the company.

of information security by demonstrating the value of security to the practice, weaving it into office discussions and meetings as applicable, and being transparent about security practices to the extent appropriate. In a culture of information security, those in authority adhere to the rules themselves, setting an example for others to follow. Such a culture lessens the likelihood that someone will intentionally do the wrong thing. It also increases the likelihood that members of the workforce would seek help in managing access to PHI if there are questions. Members of the workforce should be encouraged to report unusual or suspicious activities, such as a screen that suddenly goes blank, which could be a result of malware infecting a system with a virus or other malicious software. Finally, because such a culture is created by sensitivity to workforce needs and concerns as a result of management being engaged in everyday activities, managers will likely have a heightened sense of awareness when something is amiss.

Certain members of your workforce may be granted special authority with respect to PHI. An especially sensitive function is that of establishing a unique user identification and password for a new member of the workforce. This is typically a system administration function. Some highly sensitive security functions may require a system of checks and balances. For example, the workforce member who establishes the technical access should not also be the same person who authorizes access, who is usually a manager.

In addition to PHI in your information systems, your office is likely to have both PHI and other confidential information in paper or electronic format that should be included in your authorization and supervision policy. For example, you may want to specify who is authorized to obtain charts from off-site storage or who has access to a fireproof safe for archives and backups stored on tape or disks. You may even want to specify who has authority to open mail and receive incoming faxes. Ideally the office should be moving to electronic funds transfer (EFT) at least as required by January 1, 2014, for Medicare reimbursement, so that checks are not being received, but certainly patient accounts and other financial information are confidential as well.

The Authorization and/or Supervision implementation specification should also address outside contractors and others outside your workforce who have access to PHI. Evidence from various reports and surveys show both an increasing dependence on contractors— whether working in the office or external to the office—and an increasing amount of breaches by business associates.

In contrast to the computer technician who has access to PHI by virtue of the nature of the work performed, there are other service professionals who visit the office who should not be allowed access to PHI or areas where there is PHI. Pharmaceutical representatives and salespeople are good examples. Because they are not members of your workforce and unless you have business associate contracts with their companies, they should be escorted through your office and not permitted in areas where incidental disclosure of PHI may occur.

A form like the one shown in Figure 6.2 can be used to document how you authorize and supervise access to PHI. This form can be used to identify the person or persons in your office responsible for authorizing and supervising various types of access. Because it is usually desirable to have a backup individual in charge of access when the primary person is not available, a column for recording this is included. Examples are identified in italics.

Following rules.

FIGURE 6.2

Workforce Security Functions

Date Last Revised:		
Function	**Person Assigned**	**Backup Person**
Supervise visitors with no access to PHI	*Receptionist*	*Office manager*
Supervise members of workforce who have "limited access" to PHI	*Office manager*	*Nurse manager*
Supervise business associates who have "limited access" to PHI	*Receptionist*	*Office manager*
Approve relationship with hospital, health plan, others who permit your workforce access to their PHI	*Chief medical officer (CMO)*	*None*
Appoint information security official (ISO)	*CMO*	*None*
Appoint system administrator	*CMO*	*None*
Authorize establishment of staff access privileges to external patient data sources	*Office manager*	*Nurse manager*
Authorize establishment of staff access to network and applications	*Office manager*	*CMO*
Establish access privileges to the network and applications	*System administrator*	*ISO*
Initiate termination of access privileges to external patient data sources	*Office manager*	*Nurse manager*
Initiate termination of access privileges to network and applications, including keys, badges, tokens, devices, and media as applicable	*Office manager*	*Assistant office manager*
Terminate access privileges to the network and applications	*System administrator*	*ISO*
Perform periodic audits of authorized access	*ISO*	*Supervisor, as needed*

Note: Examples are identified in italics.

Reprinted with permission from Boundary Information Group.

Workforce Clearance Procedures

Workforce clearance procedures "determine that the access of a workforce member to PHI is appropriate." At a minimum, evaluate potential members of your workforce to determine if their character is suitable to adhering to your policies and procedures for protecting PHI. Because this is an addressable implementation specification, you may implement formal clearance procedures or background investigations, or you may use some other mechanism for screening candidates to determine their suitability. Possible mechanisms are described here.

The lowest cost procedure, but perhaps not the most effective, is to have every applicant attest to information regarding education, credentials, criminal background history, and credit history included on the employment application. Be sure to verify the individual's education and credentials. If these are not as expected, you may choose not to hire the individual due to lack of qualifications. Be sure to obtain an authorization from the applicant to allow you to investigate credit and criminal backgrounds. Also, ask the applicant to supply previous addresses and telephone numbers to assist in these investigations.

A better practice is to make any job offer contingent on the actual results of a criminal and/or credit background check. Clearance procedures are included in HIPAA because individuals with a history of criminal activity and/or credit problems are thought to be those most likely to breach confidentiality or cause security incidents that result in data diversion, alteration, or loss. However, there are other reasons for screening out these individuals. For example, you may have drugs, cash/credit card information, and certainly health insurance information in your office that could be stolen and illegally used or sold. You will also want to screen out candidates who would be likely to embezzle from you if they were to have access to accounting records and/or cash.

You will also need to consider whether these investigative procedures are applicable to all or only some candidates and when they should be performed. Some organizations perform criminal and/or credit checks only for those who work in financial areas or serve as information system administrators. Other organizations perform clearance checks only of those who joined the workforce after the HIPAA compliance deadline, whereas others conduct these investigations for transfers as well. Alternatively, some organizations perform clearance checks on all members of their workforce as part of HIPAA compliance.

Termination Procedures

Termination procedures direct you to "implement procedures for terminating access to PHI when the employment of a workforce member ends or as required by determinations made as [part of the workforce clearance procedure]" (§164.308[a][3][ii][C]).

Whether someone leaves voluntarily or involuntarily, it is a good practice to remove access privileges immediately upon termination. Remember, a voluntary termination, even of someone considered a model employee, is not necessarily a friendly termination. And someone leaving on even the friendliest of terms can be the subject of coercion once employment is terminated.

The specifics of the termination procedures you adopt will vary based on the complexity of your office and the sophistication of your information systems. Figure 6.3 provides a sample list of items to include in your termination procedures. A checklist with this information can be used to make sure you have covered everything. The same checklist can be used when hiring an employee and/or granting access to PHI in order to acknowledge receipt and the obligation to safeguard your property.

F I G U R E 6.3

Items to Address When a Member of the Workforce Is Terminated

Items to Be Returned
- Keys
- ID badge
- Key cards for parking/door access
- Parking passes
- Mobile/smart phones
- Laptops/tablets
- Digital access password cards, tokens, or other access devices

(continued)

FIGURE   6.3 (continued)

Items to Address When a Member of the Workforce Is Terminated

- Remote access personal computers (PCs)
- Printouts, electronic media with PHI
- Uniform/work clothes (supplied by employer)
- Pagers

Tasks to Be Performed

- Remove information system(s) access privileges, including the individual's user ID on directories and in e-mail
- Remove physical access privileges (eg, reprogram digital access or change combination locks)

Reprinted with permission from Boundary Information Group.

   Your policies and procedures should specifically assign responsibility for retrieving property and removing information system access privileges and/or physical access to the system. You can be at risk if your policies are unclear as to who is responsible for what actions. This is especially true in larger practices where the following is likely to happen: a supervisor terminates a member of the workforce, believing that the human resources department will retrieve property and remove access; however, the human resources department assumes the supervisor took care of this. If allowed by state law, consider making the last paycheck conditional upon receipt of all items listed in Figure 6.3 and completion of all applicable actions listed in Figure 6.4.

   Although not required by HIPAA, it is a good practice to remind the workforce member who is terminating or changing job functions about the confidentiality of PHI (and your business information) learned while on the job and that termination or role change requires that information remain confidential. Include language to this effect in a confidentiality statement to be signed by the workforce member at the start of the working relationship as well as in an acknowledgment upon termination.

FIGURE   6.4

Steps to Take at Termination or Job Change

Action	Initiated By	To Whom
Workforce member terminates employment, is terminated, or changes job functions	Workforce member Supervisor/human resource department/office manager	Supervisor/human resource department/office manager Workforce member
Terminate/change network, Internet, and application accesses	Supervisor or office manager	Information technology (IT) department
Terminate/change key card/ID badge, access to doors, devices, etc	Supervisor or office manager	Physical security or information security official (ISO)
Retrieve remote access devices (PDA, PC) owned by the practice	Supervisor or administrator	IT department

Reprinted with permission from Boundary Information Group.

You should also consider whether it is a serious risk to allow a workforce member who has given notice of termination to have access to PHI until the last day on the job. If the worker has a highly sensitive position with respect to your information systems and you have reason to believe there could be some risk associated with continued access, you can:

- Have the individual leave immediately. Compensating the individual for the two-week notice period may be a small price to pay to avoid problems.
- Change the person's access privileges to be less sensitive until he or she actually leaves.
- Continue access privileges but make an exact copy of the worker's desktop as evidence in case there is any suspicion of malicious activity during the time the worker remains actively employed.

You also need to consider how to handle temporary workers or locum tenentes. Generally, these individuals are provided access to PHI for the duration of a contract, even if their services are not used for weeks or months at a time by the organization. In the past, it has not been easy to terminate access and then reinstate it each time a person returns to work. Some information systems are making this process much easier; in fact, some clinical systems can be linked to a time and attendance system where access is granted to anyone only if signed in. If your information system is not yet enhanced to make this process easier, take the following precautions:

- Ensure that your contract stipulates when access to PHI is permitted and spells out specific sanctions for any misuse of information systems resources. A confidentiality statement is important, but the contract should be more specific with respect to access privileges and sanctions.
- Ensure that each contract worker has a unique user identification and strong password or other form of authentication and that it is not shared among several contract workers from the same company.
- Ensure that you have access controls (see Chapter 9) that prevent such individuals from gaining remote access to your information systems. You might consider adopting security tokens that would be given to temporary workers only when they are present in your office.
- Investigate the availability of a set of "temporary" logins to be assigned at the time of arrival and that rotate among temporary users.

INFORMATION ACCESS MANAGEMENT STANDARD

The Information Access Management standard requires you to implement policies and procedures for authorizing access to PHI that are consistent with the applicable requirements of the Privacy Rule, in particular the Minimum Necessary standard. As a reminder, the Minimum Necessary standard requires covered entities to identify "(A) Those persons or classes of persons, as appropriate, in its workforce who need access to PHI to carry out their duties, and (B) For each such person or class of persons, the category or categories of PHI to which access is needed and any conditions appropriate to such access," and also "to make reasonable efforts to limit the access of such persons or classes identified to PHI consistent with the category of categories of PHI to which access is needed" (§164.514[d][2]).

The Minimum Necessary standard does not apply to disclosures to a healthcare provider for treatment, to uses and disclosures made to the individual (patient), to uses and disclosures pursuant to an authorization, or to disclosures required by law or to the Secretary of HHS in accordance with HIPAA compliance enforcement.

Information access management includes implementation specifications relative to isolating a healthcare clearinghouse function, access authorization, and access establishment and modification. The Information Access Management standard is closely related to the implementation specification of Termination Procedures in the Workforce Security standard.

Isolating Healthcare Clearinghouse Function (As Applicable)

Isolating healthcare clearinghouse functions from other functions in the organization is a required implementation specification "if a health care clearinghouse is part of a larger organization" (§164.308[a][4]). It is unlikely that a small physician practice would provide clearinghouse functions for others. If it does, the Security Rule requires you to "implement policies and procedures that protect the PHI of the clearinghouse from unauthorized access by the larger organization" (§164.308[a][4][ii][a]).

Access Authorization

Access authorization calls for you to "implement policies and procedures for granting access to PHI, for example, through access to a workstation, transaction, program, process, or other mechanism" (§164.308[a][4][ii][B]). A number of terms associated with the granting and control of access are defined below.

Understanding the Terms

Access authorization is the permission given to a person to have specific access to information, in accordance with the organization's access rules. Authorization should be performed by a supervisor and required for any new access and any change to access privileges.

Access establishment and modification is the technical process of creating the unique user identification and authentication process for a person who has been authorized to access information.

Access controls are the technology that implements the access rules (see Chapter 9). Access rules identify persons or classes of persons who need access to PHI, the category or categories of PHI to which access is needed, and any conditions appropriate to such access. Access termination is the process of removing an individual's access privileges (see the discussion of the Termination Procedures implementation specification under Workforce Security in this chapter).

Policies and procedures for authorizing access should identify who has authority to grant access privileges. Make sure that a supervisory person always authorizes access. The access authorization should be in writing. If e-mail is used, a return receipt should be requested. If such is returned and was not requested, then you know someone else is attempting to gain a login. In general, no one should authorize his or her own access, and the person who authorizes access should not be the same person who establishes access (ie, actually creates a unique user ID and sets authentication requirements). This separation of duties may not be possible in a very small office.

In authorizing access, follow the access rules established by your practice. Document any exceptions, such as for assignment of multiple roles. Figure 6.5 provides a sample set of access rules. If your practice is not organized by department, you may eliminate the first column in the table and refer only to job functions.

FIGURE   6.5

Sample Access Rules

Depart-ment	Job Function	Access to Information Systems		Privileges (See Key)	Internet Access	Remote Access
		Application	Views			
Business Office	Billing clerk	Practice management systems	Claims	C/R/W	Yes	No
Business Office	Billing clerk	Health plan	Claims status	R	Yes	No
Scheduling/ Registration	Registrar	Practice management system	Scheduling	C/R/W	No	No
Scheduling/ Registration	Registrar	Health plan	Eligibility	R	Yes	No
Nursing	Nurse	Electronic health record	Patient care	C/R/W	No	Yes
Medical Records	Contract transcrip-tionist	Practice management system	Demographic data and sub-mittal of tran-scribed reports	R	No	Limited
Key: C = create, R = read, W = write, D = delete from active view, S = system administration.						

Reprinted with permission from Tom Walsh Consulting, LLC.

Create access rules specific to your applications and requirements. You may establish a policy that allows all members of the workforce access to basic office functions on a work-station, with access to specific applications authorized based on job functions. Some offices also want to restrict access to certain sensitive information, for certain "very important per-son (VIP)" patients (such as celebrities or government officials), or for certain information specified by the patient. Although all of these forms of access controls should be feasible in your information system, the level of access control granularity varies with the product. If you do not have the type of access control capability you desire, you should contact your vendor for assistance.

In the past, access to the Internet was generally restricted quite significantly, due largely to concerns about introducing malware into your systems. Today, use of the Internet has become a way of life for all, including professionals. Software to significantly reduce the risk of malware is essential and is significantly improved over what was previously avail-able. In fact, most concerns about use of the Internet today surround productivity. There can be great value in accessing drug information, patient education materials, etc. How-ever, a lot of time can be spent "surfing the Web."

Many providers are now limiting Internet use by policy to those who must have access for business purposes. For example, registration and business office personnel, or nursing personnel involved in precertification or referrals, may use the services of a major health insurance program that provides online eligibility information via the Internet. Nurses and providers may want to access patient education online, or access clinical reference material or practice guidelines. A policy that limits Internet use for business purposes will not put actual physical or technical restrictions on Internet use, but would enable a manager or board to monitor for and sanction someone for abuse of such privileges.

Remote access, such as from the physician office to a hospital to retrieve information, could also be limited, probably to selected members of the professional staff and information technology (IT) personnel. This is relatively easy to do via giving access privileges only to certain individuals. Although contractors may need remote access (such as for troubleshooting your information systems), such access should be provided only when you are called in advance and can open a modem line or otherwise set permission.

Although access authorization (and termination, as previously discussed) and access controls (see Chapter 9) focus on PHI in electronic form, your policy should be based on the Privacy Rule's Minimum Necessary standard. This permits use of the policy for all forms of PHI and also applies to all other confidential information in your practice, whether in electronic form or not.

Access Establishment and Modification

Access establishment and modification means that you should "implement policies and procedures that, based on the entity's access authorization policies, establish, document, review, and modify a user's right of access to a workstation, transaction, program, or process" (§164.308[a][4][ii][C]).

Assign a specific person, together with one or more backup persons, to be responsible for implementing and managing the establishment and modification of access privileges that have been authorized in accordance with your policies and procedures. This is likely to be the same individual responsible for terminating access privileges for members of the workforce who leave.

An IT support person is the most likely candidate. Candidates for backing up this person, or an alternative for a small office, would be the office manager or practice administrator, business office manager, or another IT person. An outside IT contractor could also be used, providing strict policies exist that state that establishment or modification of access cannot occur without verifiable authorization. Verifiable authorization may include a fax of a signed document, a callback process followed by a fax or e-mail, an e-mail with return receipt requested, or an encrypted e-mail that affords nonrepudiation, so that no one can deny their authenticity.

Your policies and procedures for access establishment and modification should include a periodic review of all established or modified accesses to ensure they are valid and consistent with those authorized. In some cases, the records of access establishment and modification may not be maintained within your information systems. For instance, if a health plan or hospital provides the capability for a physician's practice to remotely access PHI with regard to your practice's patients, the access establishment records are normally maintained by the health plan or hospital. In this case, your policies and procedures should include the responsibility of periodically verifying the authorizations supplied to these outside organizations against their records of access establishment, modification, or termination. (The outside organization may require this of you, but if not, it is good practice for you to initiate this. It protects both parties.)

Figure 6.6 can be used by the ISO to document the periodic review of access authorization, establishment, modification, and termination. Note that the form includes internal applications and external access to hospitals, labs, and health plans. You may want to expand this to include access to other confidential business information.

Notations such as when an agreement is up for renewal, or when the hospital was notified that access for a patient should be terminated but the action has not been confirmed, can be listed in the Other Actions/Notes column. Documentation confirming actions taken, such as e-mails sent to confirm removal of access or computer printouts of access lists indicating who has been terminated, could be added to this form. These documents can be maintained in paper or electronic form. Keep them in a secure place under the management of your ISO.

FIGURE 6.6

Information Access Review Form

Date of Review:			
Information System Application	Document Produced (Date/Person)	Update Completed (Date/Person)	Other Actions/Notes
Practice management system			
Clearinghouse			
Electronic health record			
Hospital A lab results			
Hospital A census			
Hospital B lab results			
Lab A results			
Health plan A remittances			
Health plan B eligibility			
Bank: Checking account			

Reprinted with permission from Boundary Information Group.

SECURITY AWARENESS AND TRAINING STANDARD

The Security Awareness and Training standard requires you to "implement a security awareness and training program for all members of [your] workforce (including management)" (§164.308[a][5]).

Security training for all new and existing members of the workforce was required by the compliance date of the Security Rule. Periodic retraining should be given in response to environmental and operational changes affecting the security of PHI. These changes may include:

- New or upgraded software or hardware with enhanced security features and functionality
- New technologies employed to increase security protection (eg, new level of encryption or new technology to handle PHI on an open network)

- Increased threats based on experience specific to the healthcare industry or your practice
- Changes in the HIPAA security regulations
- Changes in privacy regulations that require different approaches to security to maintain privacy

As time has passed since the compliance date of the Security Rule and information systems and their technological advances change continuously, in practice, most offices find it beneficial to have more frequent formal training—certainly anytime there is a significant change, as noted above, but sometimes each year. Most importantly, however, awareness building should be ongoing. To create a culture in which people understand the importance of information security, are aware of what security incidents might arise, and are comfortable reporting security issues, you want an environment in which there is heightened awareness of potential problems, not an environment of suspicion.

The Security Awareness and Training standard includes four implementation specifications:

- Security Reminders
- Protection From Malicious Software
- Login Monitoring
- Password Management

Apply these to your office as determined by your risk analysis.

Reminders

HIPAA defines Security Reminders as "periodic security updates" (§164.308[a][5][ii][A]).

An office can address how it will provide security updates, which can take several forms. Select those that are best suited for your practice. (Don't forget to place reminders in each office if you have multiple office sites.) Examples include:

- Notices in printed or electronic workforce newsletters
- Table tents in the staff lunchroom, posters in the file room, or signs in staff workrooms
- Agenda items and specific discussion topics at monthly staff meetings (be sure to include the entire workforce impacted by the reminders in the staff meetings)
- Focused reminders posted in affected areas (eg, instructions for securely sending faxes near the fax machine, labels on wastebaskets for "general trash only")
- Formal retraining on the security policies and procedures in your practice

Security awareness building needs to be not only continual, but fresh. To keep your reminders fresh, you may want to get ideas about things to discuss, post, or retrain on by subscribing to various information security publications, periodically reviewing the Web sites of the OCR and the HHS breach list, and downloading annual reports that survey health information security. Set your Web browser to "health information security" for ideas.

Document and file all security reminders. Include the dates on which they were distributed or when they were posted; keep agendas, minutes, attendance rosters, and handouts used at staff (workforce) meetings; and document the completion of each security training program and its content.

HIPAA specifically calls out three topics to cover in security awareness and training. These include protection from malicious software (malware), login monitoring, and password management.

Protection From Malicious Software

Protection from malicious software includes "procedures for guarding against, detecting, and reporting malicious software" (§164.308[a][5][ii][C]).

Malicious software is any program that harms your information systems. There are many types of malicious software, such as viruses and worms, with new types being created all the time. The federal government uses the term *malicious software* to be general enough to encompass future technologies that will likely appear.

Although malicious software is frequently introduced through e-mail attachments, programs downloaded from the Internet, or other intrusions through an open network connection, be aware that malicious software can also be brought into your information systems on portable media, such as a CD, or devices, such as a USB drive, or from an infected PC or other mobile device that connects to your internal network through infrared, wireless, or cable connections. Malicious software typically is created for the purpose of causing harm. However, computer files can become corrupt through other means and result in additional problems. Antivirus software and other technical controls should be implemented on all workstations in your office, including desktops, laptops, tablets, servers, and any other devices that connect to your network. See Chapters 9 and 10 for additional information. (Note that the term *antivirus software* is still frequently used to describe software that protects against many forms of malware.)

Having antivirus software, even when automatically updated and distributed throughout your network to all connected devices on a daily basis, does not mean that you are totally safe. You can acquire malicious code before your antivirus software gets updated. Devices that are not directly connected to the network should either be connected regularly (even if by a wireless connection) to receive the update or be updated manually. If such devices permit the user to bypass or postpone an upgrade, this functionality should be turned off. Periodically remind members of the workforce about:

- The importance of updating antivirus software
- How to check a workstation or other device to determine if virus protection is current
- Recognizing signs of a potential virus that could sneak past antivirus software or come in prior to receiving an update
- How to quarantine a file and manually check it for viruses

A virus that successfully invades your information system can cause significant damage that will be expensive to repair and could cause loss of data.

Login Monitoring

Login monitoring refers to "procedures for monitoring log-in attempts and reported discrepancies" (§164.308[a][5][ii][C]).

Typically, one thinks of an attempted login as someone entering multiple potential passwords to attempt unauthorized access. Many information systems can be set to identify multiple attempts to log in. The software can either record these attempts in an audit trail or require resetting of a password after a specified number of unsuccessful login attempts. Login monitoring applies at multiple points in information systems, as described in Table 6.2. Although the Security Rule only addresses PHI, some offices may extend monitoring to phones and faxes as well.

TABLE 6.2

Types of Login Attempts to Monitor

Type of Security Incident	Samples of Monitoring
Network access without authorization	■ Network monitoring software that tracks number of failed logins and requires password resetting ■ Network audit trail
Impersonation within organization	■ Awareness training ■ Help-desk personnel and logs
External access through Internet portal	■ Firewall and monitoring software
External access through phone modem	■ War dialer (for a very large facility, software that helps identify where all active modems are located)
Unauthorized printer usage	■ Audit trail of print requests
Unauthorized paper record access	■ File area ID verification
Unauthorized phone calls	■ Phone call logs
Unauthorized fax usage	■ Fax call logs

Reprinted with permission from Boundary Information Group.

Password Management

Password management covers "procedures for creating, changing, and safeguarding passwords" (§164.308[a][5][ii][D]). A password is one way to authenticate a user. Note that a password authenticates a user, while a user ID specifies the nature of the access the user may have. Other mechanisms to authenticate users who have authority to access an information system include physical devices, such as smart cards or tokens, or biometrics (ie, fingerprint recognition, retinal scan).

Every workforce member assigned a password should know how to safeguard it. If multiple information systems each require their own password, train users on how to synchronize their multiple passwords so that only one, strong password is used (see Figure 6.7).

FIGURE 6.7

Strong Passwords

Strong passwords are:

■ At least six characters, preferably seven to nine; a mixture of alpha, numeric, and/or special characters; not dictionary words and do not contain dictionary words; and something that is not easily guessed by others. For example, relative or pet names and birth or anniversary dates should not be used; these are known by hackers to be commonly used passwords.

■ Unique each time they are created. Do not use a password that is a series, even if the initial password was strong. For example, 67A34B may be a strong password the first time it is used, but 67A34C is not appropriate for the next password.

■ Committed to memory. They should never be written down, such as on a Post-It Note placed under the keyboard, in a drawer in the workstation area, or even on the back of your badge. They should not be stored in a mobile device or saved in any program.

(continued)

F I G U R E 6.7 (continued)

Strong Passwords

- Changed whenever compromised. If you have any reason to believe that someone knows your password by observing your entry or guessing it, change it immediately.
- Changed periodically. Your practice may identify a frequency with which all passwords must be changed.
- Not reused. Information systems should be able to prevent reuse of a password.
- Not be shared with anyone, including anyone claiming to need a password to fix your computer or for an emergency. The requirement for access controls includes an emergency access procedure (see Chapter 9). Ideally, this should be the technical capability of overriding an existing access privilege on an exception basis, with an audit trail or other notification generated as a result.

Reprinted with permission from Tom Walsh Consulting, LLC.

SECURITY INCIDENT PROCEDURES STANDARD

The Security Incident Procedures standard requires you to "implement policies and procedures to address security incidents" (§164.308[a][6]). Typically, security incident procedures involve:

1. Identifying suspected or known security incidents.
2. Reporting security incidents to the appropriate person.
3. Responding to a security incident, which includes:
    a. Preservation of evidence, if applicable.
    b. Correction of the situation that caused the incident.
    c. Mitigation, to the extent practicable, of any harmful effects.
4. Documenting security incidents and their outcomes.
5. Evaluating security incidents as part of ongoing risk management.

The implementation specification required for this standard is Response and Reporting. The standard states: "Identify and respond to suspected or known security incidents; mitigate, to the extent practicable, harmful effects of security incidents that are known to the covered entity; and document security incidents and their outcomes" (§164.308[a][6][ii]).

An incident is a situation where a threat exploits a vulnerability. Although many incidents cause harm, not all do. For example, a network may be pinged (ie, one computer has reached another across the Internet), but this ping may not cause a problem, or it may introduce a virus or other form of hack attack. Figure 6.8 provides a list of some security incidents that can occur in a physician's office. All members of the workforce should be taught to recognize and report these.

FIGURE 6.8

Sample Security Incidents in Physician Offices

- Use of someone else's password
- Visible reminder of password
- Copies of printouts or notes with PHI in unsecured trash
- Corrupt backup media
- Malicious code and/or virus attack
- Physical break-in with patient information copied or stolen (paper or electronic)
- PHI posted on the Internet from a Web portal
- Misdirected e-mail
- Patient charts left unsupervised in a place accessible to patients or others
- Workstation monitors left logged on when not in use
- System access to patient data down and no operational plan to have the information to treat patients
- Unencrypted or otherwise unsecured e-mail or file attachments containing PHI
- Former employee using old ID and password to access PHI
- PC hard drive, CDs, USB drive, or mobile devices including PHI discarded (including donated or sent to a special collection agent) without physical destruction
- Terminated employee keeping copies of records with PHI
- Maintenance personnel fixing equipment with PHI without supervision by your workforce
- Someone impersonating an IT technician asking for a password

Reprinted with permission from Boundary Information Group.

Although some of the incidents listed in Figure 6.8 are always a concern and do get reported, some have actually been normal practice pre-HIPAA, such as discarding notes in unsecured trash and sharing passwords. To this day, it requires regular reminders to urge everyone to report all security incidents. Such reporting should be viewed as part of awareness building and should not be performed in an accusatory manner. Also, there should be no retaliation for reporting security incidents.

Your practice needs to develop a process to manage the reporting of security incidents. Identify to whom (supervisor, ISO, and/or office manager) and how (via phone, e-mail, written memo) security incidents should be reported. Responding to an incident involves first determining if the incident involves a breach as defined under the HITECH Act and taking applicable notification steps (see Chapter 10 for a comprehensive description of these requirements), then investigating what caused the incident, repairing any harm caused by the incident, taking steps to ensure the incident does not occur again, mitigating any harmful effects of the incident to the extent practicable, and applying sanctions if necessary.

To determine cause and repair results, it may be necessary to preserve evidence. Although it probably won't be necessary to call in a forensic security specialist, any evidence of wrongdoing must be preserved. This is one reason why all security incidents must be reported to the ISO, even if the report is made through a supervisor. Remediation for security incidents varies with the type of incident and may involve retraining, revising procedures, or instituting a new technical control.

Any harmful effects of a security incident must also be mitigated. For example, if the inability to access information results in delayed treatment or corrupt data that cause a treatment error, clinical risk management procedures must be applied. If an attack on your information system results in theft of credit card information, you will probably have to support your patients in correcting their credit history.

Prior to HIPAA, many security incidents, such as improper access to PHI, were handled simply in a conversation between a supervisor and the workforce member regarding the inappropriate behavior. Often, there was a verbal warning with no documentation in the employment file and no formal reporting to anyone else. Today, there are sanctions if incidents are found to be intentional or due to laxity in following policies and procedures, and notifiable breaches are reported to the federal government.

In addition to the regulatory requirement for documentation, recognizing repeated incidents will alert you to a potentially more serious problem that may require revision of policy or adoption of stronger technical controls. If all incidents are not reported and included in a security incident analysis, it may be impossible to identify the significance of an isolated incident. Treat the security incident documentation as confidential business information and maintain it in a secure manner.

CONTINGENCY PLAN STANDARD

HIPAA requires contingency planning in which you "establish (and implement as needed) policies and procedures for responding to an emergency or other occurrence (eg, fire, vandalism, system failure, and natural disaster) that damages systems that contain ePHI" (§164.308[a][7]).

The standard includes five implementation specifications:

■ Data backup plan
■ Disaster recovery plan
■ Emergency mode operation plan
■ Testing and revision procedures
■ Applications and data criticality analysis in support of the other contingency plan components

Data Backup Plan

The Data Backup Plan specification requires you to "establish and implement procedures to create and maintain retrievable exact copies of ePHI" (§164.308[a][7][ii][A]).

Although it would seem obvious that all PHI should be backed up, you may find you are in a hybrid environment where some data are on paper and other data are electronic. Even if you are fully electronic, there may be multiple sources, which do not necessarily reside in the same database. There are also other important data to back up. Figure 6.9 provides examples of data that need to be backed up.

FIGURE 6.9

Examples of Data to Be Backed Up

- Patient accounting data, including claims, remittances, etc
- Transcribed documents, including history and physical examination notes, records of phone calls, etc
- Scanned documents about patients, such as those from other physicians, consents for specific treatments, etc
- All e-mail, whether containing PHI or not
- Electronic health record (EHR) data
- Health maintenance, case management, and disease management information
- Diagnostic test results obtained from your practice or another provider
- Digital recordings of diagnostic images, such as ultrasound recordings, x-rays, etc
- Research data in databases or spreadsheets
- Any other documents created or used in the practice with PHI
- Appointment scheduling and registration (although this may not include PHI, it may be critical to your office functions)

Reprinted with permission from Boundary Information Group.

Once you know what you are going to back up, you should document a backup plan.

The first step in creating a backup plan is to determine who will be responsible for creating and maintaining the plan. Typically, the IT department, person, or contractor is responsible for performing the backup for your office's data. However, there may not be a formal, documented plan; or the plan may not fully address all elements of an appropriate backup strategy. Ideally, your ISO should coordinate with IT to assure that a backup plan is in place and that it is being performed as intended.

Next you will need to establish policies and procedures for how frequently the backup is performed, what media are used and a rotation schedule, where backups will be stored, and the process to place backups in the backup location.

Tapes have been the most common backup medium, although they are being widely replaced with CDs or other media, or direct transmission of data to a backup location. If you are backing up on media, the backup process is similar regardless of the media used. Figure 6.10 provides backup, rotation, and storage procedures for backup media.

F I G U R E 6.10
Backup, Rotation, and Storage Procedures for Backup Media

Frequency of Backups

Perform backups when they are least likely to impact office operations. Typically, this means setting up the backups to run automatically at night after the office closes. If you do not yet have an EHR system, configure information systems to run incremental backups four times each week and a full backup at least one day each week. The fourth weekly backup each month is considered a monthly backup.

The backup cycle initially uses 10 tapes, as follows:

- One for each of the four daily backups
- Three weekly tapes for weekly backups
- Two tapes for monthly backups
- One yearly backup tape

Daily backup: An incremental backup in which only the files that have changed since the last incremental (daily) backup was performed. The advantage is that the backup takes less time to run and uses less space on the backup medium. Daily (incremental) backup tapes are normally kept on site in a secure, fire-rated container.

Weekly backup: A backup operation that performs a full backup of all files on a drive, regardless of whether the file changed since the last full backup. These backup tapes are kept off site and are rotated back into use once a month. The advantage of full backups is that regardless of whether the entire system or only a few files need to be restored, all of the most current information is located on tape. The disadvantages are that it may take more than one tape to contain all of the files and they are time consuming.

Monthly backup: A full backup that is kept securely off site as the archive copy for the previous month.

Yearly backup: A full backup that is made once each year, usually on the last business day of the year. If the last business day is in the middle of the week, the normal rotation schedule for that week is changed. After the backup is made, the backup tape is kept securely off site as the archive for the year.

Labeling Backups

Label the tapes for each server or system, with the server or system name in ink. Use pencil to write the date of backup because the dates will change each week. Example of backup labeling initiated on Monday, June 2:

1. Server or System Name, Monday—June 2.
2. Server or System Name, Tuesday—June 3.
3. Server or System Name, Wednesday—June 4.
4. Server or System Name, Thursday—June 5.
5. Server or System Name, Weekly 1—June 6.
6. Server or System Name, Weekly 2—June 13.
7. Server or System Name, Weekly 3—June 20.
8. Server or System Name, Monthly 1—June 2.
9. Server or System Name, Monthly 2—July 25.
10. Server or System Name, Year 2XXX—December 31.

(continued)

F I G U R E 6.10 (continued)

Backup, Rotation, and Storage Procedures for Backup Media

Backup Steps

Assign someone in your office the responsibility for changing out the tapes and verifying that the backup was completed properly each day. Most offices assign this task to the ISO or an IT support person, if the office is large enough to have on-site IT support. Following are the general steps for this person to follow.

1. Remove the tape that ran the night before from the tape backup unit.

2. Label the date on the tape.

3. If the tape is a daily tape (labeled Monday–Thursday), store it in the fire-rated safe or container. Remove the tape for the current night's backup from the fire-rated container or safe.

4. Insert the tape labeled for the present day (Friday tapes are labeled as "Weekly x" or "Monthly x").

5. Log that the backup was completed and the name or initials of the person who swapped out the tapes. Note: If a tape backup does not complete properly, immediately notify your IT vendor or support person to diagnose the problem and take the necessary steps to maintain backup integrity. Backups are usually scheduled by your IT vendor or support person to run automatically. The only manual interaction that is required is changing of the tapes.

Storing Backups

On-site backups: Daily backup tapes should be stored on site in a fire-rated container or safe. Old weekly tapes that have been cycled back on site and are ready for reuse after a monthly tape has been made should be stored on site.

Replace daily and weekly backup tapes that have been in service for more than two years. Over time, the possibility of media failure from constant reuse increases. Don't cut corners on something as valuable as backups by overextending the useful life of the tapes.

Off-site backups: Weekly, monthly, and yearly backup tapes should be securely stored off site. At any given time there should be at least three to six backup tapes stored off site. Yearly backups should be kept as your archive and should not be reused. Storing backup media offsite requires moving the media from your office to another location. Because there is always the risk of loss or theft of the media—even when using the US Postal Service, a commercial carrier, or your most trusted office member, the data on the media should be encrypted prior to movement. See Chapter 10 for additional information on guidance to render portable media indecipherable. A best practice would be to encrypt media even if it will not be located out of the office, as there is always the possibility that these will be misplaced, accidentally discarded, or stolen.

Testing Backups

Test your backups regularly and document any time when files were restored from backup media. (Documentation of backup recovery can support your proof for addressing the implementation specification, ie, Testing and Revision Procedure of the Contingency Plan standard.)

Reprinted with permission from Tom Walsh Consulting, LLC.

Finally, if you have a complete EHR, your backup should essentially be continuous. If you retain servers in your office, you should have a fully redundant set of servers in the event of a server crash. These servers, however, are for processing current work. You should also have a separate storage server, storage network, or process to transmit backup data to a remote location. As data are entered into the EHR servers, they should be copied to the storage server, network, and/or remote site. Such a backup process, however, should also be documented, tested regularly, and refreshed periodically. The amount of data that will be backed up from an EHR is great. While you need to keep the data in accordance with your state's statute of limitations and any other needs you identify, such as malpractice insurance requirements, research, etc, it is possible that not all of the data will be needed immediately for the duration of the retention period. Retrieving data from a backup server can take an increasing amount of time if the backup data are not well-managed. In fact, storage management is becoming a separate IT function. It is very likely that you will want to store certain types of data separately from a primary storage server. Work with your EHR vendor or disaster recovery specialist to determine how best to manage your data storage and backup process.

Disaster Recovery Plan

The Disaster Recovery Plan specification requires you to "establish (and implement as needed) procedures to restore any loss of data" (§164.308[a][7][ii][B]).

If you already have an information systems disaster plan, review it at any time you make a major change to your systems. Many offices are actively enhancing their systems, adding an EHR, offering a patient portal and/or personal health record, and participating in a health information exchange organization (HIO). At each of these major milestones it is good to review the associated disaster plan. If you do not have an information systems disaster plan but have a general disaster plan for your practice location, review it and potentially enhance it to ensure that it meets your needs in recovering PHI. If you do not have a disaster plan at all, now is the time to develop a comprehensive one that includes recovery of PHI.

If you use hosted services for your information systems, the vendor should have a disaster recovery plan. Be sure to obtain documentation that you understand and that meets your needs. However, this does not preclude you from also having a disaster plan for the components that reside in your office or connect to your office. For instance, the hosting company may be located many miles away, but if you have only one connection to the Internet and that goes down, you have a disaster. Some practices subscribe to a second wireless service, cable, DSL, or even dial-up connection for backup connectivity. These may only afford slow service, but at least you would be able to access key information to manage until the main connectivity is restored. In fact, loss of connectivity is the most common problem associated with using a hosted service. If your office experiences a break-in and the computers you use to access your applications are stolen, you may or may not lose PHI depending on what was stored on local devices. But you will still need to operate in your environment until the devices are replaced. Storing spare computers at another location or using computers personally owned by members of the workforce may be applicable.

Whether you host your own servers or use some form of hosted service, a disaster recovery plan is still essential. It will address issues specific to your environment, including the types of disasters that could occur, from temporary loss of electricity to a fire or tornado, which could wipe out not only the data on site but also the physical facility where you see patients. If you have more than one office location and a disaster struck, you may be able to use another location for seeing patients; if you have only one location, you will need to develop a new permanent or temporary location. For practices located in a medical office building, it is probably not possible to use empty office space in the building or to double up with another physician in the building if disaster strikes the whole building. Determine whether building management has a disaster plan that you could use as an alternative.

If you are using a hosted service, your disaster recovery plan will need to address the computer you have on site, power, and connectivity to the remote site.

Figure 6.11 describes the components of a disaster recovery plan where you host your own servers. As part of your disaster planning, determine where all information systems are located. If you have multiple sites, each with its own local area network, it may be appropriate to expand the network so that you have local storage as well as a single site that serves as a primary data center and another as a backup. An alternative is to have each site serve as a backup for the others.

FIGURE 6.11

Disaster Recovery Plan Components

- Telephone numbers of all persons you should contact in the event of a disaster. This includes police, fire, rescue, and other emergency service numbers as well as contact information for your own immediate response team to investigate and secure the site as necessary. Add contact information for any ongoing physical security that may be needed if not provided by a leased building. Also include contact information for where you may be able to relocate your practice if necessary. If yours is a large enough practice, include a call tree so that all members of your office workforce can be contacted and can begin to carry out any functions they may be assigned in the event of a disaster.
- A list of tasks each person in the practice should be prepared to perform in the event of a disaster.
- Inventory of all computer hardware, including workstations, servers, printers, etc, that would need to be replaced as part of the recovery from a disaster. The inventory should include the model number of the equipment; the name, telephone number, and Web site URL of the company from which you purchased the equipment for replacement purposes; the date of equipment purchase and serial number of the equipment for recovery/insurance purposes.
- Documentation of your network configuration, and contact information for outside agencies or other resources to contact to restore or rebuild the network.
- Inventory of the software licenses and backup copies of the license agreements for all software that would need to be replaced. Include the phone numbers and the system account or contract numbers of the information systems vendors who can replace the software or restore access to a hosted environment.
- Records of the backup data that would be used in the recovery process, including their location. If stored under contract services, a copy of the contract, contact information, and hours of operation. If stored in an on-site safe, bank safety deposit box, or other private location, keys/combinations and authorization papers authorizing access.
- Record of when the disaster recovery plan was last reviewed, tested, and workforce trained.

Reprinted with permission from Margret\A Consulting, LLC.

Keep a copy of your disaster recovery plan readily accessible, either in a paper notebook or on a CD if you have access to an off-site PC. Keep one copy in the primary office location; keep another copy off site, such as at home. Do not keep the only other copy in a bank vault where you only have access during regular business hours.

Insurance coverage may be needed to pay for replacement equipment and to recreate and test the data and information system infrastructure. Your documentation will be critical for this purpose as well.

Companies that specialize in disaster recovery can assist you in understanding the type of planning and level of automation you need for your environment. Having a disaster recovery company is much like having an insurance policy.

An option other than hosting your own disaster recovery services, especially for larger offices or single-site offices, is to obtain disaster recovery services from a vendor. This may be the same vendor who performs backup for you if you transmit backup data out of your office. In general, there are three categories, or levels, of disaster recovery services. They may provide a hot site, warm site, or cold site. Figure 6.12 provides a description of each of these and advantages and disadvantages of each.

F I G U R E   6.12

Categories of Disaster Recovery Services

Hot site: A hot site is another facility that has the necessary infrastructure (power, environmental controls, network connectivity, etc) plus hardware to allow recovery of operations within a few hours by restoring the information systems from backup tapes. An even better hot site is another location that has not only the infrastructure and hardware but an exact replica of your system, including software. If a reciprocal arrangement with another practice or other type of facility is not possible for you and you want the quickest possible ability to return to normal operations, talk to your software vendor or evaluate companies that specialize in providing hot sites. A hot site:

■ Is the most expensive
■ Has the shortest recovery time
■ Supplies equipment
■ Supplies short-term use of facility
■ Is a good way to test backups and recovery plans

Warm site: A warm site has the infrastructure but not all of the computer and network hardware. It is a facility that has been designated as the location from which recovery operations will be performed. It may take a few days or more to get the necessary computer and network equipment set up at a warm site to restore operations. A warm site:

■ Is moderately priced
■ Provides at a minimum infrastructure to recover within a matter of a few days
■ Does not afford an easy way to test recovery plans
■ May not always be available

Cold site: A cold site is a facility with basic necessities of power and heating, ventilation, and air conditioning (HVAC), and empty floor space, but not much more. Getting an operation recovered from a cold site can take a long time. A cold site:

■ Is the least expensive
■ Requires the longest recovery time
■ Does not provide any equipment
■ Some desired infrastructure may not be completely in place

Reprinted with permission from Tom Walsh Consulting, LLC.

Your determination of which site will be best for your office is based on how long the practice can function without its information systems. As your office becomes more dependent on computers for automation of business processes (electronic claims processing, online scheduling, and EHRs), the more important a disaster recovery site becomes. You may consider using an application service provider (ASP), software as a service (SaaS), or other outsourcing arrangement for disaster recovery. As previously noted, however, you are ultimately responsible and should manage your relationship with an ASP, SaaS, or other host as you would any other vendor relationship.

Emergency Mode Operation Plan

The Emergency Mode Operation Plan specification requires you to "establish (and implement as needed) procedures to enable continuation of critical business processes for protection of the security of ePHI while operating in emergency mode" (§164.308[a][7][ii][C]).

Emergency mode operation planning is often called business continuity planning because it is designed to keep you functioning even when you don't have access to your computer systems or other office equipment. An example of emergency mode operation is when everything in your practice is operating normally (including electricity), but a technical failure in your information system causes downtime. Another example is a power outage.

The question to be answered is: How will I operate the practice until I can access data or my ability to enter data is restored? This answer will vary depending on your level of automation and the nature of the disaster.

CASE STUDY 6.3
Appointment Scheduling and/or Practice Management System Is Down

If the practice does not have an EHR, print out appointment lists, encounter forms, and medical record chart pull lists each day for the next day. That way, you still know what appointments have been scheduled and when, the charts can be pulled, and the encounter forms have already been printed for use in recording information for billing and other purposes. (Make sure that the practice management system is set to always print the patient balance due on the encounter form.) By handwriting appointments on blank encounter form templates that are added while the system is unavailable and keeping a manual payment log to record receipts of cash, checks, and credit card payments, the practice can keep going for a full day, which is usually adequate for an issue associated only with the information system itself. Use the paper documentation to enter the data the next day.

CASE STUDY 6.4
Practice Management and EHR System Is Down

Printing the appointment schedule and encounter forms with at least patient contact information each night for the next day is still a very good practice. In a small practice, clinicians can review the schedule and determine which patients they believe can still be seen and for which patients they will need to access the EHR, such that their appointments will need to be rescheduled. A large practice should determine from their information systems vendor or support service how long it will take to restore the system. The practice may need to call all or most patients and reschedule appointments. Obtaining patients' cell phone numbers is a good practice to avert patients arriving before they can access their voice mail at home or work. If the EHR is able to generate an encounter form in the form of a patient summary with problem list, medication list, medication allergy list, and last lab results, more—if not most—patients may be able to be seen.

Another potential alternative is to nightly load onto fully charged computers the encounter/patient summary data for the first few patients to be seen each day. This can be used as an electronic form of a paper encounter/patient summary form. (This will require an EHR system to generate such information and transfer it to laptops or tablets that have the processing capability to hold such data. Some of the hosted EHR systems do not afford such functionality.) Even if the rest of the patients need to be rescheduled, at least those that show up at the same time as you open the office and discover the down system can be seen. Most laptop or tablet computers will hold a charge for four hours at a minimum. Extra and/or long-life batteries can also be a part of your plan. Part of your emergency mode operation planning should include the nature of patient visits that can be conducted without access to the full EHR or a determination that all patients will be rescheduled. Documentation will need to be entered on the encounter form for later entry, or dictated and/or handwritten and electronically fed or scanned into the EHR.

Remember, however, that if a down computer system is the result of loss of power, the loss of power will likely necessitate shutting down the entire office because heating, cooling, lighting, some medical devices, and other factors may preclude seeing patients even if the EHR is available on a charged portable device. If alarm and locking systems are electronic and not working, alternative methods will have to be used to secure the practice and your data. Although an expensive proposition, a backup generator may be a consideration for large practices or those in locations particularly prone to power outages. In the event of an extended power outage, an emergency mode operation plan may be to see patients in another location, if one is available.

Another consideration, if the system is down due to a system crash and not a power outage, is to plan for full redundancy in all information system components (as well as power) so that if one part of a system goes down, there is immediate backup. It is common practice for EHR systems to run on two servers simultaneously—with one serving as an immediate backup for the other. Redundancy in connectivity to the Internet for a hosted environment was previously mentioned.

Your risk analysis should help you decide the extent to which your emergency mode operation plan needs full or partial redundancy in servers, connectivity, and power. Consider the emergency mode operation plan components in Figure 6.13.

FIGURE 6.13

Emergency Mode Operation Plan Components

- Printouts of patient schedules and/or encounter forms, either of which should include patient telephone or cell phone numbers.
- Inventory of hard copy forms and documents that are needed to record clinical and financial interactions with patients who may be seen without access to the EHR.
- Access to hard copy or secondary versions of electronic records that can be used to create hard copy versions of patient clinical and billing data (eg, laptop or tablet computer and extra, charged batteries).
- Written instructions in at least two separate locations about what to do and who is responsible for performing what tasks during emergency mode.
- Assigned responsibility to safeguard the hard copy transition documents until the information can be entered into and processed by the electronic systems once they have been restored to full operation.

Reprinted with permission from Boundary Information Group.

Testing and Revision Procedures

For the Testing and Revision Procedures specification, you would develop "procedures for periodic testing and revision of contingency plans" (§164.308[a][7][ii][D]).

This implementation specification applies to all contingency plans: data backup, disaster recovery, and emergency mode operation. Although the specification is addressable, it is the frequency and comprehensiveness of the procedures, rather than alternatives to testing, that will vary among covered entities.

A typical test for data backup is to use the most recent or the second most recent version of the data backup in restore mode and see if it works. Criteria for testing your backup plan appear below. Remember that if your information systems are hosted, you are still responsible for assuring that the company has contingency plans and that these are routinely tested. Request evidence of such testing as part of your routine information system management process.

Testing and Revision Criteria for Backup Plan

- Is the process for restoring data from backups documented and do the people responsible for performing the restoration know where the documentation is?
- Following the step-by-step procedures in the backup and restoration plan documents, was the data restored for all data displays to provide an exact copy?
- Did the process of restoring the data take place in a time frame that is acceptable to your practice?

Disaster recovery plans and emergency mode operations also need testing; both are frequently tested in the form of a drill or desktop scenario. You may already perform drills for other safety reasons, or your office building may have routine fire drills or even disaster recovery drills of its own. If your building performs planned power outages, use this time to test your information systems emergency mode and disaster recovery. Document the results of each test and the date when each was run; have the ISO maintain all documentation. Any problems with the backup process should be reviewed and corrected by either changing the process, changing the documentation for recovery, or changing the resources that are used to restore the data.

Consider conducting these tests on test mode servers and testing versions of the applications. If the test fails, the operational data do not become corrupt or unavailable. It may be necessary to conduct the test on a fully operational system. If this is done, conduct the test during off-hours so that there is time to recreate the data from other sources without impacting patient care if the recovery does not work correctly.

CASE STUDY 6.5
A Hospital with a Payroll System Problem

A hospital ran its biweekly payroll on Friday afternoon, with the paychecks issued to the hospital staff starting at 6:00 AM Monday morning before the nurses left their shifts that ended at 7:00 AM. One Friday the payroll system failed. The hospital had a contingency plan that included an agreement with a school system, which had the same hardware, to use their facilities during off-hours if the hospital system failed. The agreement was reciprocal.

The hospital information system staff took the payroll data tapes and payroll software over to the school system's data center on Friday evening. They loaded the payroll software, loaded the payroll data, worked all weekend to get it to work right, and on Monday morning were handing out paychecks to the nursing staff at 6:30 AM before they left work. The backup plan had been put in place and it worked, in part because every quarter they tested the backups and the disaster recovery plan for just such a contingency.

CASE STUDY 6.6
A Medical Group With a Billing System Problem

The month-end billing process from the practice management system for a medical group failed. A disk drive with the current data was thought to be corrupt. The computer night operator took the full system backup from the night before, loaded it onto the computer, and reran the billing program. However, instead of reading the data from the backup, he wrote the corrupt data onto this first backup copy. At 4:00 AM, he realized his mistake and loaded the two-day-old backup onto the computer and reran the process. Unfortunately, he made the same mistake again. This left the medical group with the current billing database and the two previous backups all corrupt.

Why did this happen? It happened for two reasons. First, they had never tested their backup recovery procedures. Second, the backup recovery procedures were not well documented. The night operator thought he knew what he was doing, but he did not. It took several weeks, with the assistance of the billing system vendor, to recover most of the billing data and restore the system with full data integrity. During that time, no billing could take place and cash flow to the practice suffered, while they also incurred the significant expense for the assistance from their software vendor.

Applications and Data Criticality Analysis

For the Applications and Data Criticality Analysis specification, you "assess the relative criticality of specific applications and data in support of other contingency plan components" (§164.308[a][7][ii][E]).

This means that your practice needs to inventory the software applications that you use and determine how important each is in order to prioritize your disaster recovery and/or emergency mode operations. In essence, you are making a priority list of which gets restored first, or which is maintained on the backup generator. This is an addressable implementation specification because if you only have one system, that system is obviously the one that is most critical! Alternatively, you may believe that the Web portal used to retrieve hospital lab results is critical. Because the hospital is able to fax you copies of the most urgently needed lab results, this turns out not to be your most critical data and application in planning for emergency mode operation. Consider the factors suggested in Figure 6.14 to prioritize your disaster recovery efforts.

Data Criticality Considerations

- Length of time you can work without access to the data (eg, 30 minutes, one day, several days)
- Archived data (eg, paper charts in your office, paper charts in a warehouse) are available within a reasonable period of time. These are not backups of your electronic data, but older records for which some of the data have been transferred to electronic form. While not containing the most current information, they can be useful if a backup system fails.
- Applications run on a hosted vendor from which access can be gained from another location (be sure your contract with the vendor guarantees 100% up-time)
- Laptop/notebook PC battery life/availability of (charged) spare batteries

Reprinted with permission from Boundary Information Group.

EVALUATION STANDARD

The standard on evaluation requires you to "perform a periodic technical and nontechnical evaluation, based initially on the standards implemented under this rule and subsequently, in response to environmental or operational changes affecting the security of ePHI, that establishes the extent to which an entity's security policies and procedures meet the requirements of [the Security Rule]" (§164.308[a][8]).

This standard has no implementation specifications. At the time when the Security Rule was first implemented, the initial evaluation was to be based on the standards in the Security Rule. The risk analysis in Chapter 5 can be used as a guide for the initial evaluation.

Any subsequent evaluations should be based on environmental or operational changes. Use the analysis of your security incidents and breaches, any changes in your practice, and information about new technology to highlight the areas needing attention. Be aware of security incidents in other practices, in health care in general, and even in other industries in your community. These can be indicative of new threats.

Although HIPAA does not specify a time frame for conducting periodic evaluation, it is a good idea to perform an evaluation annually and at the time significant changes occur in your operations, if a large number of incidents/breaches occur, or if there are sudden threats in your environment.

Evaluation can be performed internally, using external assistance, or through a combination. The evaluation process should be unbiased. To achieve this, have a small committee instead of one person conduct the evaluation. Consider using an outside expert for evaluation in areas in which you have identified problems and are not sure how to best address them in your practice.

Fully document your periodic evaluation reports, the supporting material considered in your analysis, recommendations, and subsequent changes. Again, the risk analysis form in Chapter 5 can be extended for this purpose. The evaluation is typically conducted or at least overseen by the ISO. Because periodic security evaluations often identify significant gaps that pose a high risk, limit the number of individuals involved in the evaluation process and the number of individuals that see the report to those who have a need to know before the high-risk issues have been addressed. You may need to obtain an unbiased review of the ISO's performance, which would be analyzed with the ISO but retained in a separate file.

IMPORTANCE OF ADMINISTRATIVE SAFEGUARDS

From this chapter's description of the HIPAA Administrative Safeguard standards and their implementation specifications, you can see that much of security is about garnering support from the people in your practice for attention to information security, planning and policy development, procedures and processes to carry out plans, and ensuring preparedness through testing and evaluation of the plans to ensure they work as expected.

Appropriate policies and procedures that are effectively and efficiently carried out by all members of your workforce are critical to compliance with the administrative safeguards. The Administrative Safeguards comprise over half of the HIPAA requirements for security. This clearly represents the importance HIPAA places on these safeguards.

CHECK YOUR UNDERSTANDING*

Match each item to its definition:

1. Information System Activity Review ___

2. Workforce Termination Procedures ___

3. Information Access Management ___

4. Access Establishment ___

5. Security Awareness ___

6. Security Training ___

7. Login Monitoring ___

8. Password Management ___

9. Security Incident Procedures ___

10. Evaluation ___

    a. Authorizing access according to the minimum necessary needed for PHI
    b. Periodic reminders about security
    c. Reviewing discrepancies in attempts to access information systems
    d. Documentation and evaluation of audit logs, access reports, and security incidents
    e. Requirement for changing an authentication mechanism
    f. Implementation of access based on authorization
    g. Process used to manage a situation where a threat has exploited a vulnerability
    h. Removing access to information systems
    i. Instruction on how to use security controls
    j. Periodic review of the need to update security policies and procedures

*For answers, refer to the Answer Key at the end of the book.

Business Associate Contracts and Other Arrangements Standard

While most practices have had at least a few business associates in the past, use of business associates is significantly increasing with enhanced automation, increasing use of Internet-based hosting services, greater contributions of population data to registries, advanced analytics, new cross-organizational relationships forming for health reform, and participation in electronic and formalized health information exchange. As greater use is made of business associates the risk of security incidents increases.

HOW TO USE THIS CHAPTER

This chapter covers the business associate contracts and other arrangements standard in HIPAA and more. It:

- Defines business associate and describes business associate contract provisions
- Describes changes to the business associate status from the Health Information Technology for Economic and Clinical Health (HITECH) Act of 2009
- Offers special considerations when acquiring information systems from vendors providing Internet-hosting services and other shared services
- Discusses health information exchange (HIE) participation and health information exchange organization (HIO) agreements
- Provides suggestions for managing your Web presence and social media usage

The HIPAA Security Rule requires business associate contracts and other arrangements to bind business associates to the requirements of the rule. HIPAA actually addresses business associates in four sections: first to provide a definition of business associate, then to describe what access to protected health information (PHI) a business associate is permitted, and finally to provide particulars with respect to the Security Rule and to the Privacy Rule.

BUSINESS ASSOCIATE DEFINED

HIPAA defines business associate (at §160.103) as

> a person who (i) on behalf of [a] covered entity . . . but other than in the capacity of a member of the workforce of such covered entity . . . performs, or assists in the performance of:
>
> (A) A function or activity involving the use or disclosure of individually identifiable health information, including claims processing or administration, data analysis, processing or administration, utilization review, quality assurance, billing, benefit management, practice management, and repricing

(continued)

(B) Any other function or activity regulated by [HIPAA]

   (C) . . . legal, actuarial, accounting, consulting, data aggregation, administrative, accreditation, or financial services to or for [a] covered entity . . . where the provision of the service involves the disclosure of individually identifiable health information from [the] covered entity, or from another business associate of [the] covered entity . . . to the person.

Use the checklist in Figure 7.1 to make sure all of your business associates are identified.

FIGURE 7.1

Business Associate Checklist

Person or entity who is not part of the covered entity's workforce providing the following services:

- ◻ Claims processing or administration
- ◻ Data analysis
- ◻ Utilization review
- ◻ Quality assurance
- ◻ Billing
- ◻ Benefit management
- ◻ Practice management
- ◻ Repricing
- ◻ Legal
- ◻ Actuarial
- ◻ Accounting
- ◻ Consulting
- ◻ Data aggregation
- ◻ Management
- ◻ Administrative
- ◻ Accreditation
- ◻ Financial

Under HITECH, the following are also considered business associates:

- ◻ Health information exchanges
- ◻ Regional health information organizations
- ◻ E-prescribing gateways
- ◻ Organizations that provide data transmission of PHI to a covered entity
- ◻ Vendors providing personal health record systems for covered entities

The checklist in Figure 7.1 could be made much more granular. For instance, services such as coding, transcription, record scanning, document shredding, the work of information system application vendors, and many others are considered examples of one or more of the categories in the checklist. Some terms in the checklist may need further explanation. For example, data aggregation with respect to PHI means the combining of PHI of one covered entity with PHI received from another covered entity to permit analysis of data relating to the healthcare operations of the respective covered entities. Also remember that the checklist contains services that may more likely apply to health plans as covered entities rather than providers. However, there are some persons or entities that provide services to your office (and other covered entities) that are generally not considered business associates. These include mail carriers, police and fire department personnel responding to an alarm, building contractors, or a salesperson selling soap. The idea is that if persons or entities will never have access to PHI by virtue of only being a conduit for PHI or their work never requiring access to PHI, they are not business associates for whom a business associate contract is required. Some have questioned whether janitorial service firms or garbage collectors are considered business associates. The OCR Frequently Asked Question (FAQ) Number 243 (http://www.hhs.gov/ocr/privacy/hipaa/faq/index.html) indicates that in the course of their work, those providing janitorial services are not business associates because their work does not require access to PHI, and any access would be incidental.

It is also noted in HIPAA that a covered entity may be a business associate of another covered entity. For instance, a physician who is a member of the medical staff of a hospital admits patients and obviously has access to PHI. This relationship is not one of a business associate. However, if the physician uses hospital services to prepare professional claims, this service makes the hospital a business associate of the physician with respect to the service. Similarly, if the hospital contracts with a physician who is not a member of its medical staff to assist with one-on-one physician training on the EHR, the physician is a business associate of the hospital.

BUSINESS ASSOCIATE INVENTORY

In addition to making sure that all business associates are identified, it can be helpful to maintain an inventory of business associates. This inventory might include:

- Name of the business associate
- Summary of the purposes for which the business associate uses PHI
- Description of any special provisions for permitting use or disclosure of more than a limited data set of PHI
- Date the business associate contract was offered
- Date the business associate contract was signed
- Whether the business associate contract is part of a larger contract, license agreement, or other binding arrangement
- If part of a larger contract, the date the larger contract requires renewal
- Person authorized to sign the business associate contract for the covered entity
- Location of original business associate contract

Large organizations use special contract management software for the purpose of maintaining an inventory of contracts.

BUSINESS ASSOCIATE CONTRACTS AND OTHER ARRANGEMENTS

In §164.308(b), the business associate contract is described with respect to permitting a business associate to "create, receive, maintain, or transmit PHI on the covered entity's behalf . . . if the covered entity obtains satisfactory assurances . . . that the business associate will safeguard the information." This business associate standard does not apply to the following three situations specified in the Security Rule:

- Transmission by a covered entity of PHI to a healthcare provider concerning the treatment of an individual

- Transmission of PHI by a group health plan (or specified others) to a plan sponsor (this would not apply to most physician practices, except perhaps in their role as the sponsor of a health plan for the organization's workforce)

- Transmission of PHI from or to other agencies providing certain specified services when the covered entity is a health plan that is a government program providing public benefits (usually this does not apply to a physician practice)

It should be clear from both the definition of business associate and the exclusions that the relationship of two treating providers to a specific patient is not a business associate relationship. However, you should be aware that some hospitals are expecting treating providers to sign a business associate contract. In many instances this practice has arisen out of concerns that another provider is not following the HIPAA Privacy Rule and Security Rule in perhaps the same manner as the hospital. Case Study 7.1 provides an example. There is certainly no harm in different providers entering into a dialogue about strengthening their respective privacy and security practices. Organizations are also free to require a contract to engage in certain activities. However, in addition to HIPAA not requiring a business associate contract among treating providers, members of the medical staff are also bound by medical staff bylaws to comply with applicable rules and regulations. It seems (to this author at least) that there are better ways to ensure privacy and security compliance among treating providers where there may be concerns than via a business associate contract.

CASE STUDY 7.1
A Treating Provider as a Business Associate

A hospital opened a provider portal so that members of its medical staff would have access to lab results and eventually other information about their patients. After some period of time, an incident arose where the hospital noticed that a particular user ID and password was being used to gain access to the portal although it was known that the individual was no longer employed by the physician's office. As a result, the hospital decided to require all members of its medical staff who would access the provider portal to have a business associate contract with the hospital. Reactions were mixed, but many physicians signed the contract while wondering why it was required. When the hospital was asked about this at a meeting of the medical staff, it indicated that "there have been instances of inappropriate access by physician offices." The hospital never reported directly to the physician office involved that the user ID and password were still being used. Although many offices "recycle" user IDs and passwords as staff changes, the hospital never sent out a reminder to physician offices to be sure to notify the hospital of any terminations and new hires so that new user IDs and passwords could be assigned. While the physician office should have known to require a unique user ID and password for each member of its workforce, the hospital apparently thought that the practice would stop once a business associate contract was signed—even though, of course, it did not since there was no explicit action taken to correct the problem.

Contract vs Arrangement

The official term for the contractual arrangement between a covered entity and business associate is *business associate contract*. However, because the federal government uses *contract* in a more limited sense and has restrictions on who may enter into contracts, the alternate term *business associate agreement* is used synonymously to accommodate such federal government and private sector relationships.

Some covered entities seem to prefer the term *arrangement* over *contract*. This book uses the term *contract* both as a matter of convenience and to emphasize the contractual nature of the document.

Business Associate Contract Requirements

In §164.314, the business associate contract with respect to the Security Rule is described. In §164.504(e), the business associate contract with respect to the Privacy Rule is described. Both of these sections provide essentially the same information, with differences only in respect to requirements that are unique to privacy or to security. The language from these sections could be combined and used directly to serve as your business associate contract. In fact, many covered entities do this in order to avoid repercussions from including additional clauses or different language that may impose additional terms or convey a different meaning.

The Security Rule standard for Business Associate Contracts and Other Arrangements is consistent with the Business Associate Contract in the Privacy Rule. It allows a covered entity to "permit a business associate to create, receive, maintain, or transmit PHI on the covered entities' behalf only if the covered entity obtains satisfactory assurances in accordance with the Security Rule standard on Business Associate Contracts or Other Arrangements specifying the requirements of the business associate contract or other arrangements that the business associate will appropriately safeguard the information" (§164.308[b]).

Model Business Associate Contract

The model business associate contract in Figure 7.2 is taken directly from and integrates the Security Rule and Privacy Rule requirements. It also includes language that addresses the HITECH breach notification requirements that became effective on September 23, 2009, and limitations on uses and disclosures of a limited data set of PHI unless a greater amount of PHI is the minimum necessary required to perform the purposes of the contract (effective February 17, 2010). A limited data set is PHI that excludes certain direct identifiers of the individual or of relatives, employers, or household members of the individual. The list of identifiers includes most, but not all, of the identifiers required to be removed to de-identify data. These include names, address (but the limited data set may include city, state, and zip code), telephone and fax numbers, e-mail addresses, social security numbers, medical record numbers, health plan beneficiary numbers, account numbers, certificate/license numbers, vehicle identifiers, universal resource locators (URLs), Internet protocol (IP) addresses, biometrics, and full-face photos or comparable images. In addition to city, state, and zip codes, birth dates and dates of service are also permitted to be in a limited data set.

FIGURE 7.2

Business Associate Contract

Business Associate Contract

THIS CONTRACT is entered into on this _____ day of _____, year of _____, between _____ ("COVERED ENTITY") and _____ ("BUSINESS ASSOCIATE").

****

WHEREAS, COVERED ENTITY will make available and/or transfer to BUSINESS ASSOCIATE Protected Health Information, in conjunction with goods or services that are being provided by BUSINESS ASSOCIATE to COVERED ENTITY, that is confidential and must be afforded special treatment and protection.

WHEREAS, BUSINESS ASSOCIATE will have access to and/or receive from COVERED ENTITY Protected Health Information that can be used or disclosed only in accordance with this Contract and the Privacy Rule.

NOW, THEREFORE, COVERED ENTITY and BUSINESS ASSOCIATE agree as follows:

1. **<NL>Definitions**. The following terms shall have the meaning ascribed to them in this Section. Other capitalized terms shall have the meaning ascribed to them in the context in which they first appear.

   - **<BL>Contract** shall refer to this document.
   - **BUSINESS ASSOCIATE** shall mean _____
   - **COVERED ENTITY** shall mean _____
   - **Privacy Rule** shall mean the Code of Federal Regulations ("C.F.R.") at Title 45, Sections 160 and 164.
   - **Security Rule** shall mean the Code of Federal Regulations ("C.F.R") at Title 45, Sections 160 and 164.
   - **Individual** shall mean the person who is the subject of the Protected Health Information, as defined by 45 C.F.R. 164.501.
   - **Protected Health Information** shall mean a "limited data set" of Protected Health Information as defined by 45 C.F.R. 164.514(e) unless a greater amount of PHI, as specified in this Contract, is the minimum necessary required to carry out the purposes of this contract. **Parties** shall mean BUSINESS ASSOCIATE and COVERED ENTITY.
   - **Secretary** shall mean the Secretary of the Department of Health and Human Services ("HHS") and any other officer or employee of HHS to whom the authority involved has been delegated.

2. <NL>**Regulatory References.** A Reference in this Contract to a section in the Privacy Rule or Security Rule means the section as in effect or as amended.

OBLIGATIONS OF BUSINESS ASSOCIATE

3. **Limits on Use and Disclosure Established By Terms of Contract**. BUSINESS ASSOCIATE hereby agrees that it shall be prohibited from using or disclosing a "limited data set" of Protected Health Information as defined by 45 C.F.R. 164.514(e) unless a greater amount of PHI, as specified below, is the minimum necessary to accomplish the purposes of the use, disclosure, or request

---

(continued)

Business Associate Contract

provided or made available by COVERED ENTITY for any purpose other than as expressly permitted or required by this Contract or as required by law:

_____

4. **Stated Purposes for Which BUSINESS ASSOCIATE May Use or Disclose Protected Health Information.** Except as otherwise limited in this Contract, BUSINESS ASSOCIATE may use, disclose, or respond to a request for a "limited data set" of Protected Health Information unless a greater amount of PHI, as specified in this Contract, is the minimum necessary to accomplish the purposes of the use, disclosure, or request on behalf of, or to provide services to, COVERED ENTITY for the following stated purposes:

_____

5. **Use of Protected Health Information for Management, Administration, and Legal Responsibilities**. BUSINESS ASSOCIATE is permitted to use a "limited data set" of Protected Health Information unless a greater amount of PHI, as specified in this Contract, is the minimum necessary for the proper management and administration of BUSINESS ASSOCIATE or to carry out legal responsibilities of BUSINESS ASSOCIATE.

6. **Disclosure of Protected Health Information for Management, Administration, and Legal Responsibilities.** BUSINESS ASSOCIATE is permitted to disclose a "limited data set" of Protected Health Information unless a greater amount of PHI, as specified in this Contract, is the minimum necessary for the BUSINESS ASSOCIATE or to carry out legal responsibilities of BUSINESS ASSOCIATE, provided:

    a. <AL>The disclosure is required by law; or

    b. The BUSINESS ASSOCIATE obtains reasonable assurances from the person to whom the Protected Health Information is disclosed that it will be held confidentially and used or further disclosed only as required by law or for the purposes for which it was disclosed to the person, the person will use appropriate safeguards to prevent use or disclosure of the Protected Health Information, and the person immediately notifies the BUSINESS ASSOCIATE of any instance of which it is aware in which the confidentiality of the Protected Health Information has been breached.

7. <NL>**Data Aggregation Services.** BUSINESS ASSOCIATE [*is/is not*] permitted to use or disclose a "limited data set" of Protected Health Information unless a greater amount of PHI, as specified in this Contract, is the minimum necessary to provide data aggregation services, as that term is defined by 45 C.F.R. 164.501, relating to the health care operations of COVERED ENTITY.

8. **Report Violations of Law.** BUSINESS ASSOCIATE may use a "limited data set" of Protected Health Information unless a greater amount of PHI is the minimum necessary to report violations of law to appropriate Federal and State authorities, consistent with 45 C.F.R. 164.502(j)(1).

9. **Limits on Use and Further Disclosure Established by Contract and Law.** BUSINESS ASSOCIATE hereby agrees that the Protected Health Information provided or made available by COVERED ENTITY shall not be further used or disclosed other than as permitted or required by the Contract or as required by law.

(continued)

Business Associate Contract

10. **Appropriate Safeguards**. BUSINESS ASSOCIATE will establish and maintain appropriate administrative, physical, and technical safeguards that reasonably and appropriately protect the confidentiality, integrity, and availability of the Protected Health Information it creates, receives, maintains, or transmits and to prevent use or disclosure of the Protected Health Information other than as provided for by this Contract.

11. **Reports of Any Security Incident or Improper Use or Disclosure.** BUSINESS ASSOCIATE hereby agrees that it shall report to COVERED ENTITY [*within five (5) business days of discovery*] any security incident of which it becomes aware or any use or disclosure of Protected Health Information not provided for or allowed by this Contract. [*It is further the obligation of the business associate to:*

    a. *<AL>Render PHI unusable, unreadable, or indecipherable to unauthorized individuals through the use of a technology or methodology specified by the Secretary of HHS in Guidance Specifying the Technologies and Methodologies that Render PHI Unusable, Unreadable, or Indecipherable to Unauthorized Individuals for Purposes of the Breach Notification Requirements under HITECH, issued on April 27, 2009, including use of encryption when transmitting PHI or maintaining PHI on portable devices or media, or destruction when discarding any PHI in electronic or paper form.*

    b. *Provide a description of the nature of the security incident or privacy breach, including (1) the date the breach occurred, (2) the date of discovery or the date on which the BUSINESS ASSOCIATE should have known of the incident or breach, (3) the categories of PHI involved in the breach including the manner in which the PHI was secured, and (4) the nature of the incident or breach, including if it was an unintentional access by a member of the BUSINESS ASSOCIATE's workforce, an inadvertent disclosure to a person at the same BUSINESS ASSOCIATE and no further use or disclosure in violation of the HIPAA Privacy Rule was made, or a disclosure where the BUSINESS ASSOCIATE believes the unauthorized recipient would be unable to retain the PHI. In addition, the BUSINESS ASSOCIATE must describe (5) the status of its investigation into the incident or breach, (6) steps taken to mitigate the harm caused by the security incident or privacy breach, and (7) the steps taken or will be taken to prevent a recurrence.*

    c. *Pay the COVERED ENTITY any expenses associated with investigation, notification, and mitigation of the security incident or privacy breach, including attorneys' fees, consultants' fees, the costs of delivering notice to individuals, the cost of any notice published in the media, the cost of services offered to affect individuals, and the cost of responding to any audit triggered by the security incident or privacy breach.*

12. **<BL>Subcontractors and Agents**. BUSINESS ASSOCIATE hereby agrees that anytime Protected Health Information is provided or made available to any subcontractors or agents, BUSINESS ASSOCIATE must enter into a contract with the subcontractor or agent that contains the same safeguards, terms, conditions and restrictions on the use and disclosure of Protected Health Information as contained in this Contract. [*No subcontractor or agent may be used that is an "offshore" contractor or otherwise does business with contractors not based in the United States/without the express written consent of the COVERED ENTITY.]*

13. **Right of Access to Protected Health Information.** BUSINESS ASSOCIATE hereby agrees to make available and provide a right of access to Protected Health Information by an Individual if it maintains Protected Health Information in a designated record set. This right of access shall conform

(continued)

F I G U R E   7.2 (continued)

Business Associate Contract

---

with and meet all of the requirements of 45 C.F.R. 164.524, including substitution of the words "Covered Entity" with BUSINESS ASSOCIATE where appropriate.

14. **Amendment and Incorporation of Amendments.** BUSINESS ASSOCIATE agrees to make Protected Health Information available for amendment and to incorporate any amendments to Protected Health Information if it maintains Protected Health Information in a designated record set in accordance with 45 C.F.R. 164.526, including substitution of the words "Covered Entity" with BUSINESS ASSOCIATE where appropriate.

15. **Documentation and Provision of Accounting of Disclosures.** BUSINESS ASSOCIATE agrees to document such disclosures of Protected Health Information and information related to such disclosures as would be required for COVERED ENTITY to respond to a request by an Individual for an accounting of disclosures of Protected Health Information in accordance with 45 C.F.R. 164.528, and to provide to COVERED ENTITY or an Individual, as designated by COVERED ENTITY within 10 days of request, an accounting of such disclosures. (ref. 164.504(e)(2)(ii)(G))

16. **Access to Books and Records.** BUSINESS ASSOCIATE hereby agrees to make its internal practices, books, and records relating to the use or disclosure of Protected Health Information received from, or created or received by BUSINESS ASSOCIATE on behalf of the COVERED ENTITY, available to the Secretary or the Secretary's designee, in a time and manner as designated by the Secretary, for purposes of the Secretary determining COVERED ENTITY'S compliance with the Privacy Rule.

17. **Return or Destruction of Protected Health Information.** At termination of this Contract, BUSINESS ASSOCIATE hereby agrees to return or destroy all Protected Health Information received from, or created or received by BUSINESS ASSOCIATE on behalf of COVERED ENTITY. BUSINESS ASSOCIATE agrees not to retain any copies of the Protected Health Information after termination of this Contract. If return or destruction of the Protected Health Information is not feasible, BUSINESS ASSOCIATE agrees to extend the protections of this Contract for as long as necessary to protect the Protected Health Information and to limit any further use or disclosure. If BUSINESS ASSOCIATE elects to destroy the Protected Health Information, it shall certify to COVERED ENTITY that the Protected Health Information has been destroyed.

18. **Mitigation Procedures.** BUSINESS ASSOCIATE agrees to mitigate, to the extent practicable, any harmful effect that is known to BUSINESS ASSOCIATE of a use or disclosure of Protected Health Information by BUSINESS ASSOCIATE in violation of the requirements of this Contract.

19. **Sanction Procedures**. BUSINESS ASSOCIATE agrees and understands that it must develop and implement a system of sanctions for any employee, subcontractor, or agent who violates this Agreement or the Privacy or Security Rule.

20. **Property Rights.** The Protected Health Information shall be and remain the property of COVERED ENTITY. BUSINESS ASSOCIATE agrees that it acquires no title or rights to the Protected Health Information, including any de-identified Protected Health Information, as a result of this Contract.

OBLIGATIONS OF COVERED ENTITY

21. COVERED ENTITY shall notify BUSINESS ASSOCIATE of any limitation(s) in its notice of privacy practices of COVERED ENTITY, in accordance with 45 C.F.R. 164.520, to the extent that such limitation may affect BUSINESS ASSOCIATE'S use or disclosure of Protected Health Information.

(continued)

FIGURE 7.2 (continued)

Business Associate Contract

22. COVERED ENTITY shall notify BUSINESS ASSOCIATE of any changes in, or revocation of, permission by Individual to use or disclose Protected Health Information, to the extent that such changes may affect BUSINESS ASSOCIATE'S use or disclosure of Protected Health Information.

23. COVERED ENTITY shall notify BUSINESS ASSOCIATE of any restriction to the use or disclosure of Protected Health Information that Covered Entity has agreed to in accordance with 45 C.F.R. 164.522, to the extent that such restriction may affect BUSINESS ASSOCIATE'S use or disclosure of Protected Health Information.

24. COVERED ENTITY shall not request BUSINESS ASSOCIATE to use or disclose Protected Health Information in any manner that would not be permissible under the Privacy Rule if done by COVERED ENTITY, except if the BUSINESS ASSOCIATE will use or disclose Protected Health Information for data aggregation or management and administrative activities of BUSINESS ASSOCIATE.

TERM AND TERMINATION OF CONTRACT

25. **Term**. The term of this Contract shall be effective as of _____, and shall terminate when all of the Protected Health Information provided by COVERED ENTITY to BUSINESS ASSOCIATE is destroyed or returned to COVERED ENTITY, or, if it is infeasible to return or destroy Protected Health Information, protections are extended to such information, in accordance with the following termination provisions:

_____

26. **Termination for Cause**. Upon COVERED ENTITY'S knowledge of a material breach by BUSINESS ASSOCIATE, COVERED ENTITY shall:

    a. Provide an opportunity for BUSINESS ASSOCIATE to cure the breach or end the violation and terminate this Contract if BUSINESS ASSOCIATE does not cure the breach or end the violation with the time specified by COVERED ENTITY, or

    b. Immediately terminate this Agreement if BUSINESS ASSOCIATE has breached a material term of this Contract and cure is not possible, or

    c. If neither termination nor cure is feasible, COVERED ENTITY shall report the violation to the Secretary.

27. **Effect of Termination**. Except as provided in Clause 28, upon termination of this Contract, for any reason, BUSINESS ASSOCIATE shall return or destroy all Protected Health Information received from COVERED ENTITY, or created or received by BUSINESS ASSOCIATE on behalf of COVERED ENTITY. This provision shall apply to Protected Health Information that is in the possession of subcontractors or agents of BUSINESS ASSOCIATE. BUSINESS ASSOCIATE shall retain no copies of the Protected Health Information.

28. In the event that BUSINESS ASSOCIATE determines that returning or destroying the Protected Health Information is infeasible, BUSINESS ASSOCIATE shall provide to COVERED ENTITY notification of the conditions that make return or destruction infeasible. Upon receipt within 10 days of request of that notice that return or destruction of Protected Health Information is infeasible, BUSINESS ASSOCIATE shall extend the protections of this Contract to such Protected Health

(continued)

Business Associate Contract

Information and limit further uses and disclosures of such Protected Health Information to those purposes that make the return or destruction infeasible, for so long as BUSINESS ASSOCIATE maintains such Protected Health Information.

29. **Governing Law.** *This Contract shall be governed by the law of the state of* _____.

30. **Amendment.** *The Parties agree to take such action as is necessary to amend this Contract from time to time as is necessary for COVERED ENTITY to comply with the requirements of the Privacy and Security Rules and the Health Insurance Portability and Accountability Act of 1996, Pub. L. No. 104-191.*

31. **Survival.** *The respective rights and obligations of BUSINESS ASSOCIATE under Clause 28 of this Contract shall survive the termination of this Contract.*

32. **Interpretation.** *Any ambiguity in this Contract shall be resolved to permit COVERED ENTITY to comply with the Privacy and Security Rule and the Health Insurance Portability and Accountability Act of 1996, Pub. L. No. 104-191.*

33. **Injunctive Relief.** *Notwithstanding any rights or remedies provided for in this Contract, COVERED ENTITY retains all rights to seek injunctive relief to prevent or stop the unauthorized use or disclosure of Protected Health Information by BUSINESS ASSOCIATE or any agent, contractor, or third party that received Protected Health Information from BUSINESS ASSOCIATE.*

34. **Binding Nature and Assignment.** *This Contract shall be binding on the Parties hereto and their successors and assigns, but neither Party may assign this Agreement without the prior written consent of the other, which consent shall not be unreasonably withheld.*

35. **Notices.** *Whenever under this Contract one party is required to give notice to the other, such notice shall be deemed given if mailed by First Class United States mail, postage prepaid, and addressed as follows:*

COVERED ENTITY:

_____

BUSINESS ASSOCIATE:

_____

Either Party may at any time change its address for notification purposes by mailing a notice stating the change and setting forth the new address.

37. **Article Headings.** *The article headings used are for reference and convenience only, and shall not enter into the interpretation of this Contract.*

38. **Entire Agreement.** *This Contract consists of this document, and constitutes the entire agreement between the Parties. There are no understandings or agreements relating to this Contract which are not fully expressed in this Contract and no change, waiver, or discharge of obligations arising under this Contract shall be valid unless in writing and executed by the Party against whom such change, waiver, or discharge is sought to be enforced.*

(continued)

FIGURE 7.2 (continued)

Business Associate Contract

IN WITNESS WHEREOF, BUSINESS ASSOCIATE and COVERED ENTITY have caused this
Contract to be signed and delivered by their duly authorized representatives, as of the date set forth above.

BUSINESS ASSOCIATE   COVERED ENTITY
By:_____   By:_____
Print Name:_____   Print Name:_____
Title:_____   Title:_____

Note: This model business associate contract does not constitute legal advice. If legal advice is required, the services of a competent professional should be sought. The model contract includes all required language from both the HIPAA Privacy Rule and Security Rule as well as changes that have already gone into effect from the HITECH Act. It also includes, as indicated by italics, some optional language frequently recommended for inclusion in business associate contracts. Blanks are inserted for the parties to complete. The contract does not address changes that are pending final regulations to be promulgated from the HITECH Act with respect to changes in the business associates' status with respect to the Privacy Rule and Security Rule or changes anticipated to the accounting for PHI disclosures standard in the Privacy Rule that may apply to business associates.

Reprinted with permission from Margret\A Consulting, LLC.

Managing Business Associates

Many vendors have drafted their own business associate contracts and include them in their service contracts, licenses, or maintenance agreements. If they meet the criteria established in your policies and procedures, you may accept the contract. It is a good idea to have a checklist or use your own contract as a guide in reviewing a business associate contract offered by a business associate. Be sure every required clause is included and no clauses you do not want are included. If the vendor's contract does not meet your criteria or includes clauses you do not want, you will need to negotiate an acceptable contract with the vendor before agreeing to its provision of services involving PHI.

Remember, as the covered entity, you will be found to be in noncompliance with the Privacy Rule and Security Rule if you do not take steps to cure the breach or terminate the contract if the business associate has violated a material term of the contract. As such, the burden to assure that the contract terms meet HIPAA requirements is on you, not the business associate.

Other Provisions in Business Associate Contracts

As noted regarding Figure 7.2, some provisions in addition to those required by HIPAA are often included in business associate contracts. These provisions are those typically included in any contract for services. However, some covered entities and business associates seek to include other indemnification provisions and various warranties and liabilities. The potential for inclusion of such terms should be discussed with legal counsel.

Another common practice is for vendors to include business associate terms within their broader contract, license agreement, or other binding arrangements. As noted above, if the business associate terms are complete and consistent with those in your covered entity business associate contract, you may wish to accept that structure. However, you should be aware that increasingly business associates seek to use or disclose PHI for a wide range of purposes. Many business associate contracts offered by the business associate do not spell out these uses or disclosures. This situation will be critical for you to negotiate. There are also some optional terms included in Figure 7.2 that were not included in HIPAA but are very important. For instance, the clause on amendment of the contract is necessary to assure that any future regulatory modifications can be incorporated into an amended contract.

Establishing an explicit chain of trust through the business associate contract may also be something you want to consider. This entails spelling out in much more detail specific security controls. Sometimes such information is placed in a trading partner agreement (TPA). Having a separate TPA makes it easier to manage changes over time, rather than having to open the full contract and risk having unanticipated changes added. Whether security controls are addressed as part of the business associate contract or in a separate TPA, be sure to avoid vague language such as "best security practices," which should be replaced with specific language to:

■ Describe the controls, procedures, or processes associated with an authorized connection in sufficient detail so that each party can assess its risk in making the connection.

■ Define any external connections to the network that bypass your firewall.

■ Verify the use of authentication procedures such as passwords, personal identification numbers (PINs), or one-time password technologies. Encourage the use of digital signatures to ensure the authenticity of messages.

■ Require secure data transfers by using some type of encryption. Specify the type of encryption and how it will be kept up to date.

■ Verify that neither organization will engage in security probing of the other's site without advance notification.

Special Considerations for Shared Services Vendors and Other Arrangements

Shared services refers to the consolidation of business operations and/or purchasing of products or services used by multiple parts of the same organization. Such services enable an organization to take advantage of economies of scale, eliminate redundancy, and reduce productivity demands on contract maintenance. If your office is large enough, or part of a larger organization, it is possible that the large organization seeks to take advantage of the benefits of shared services. If this is the case, you may want to assure yourself that the centralized contracting aspects of this structure meet your specific needs. For example, you may be a behavioral health specialist who wants further protections on the PHI, or you may be an occupational health specialist who has special requirements for sharing worker data with the employer.

Other arrangements that may need special attention include contracts involving acquiring product licenses and/or services from hosting companies, an application service provider (ASP), or a software as a service (SaaS) vendor. These are becoming increasingly common, especially for EHR systems. It may be helpful to define associated terms:

■ Straight licensure is a financial strategy where an office acquires a license to use software. Most often, the software is implemented on servers maintained in the office. With respect to EHR systems, the architecture of the software is typically "client/server." This means that the software is housed on a server and clients (desktops, laptops, tablets, etc) access the software and data from the server. Although the clients may be "thin clients," ie, with minimal processing capability of their own, there is no implication in either straight licensure or client/server arrangements that thin clients are necessary or usual. In a straight licensure client/server arrangement, the office typically has considerable flexibility to configure the software as desired. As a result, there is often a very large setup and/or implementation fee. The license may also be paid for entirely up front, with only maintenance fees ongoing. The primary business associate in this situation is the software vendor. Other business associates may be hardware vendors if they have access to PHI, consultants, etc.

- A hosting company is a company that typically hosts servers for others and often provides contracted IT support, but does not sell software. In this arrangement, an office may have acquired software under straight licensure, but the software is delivered to the hosting company's servers. The servers are maintained by the hosting company's staff, and access to the software by your office is provided by a secure Internet arrangement, direct cabling, or wide-area wireless connection. While costs of maintaining servers are reduced in this arrangement, the upfront costs of the software license, setup/implementation fees, and ongoing maintenance are the same as in an internally hosted client/server environment. However, in addition to the software vendor being a primary business associate, the hosting company is also a primary business associate. There may or may not be other business associates with respect to the acquisition of hardware, etc.

- Using an ASP is both a financial strategy and an acquisition strategy. Typically the ASP charges a smaller setup/implementation fee, no upfront license fee, and an ongoing usage fee that also includes maintenance. There are no requirements for hosting servers in the office or at a hosting company because the servers are located at the ASP. The result is a low upfront cost and a moderate ongoing fee. With respect to the nature of the software product, the ASP is typically client/server architecture with a Web front end. This means that it is very much like the straight licensure client/server model in design, but access is provided via the Internet. Sometimes ASP products are referred to as Web-based. However, the term *Web-based* should be reserved to describe when service is actually delivered over the Web vs a virtual private network or other transmission not entailing the Web. Although any services can be delivered over the Web, a Web service architecture (WSA) implies that the underlying software is constructed using XML and browser-based technologies. Most ASPs today, even if delivered over the Web, are not WSA. As a result, the ASP model, while generally less customizable than the straight licensure client/server model, is somewhat customizable and interoperable with other, often older, applications an office may already have. The degree of customization permitted determines the price. Similar to the straight licensure client/server model, however, the ASP is the one primary business associate. The ASP may be located entirely within the United States or may have locations in other parts of the world—but these are known up front and are all part of one company.

- SaaS is also a financing and acquisition strategy, but it differs from the ASP model of acquiring an information system in several ways. First, SaaS typically offers a true WSA. The software offers browsing and other features of the Web. This is very appealing, especially to younger clinicians who have grown up using the Web and find the client/server architecture of either the straight licensure client/server or ASP offerings limiting in usability. Another key difference is that the SaaS offering is typically lower in price than the ASP offering. There are two reasons for this. First, the SaaS typically is one size fits all. In order to offer the service to many at a very low price, SaaS vendors severely limit or do not provide any customization. As a result, there may be no or minimal setup fees, and low ongoing fees. In fact, in other industries, SaaS is often referred to as on-demand computing. If you only use the system once a month for 5 hours, that is all you pay for. If you also need it quarterly for 10 hours, your fee is increased accordingly just for that time period. The second reason the SaaS fee is low is that the SaaS structure is very easily offered through cloud computing. Cloud computing refers to the use of ubiquitous, convenient, on-demand network access to a shared pool of configurable computing resources (eg, networks, servers, storage, applications, and services) that can be rapidly provisioned and released with minimal management effort or service provider interaction.

Cloud computing takes advantage of virtualization. Virtualization refers to a conceptual, rather than real, version of a device or resource, such as a server, storage device, network, or operating system. For example, a hard drive on a computer can be partitioned such that the one drive is conceptually two or more separate hard drives, each with different operating systems and used by different applications or companies. As a result, data can be located literally anywhere and everywhere in the world where computing resources are plentiful and cheap. The advantage to this is that it is easier to backup, move, and copy files among multiple servers, and the multiple servers already in use can supply automatic failover, where if one server fails a second server continues to support processing without interruption.

While on first blush, the SaaS would seem very similar to the ASP with respect to business associates, the concern is that the computing resources used are agents of the SaaS vendor, there can be very many of them, and they may change rapidly. While an office is not required to have a business associate agreement with the agents of a business associate, the business associate is required by the covered entity's business associate contract to "ensure that any agent, including a subcontractor, to whom it provides such information agrees to implement reasonable and appropriate safeguards to protect it" (§164.314[a][2][i][C]). Some providers have concerns about the extent to which a SaaS vendor can manage its agents.

Suffice it to say, in any form of software acquisition, there is a great need to review the license agreement thoroughly. In addition to the standard contract issues surrounding health information technology, some soul searching with respect to the level of customization and usability is desired (often resulting in a trade-off), and the business associate arrangements and service-level agreements are extremely important. Recall that availability is one of the three key elements of security's confidentiality-integrity-availability triad. As you consider availability, be aware that you are not only relying on another company to provide access to your PHI, but you are also introducing one or more third parties, which are the connectivity providers. While your office will have a primary connection service (eg, dedicated T1 or cable service) and maybe a backup (eg, DSL), connecting to the World Wide Web may be fine at your end, but the connection at the hosting company, ASP, or any one of the virtual servers in the cloud could be down. Service-level agreements go a long way to assuring better availability, yet contingency planning is even more vital than ever before because neither you nor your business associate has total control over connectivity.

HIE PARTICIPATING AGREEMENTS

The federal government is promoting health information exchange (HIE) in many formats—from local exchange of the Continuity of Care Record (CCR) with other providers or providing patients a clinical summary or access to EHR data via a portal, to the Nationwide Health Information Network, and in between, exchange via health information exchange organizations (HIOs). Each type of HIE calls for security considerations.

HIE Among Treating Providers and With Patients

With respect to the need for business associate contracts, it was noted in this chapter that there is no need for a business associate contract when exchanging health information among treating providers. (The HIPAA Privacy Rule does not require an authorization from the patient for this purpose either, although some states require a consent form to be signed.)

Certainly patients are not business associates. The HIPAA Privacy Rule permits, but does not require, a request for access to health information to be in writing. In the past, many providers did require a patient to document the request for access in writing. The primary purpose of such a written request would be to assure that you are providing information to the right patient and that you have a record of such provision. Unfortunately, patients sometimes viewed such a written request as obstructing their right to obtain a copy of their chart or otherwise access their health information. One of the most frequent complaints to the Office for Civil Rights is about small physician offices not providing access.

Today, the federal incentive program for making meaningful use of EHR technology requires providers to supply patients a clinical summary for each office visit. Though not stated, it is implied that the provision of this summary does not require a written request for access. The summary should contain the content specified in the ASTM Continuity of Care Record (CCR) standard. It may be supplied to patients in PDF format on a compact disk (CD) or exchanged using the Health Level Seven (HL7) Continuity of Care Document (CCD) standard, which provides the CCR content in a document mark-up structure. For patient access to health information via a portal, office may find it more practical to have the patient complete a form (online or offline) that would generate a unique and password for the patient. This form or the portal itself might also supply information about good privacy and security practices about which the patient should be aware.

HIE Through a Health Information Exchange Organization

A health information exchange organization (HIO) is an organization that facilitates exchange of health information. The organization generally has a governance structure and technology services, and provides specific HIE functions. There are different governance structures, where sometimes a hospital serves as an HIO, a separate company may be formed to serve as an HIO, or a vendor may be an HIO. There are also different architectures, where some HIOs serve only as a central hub for point-to-point exchange of data, and others maintain a repository of some or all of the health information that will be exchanged.

Functions of HIOs vary tremendously. One of the most well-known HIOs is Surescripts, which serves as a gateway for the exchange of prescriptions sent by providers to retail pharmacies. Other HIOs are local or regional. They may provide very limited exchange of data at this time, such as only lab results or clinical summaries. Other HIOs provide clearinghouse services for financial transactions. Still others offer a wide range of exchange services as well as data warehousing where aggregated data are analyzed and benchmarked for population health analysis. Some providers may participate in only one or two HIOs; other may participate in more depending on their location and HIE needs.

The HIO Is a Business Associate

Irrespective of the architecture, functionality, or management of the HIO, the HIO is considered a HIPAA business associate under the HITECH Act. All participants in an HIO must, therefore, have a business associate contract with the HIO. The business associate contract may be exactly like that used with any other business associate, or it may be part of a broader participation agreement and/or data use agreement, and may require consent management.

Participation Agreement

Many HIOs require a participation agreement. Such agreements are more like business contracts for any type of service. They specify the business terms under which the service will be provided. This may include things such as hours of operation, fees, and other business-related matters. In addition, many states have adopted consent requirements where patients may opt in or opt out of participation in an HIO.

Consent Management and Sensitive Data

Most HIOs are still relatively early in their operations and exchange only limited types of data. Most often this exchange occurs under an opt-out arrangement, where patients may choose not to participate. However, a full-blown consent management process can be highly complex, especially where the opt-in arrangement is used or where there are requirements to treat certain data as especially sensitive. In the opt-in arrangement, only patients who explicitly choose to participate may have their data exchanged via the HIO. Although no HIO at the time of this writing is known to be using a full "matrix" consent management arrangement (ie, where each type of data is tagged to identify to whom it may or may not be shared), it is conceivable that patients may choose to opt in to have only certain data exchanged with certain entities. At this time, there is no guidance in either HIPAA or HITECH as to the nature of types of consent structures required or permitted, or with respect to defining data sensitivity. Each HIO, through its governance body, makes these decisions. The HIO's participation agreement, then, specifies the requirements for providers to obtain and honor such consent requirements.

Data Use Agreement

When an HIO provides more than simply the exchange of data, a data use agreement may be incorporated into the participation agreement or provided separately for only those participants who want to take advantage of this additional service. In this case, the data use agreement spells out what data are covered, what uses will be made of the data, and technical considerations, such as the format in which the data must be supplied, perhaps the vocabulary in which the data must be coded, etc.

Nationwide Health Information Network

As of this writing, the Nationwide Health Information Network is still in limited production mode. A number of pilot tests have been conducted over the past several years with federal agencies and several state HIOs exchanging data within limited confines of the pilots. If you are in a state with such a pilot, you may be participating in the Nationwide Health Information Network via your HIO. One of the more recent pilots underway includes the Centers for Medicare and Medicaid Services (CMS) using the Nationwide Health Information Network for submission of documentation for Medicare claim auditing purposes. This is called Electronic Submission of Medical Documentation (esMD) and is available via Recovery Audit Contractors (RACs) and other programmatic contractors who are enrolled.

It is anticipated that by early in 2013, the Nationwide Health Information Network will become a stand-alone, nonprofit organization without direct oversight from the HHS Office of the National Coordinator for Health Information Technology (ONC). Providers who already exchange data via an HIO should see no difference, but providers who do not may have more opportunities open for HIE. This will become increasingly important as the incentive program for making meaningful use of EHR technology is anticipated to require increasing HIE as time goes on, and providers who participate in an accountable care organization under the Affordable Care Act (ACA) will certainly benefit by having connectivity with other providers via an HIO or the Nationwide Health Information Network.

Participation in the Nationwide Health Information Network requires a Data Use and Reciprocal Support Agreement (DURSA). This is a multiparty agreement that every participant must sign. It describes the privacy and security obligations of each participant, describes requests for information based on permitted purposes, provides for a duty to respond to any such request, identifies required authorization, requires participant breach notification, and specifies legal requirements, dispute resolution, and allocation of liability risk. The DURSA currently being used is available from http://www.healthit.hhs.gov. It is unknown at this time whether the content of the DURSA will change as the Nationwide Health Information Network becomes privatized.

YOUR WEB PRESENCE

Many providers now have a Web site. While some of these sites are primarily informational and are not interactive, it is still important to manage the security of the site. For Web sites that are interactive, permitting requests for appointments, bill paying, access to health information, and potentially access to a personal health record, it is very important to use a reputable Web site development company or Webmaster.

For noninteractive sites, perhaps the primary security concern about a Web site is the unlikely risk of vandalism of the site, where legitimate graphics and titles can be modified by an attacker. To reduce the likelihood of vandalism, your Web site should be constructed outside of your internal server network. This is typically called the demilitarized zone (DMZ), where traffic from the outside can be analyzed before allowing it to come into your network. A firewall specific to Web applications, not a general, all-purpose firewall, should be installed.

Web sites that are interactive will require further security services. A best practice is to encrypt the login page. Many Web sites allow a user to login and only use encryption (SSL or TLS with https) for certain functions, such as exchanging credit card information.

Another important practice where physicians or others are provided remote access to the practice management system or EHR via a provider portal is to ensure that such users connect from a secured network. Most open wireless access points, such as in coffee shops, airport terminals, or hotel lobbies, are not secure networks. If you must connect via such a network, a secure proxy should be used. Your Web developer should be able to set up an easy-to-use proxy that will ensure not only confidentiality but generally better availability. As with any login credentials, logins to your Web site should never be shared. Do not store your login credentials on the device, on any other mobile device, or anywhere else. Do not allow the Web site to store your credentials. Key-based authentication is better than password authentication. If you prescribe controlled substances, and you wish to do so via your e-prescribing gateway, and your state board of pharmacy permits this, the Drug Enforcement Administration (DEA) now permits e-prescribing of controlled substances only via a key-based hard token. (See Chapter 9 for information on use of tokens.) Instead of reserving use of such a token only for such prescriptions, a best practice is to use it for all remote access. (Some hospitals are also requiring use of a hard token for access to their EHR systems.) Finally, just as with all systems, make sure there is a backup of the Web site.

Patient portals are a means for patients to access certain limited functions to which you afford rights. These often include the ability to request an appointment or even make an appointment, information about lab results, bill payment, and so on. Remember that a portal is an entranceway. But the entranceway can be restricted. Portal access to lab results, for instance, does not mean the patient has the ability to enter lab results, change them, or do anything but view them and potentially only view them after they have been "translated" into a message you wish the patients to receive. This is also true for any other information to which you afford access. Many providers seem to be under the impression that a portal enables direct access to the practice management system or EHR, including the ability to make changes. This is not at all the intent of the patient portal.

Patient portals may also serve as an entranceway to a personal health record (PHR) that you support. In this case, the personal health record is not the same as your EHR, but you may set up your EHR to automatically copy certain data to the patient's PHR or you may direct certain data to be copied to the patient's PHR. However, most such PHRs also allow the patient to enter data into the PHR. Whether you review such data or not should be a matter of policy that you establish with the patient before arranging for the patient to have a PHR. Some providers find that certain data recorded by the patient, perhaps in a diary mode, can be helpful for patients with certain conditions. Ideally, patients should include data from other providers in their PHR as well, and in this way, the PHR serves as a means of HIE—again with applicable policies and patient consent.

With respect to business associates, your Webmaster should be considered a business associate, especially if your Web site is interactive in any way—whether by providers in the practice only, other providers, or patients. You should also be aware that if *you* offer and supply a PHR, any security incident or privacy breach of the PHR is your responsibility. The PHR vendor (which is typically also your EHR vendor) is a business associate of yours. Alternatively, if your patients use their own PHR vendor, even if you may be provided access to contribute data to it, the PHR vendor is not a business associate. Breaches that occur from such a PHR vendor are then covered under the consumer protection functions of the Federal Trade Commission (FTC) Health Breach Notification regulations.

SOCIAL MEDIA

While not directly related to business associates, social media are an increasingly popular form of communications with the external world and certainly have policy ramifications for your office. The topic is included here both because it may have privacy and security policy implications within your office and because some providers have questioned whether the social media sites they use are business associates.

Social media are defined in Wikipedia as "Web- and mobile-based technologies, which are used to turn communication into interactive dialogue among organizations, communities, and individuals." Social media have grown extremely rapidly, with more than 234 million people age 13 and older in the United States using mobile devices in December 2009. In the same time period Twitter averaged almost 40 million tweets per day. In May 2012 there were 901 million users on Facebook, and one in four people age 65 and older are now part of a social networking site. Social media technologies take on many different forms such as Internet forums, blogs, wikis, social networks, podcasts, and more. Wikipedia also describes six different types of social media: collaborative projects (eg, Wikipedia, Healthcare Information and Management Systems Society [HIMSS] clinical decision support wiki), blogs (eg, Twitter, Life as a Healthcare CIO by John Halamka, MD), content communities (eg, YouTube), social networking sites (eg, Facebook [connecting friends], LinkedIn [connecting professionals]), virtual game worlds (eg, FamScape, a game that motivates families to achieve healthy living goals), and virtual social worlds (eg, Etsy, an e-commerce site for handmade and vintage crafts). Technologies range from e-mail and instant messaging to picture sharing, video blogs (vlogs), wall postings, music sharing, crowdsourcing, and voice over IP (VoIP). Many of these social media services can be integrated via social network aggregation platforms.

There are a number of benefits of social media, including findings reported by the US Department of Education in June 2011 that online students outperformed those receiving face-to-face instruction. For health care, patients use social media to find streamlined information quickly, social media encourages patient engagement in their health care, and many turn to social media to help the healing process. Physicians find social media a way to tell their story to patients and form a community with other providers. You can also monitor the social Web for discussions about the industry and patient concerns. It can also be an outlet for everyday stress. Risks of social media probably include as many sociological, reputational, and economic issues as privacy and security issues. Because of the ubiquity of social media, it would be impractical to consider any social media site a business associate. But that does not mean precautions should not be taken in use of social media with respect to your office. The American Medical Association has a policy on Professionalism in the Use of Social Media, which is a good place to start when addressing these issues. Some additional tips to consider for your practice are provided in Figure 7.3.

FIGURE 7.3

Social Media Policy Considerations

1. Recognize that blanket bans on social media use are not a good idea and are essentially impossible to enforce.

2. Adopt as part of your security policy an acceptable use policy that addresses social media as well as all other aspects of Internet, e-mail, and property use. A good practice is to acknowledge the value of social media for professional activities while emphasizing that personal use that becomes a distraction or impacts productivity is considered theft of office resources.

3. When adopting social media for the office, understand your objectives and develop a strategy that prioritizes those objectives.

4. Mitigate risks by engaging legal counsel and insurance professionals in reviewing policies and potentially updating insurance coverage.

5. Establish professional boundaries. Although the general advice is to include more "do's" than "don'ts" in your policies, the National Council of State Boards of Nursing (2007) offers the following practical "don'ts" that you may want to include in training materials and education:

   a. Don't violate patient confidentiality (and the HIPAA Privacy Rule) by disclosing any patient information, pictures, or discussions about clinical situations of staff on social networking sites.

   b. Don't communicate with or "friend" past or present patients, even if the patient initiates the communication. Perception is reality, and it is conceivable that the conversation could turn in different directions than intended and be misinterpreted by patients, their family, or even the public, who may come to believe your office does not value patient privacy and confidentiality.

   c. Don't provide any healthcare advice on social networking sites.

   d. Don't post any personal information, photographs, or other items that could reflect negatively on your employer or your own professional image and conduct.

   e. Don't assume that with privacy and security settings your profile might not be seen by an employer or patient, whether using your own device or your employer's device.

   f. Don't violate any terms of use/user agreements in the social media sites themselves, or any other copyright policies, antitrust guidelines, or professional or employee codes of conduct.

   g. Don't ignore the warning signs of a potential incident. These might include patient complaints about their privacy or concerns about others' privacy being violated as a result of healthcare professionals' "friending" patients. All of the concerns about never sharing a password, personal information, or PHI must be heeded. Know the warning signs and how to report them to your information security official or information privacy official.

IMPORTANCE OF BUSINESS ASSOCIATE AND OTHER RELATIONSHIPS

This chapter has covered everything from the traditional business associate and the business associate contract, to the broader context of health information exchange and an HIO as a business associate, and even beyond to informal relationships that arise out of the use of social media. Physician offices need to be aware of these and take proactive steps to assure that all such relationships are appropriately documented and policies complied with. It is often suggested that a chain is only as strong as its weakest link. Business associate contracts, other agreements, and even social media policies are intended to strengthen each link in the chain from your office to your business associate, to the business associate's agent, to the agent's agent, and on.

CHECK YOUR UNDERSTANDING*

For each of the following, specify if a business associate contract is needed (Yes or No):

1. Yes/No　　Hospital where your office admits patients

2. Yes/No　　Provider to whom you are referring a patient

3. Yes/No　　Health information exchange organization

4. Yes/No　　EHR vendor

5. Yes/No　　Accountant

6. Yes/No　　Patient

7. Yes/No　　E-prescribing network

8. Yes/No　　Drug store where your patient is getting your prescription filled

9. Yes/No　　Fire department

10. Yes/No　　Accreditation organization

Define the following terms:

11. Data aggregation

12. Limited data set

13. Application service provider (ASP)

14. Software as a service (SaaS)

15. Hosting company

*For answers, refer to the Answer Key at the end of the book.

HIPAA Security Physical Safeguards

An important step in protecting your protected health information (PHI) is to restrict physical access to the information and systems you use to access, store, and transmit PHI. The ultimate physical security control would be something akin to encapsulating your computers in concrete. The only problem with this method is that while it protects against thieves, it also presents a complex barrier for you as well. The key is to find a balance between security and ease of use. Too much security becomes a barrier to getting the job done. As a result, people bypass security. Too little security, however, puts your office at risk.

HOW TO USE THIS CHAPTER

This chapter covers the Physical Safeguards standards of the HIPAA Security Rule. It:

- Describes physical security vulnerabilities and their potential threats
- Explains what each Physical Safeguard standard and implementation specification means
- Provides ideas for the most appropriate physical controls for your environment.

The Security Rule defines physical safeguards as "security measures to protect a covered entity's electronic information systems and related buildings and equipment, from natural and environmental hazards, and unauthorized intrusions" (§164.302). The Physical Safeguards standards and their implementation specifications, listed in Table 8.1, are covered here in the order in which they are listed in the Security Rule. (Not all standards have implementation specifications.)

TABLE 8.1

Physical Safeguard Standards and Implementation Specifications

Security Standard	Code of Federal Regulations Section	Security Implementation Specifications (R) = Required, (A) = Addressable
Physical Safeguards		
Facility Access Controls	§164.310(a)(1)	Contingency Operations (A)
		Facility Security Plan (A)
		Access Control and Validation Procedures (A)
		Maintenance Records (A)
Workstation Use	§164.310(b)	(R)
Workstation Security	§164.310(c)	(R)

(continued)

T A B L E   8.1 (continued)

Physical Safeguard Standards and Implementation Specifications

Security Standard	Code of Federal Regulations Section	Security Implementation Specifications (R) = Required, (A) = Addressable
Physical Safeguards		
Device and Media Controls	§164.310(d)(1)	Disposal (R) Media Reuse (R) Accountability (A) Data Backup and Storage (A)

PHYSICAL VULNERABILITIES AND THREATS

Physical safeguards are the security measures used to protect employees, buildings, and information systems from external and internal environmental and human threats. While more computing is occurring in the cloud, at an application service provider (ASP), or at a hosted facility, there remain both devices and media used in your office and the need to assure yourself that any vendor that provides remote support is also providing physical safeguards. This discussion, therefore, assumes that all of your computing resources are in your office and/or under your control.

Any threat that exploits a vulnerability is an incident. Recovery from physical security incidents can be expensive in terms of direct monetary costs, the office's reputation in the community, emotional stress, and the time it takes to return to pre-incident productivity levels. People who have been burglarized at home often feel more pain as a result of the invasion of their privacy and the violation of their security than they do as a result of the actual loss of property, especially if the property had little or no sentimental value. It takes time to once again feel comfortable after any security incident.

The HIPAA Physical Safeguards section includes four standards. These address facility access controls, workstation use, workstation security, and device and media controls. These are the first lines of defense for protecting against threats to vulnerabilities in the physical environment or vulnerabilities in the physical environment that can be exploited by humans. Physical safeguards protect your information assets from damage, unauthorized disclosure, compromise in data integrity, and theft of property; however, physical safeguards also protect human safety.

FACILITY ACCESS CONTROLS STANDARD

The first HIPAA Physical Safeguard standard is Facility Access Controls. The standard requires the practice to "implement policies and procedures to limit physical access to its electronic information systems and the facility or facilities in which they are housed, while ensuring that properly authorized access is allowed" (§164.310[a]).

Your practice includes your office and any other locations where members of your workforce work and extends to your home or other physical locations under your control from which you may access PHI.

Facility refers to physical premises, including:

- Interior and exterior of an office building, including its construction, design, landscaping, fire protection, electrical wiring, etc

- Access points, such as doors, windows, cables, wireless/broadband services, and other means by which people or information may enter or exit
- Equipment and media contained within the office and/or transmitted out of the office

There are four implementation specifications within the Facility Access Controls standard:

- Contingency Operations
- Facility Security Plan
- Access Controls and Validation Procedures
- Maintenance Records

Contingency Operations

Contingency Operations refer to the steps you take to carry out the plans you created in order to comply with the Contingency Plan standard under Administrative Safeguards (see Chapter 6). This implementation specification requires you to decide how you will "establish (and implement as needed) procedures that allow facility access in support of restoration of lost data under the disaster recovery plan and emergency mode operations plan in the event of an emergency" (§164.310[a][2][i]).

Contingency operations allow access to your facility during disasters and emergency situations. Firefighters, insurance claims adjusters, and building contractors may need facility access after a disaster or in an emergency situation. They may have to temporarily compromise your normal security controls and procedures in order to restore your operations.

For small offices, you and your staff may be the key persons involved in the recovery process. For offices of any size, make sure you have the names and phone numbers of staff and others to contact in an emergency. Each staff member must know what to do in the event of an emergency. Periodically conduct disaster drills. During the drills, make sure your contact list is current and confirm that staff remember how to implement all phases of your contingency plans.

For larger offices or in the event of significant destruction, you may need to obtain outside assistance. For example, you may need to post a guard at your facility or have guards escort individuals who need access to your office as they perform their functions. If your information systems are destroyed, it may be necessary to send all backups to your vendor for restoration, or contact your backup and disaster recovery vendor to activate recovery. If an information system vendor is out of business or no longer supports your system, identify a third party to help you convert your data from backups so it is accessible or usable in another system. Don't forget to create a business associate contract if one does not exist.

Periodic testing of your contingency plans, including backups, should have identified the loss of a vendor to support you, at which time you would have made new arrangements for disaster recovery. As electronic health record (EHR) and other mission critical information systems are being adopted, many offices are adopting full redundancy with a second, failover server, network redundancy, and power redundancy. A daily backup of an EHR is not sufficient to ensure availability of the information directly entered in the EHR throughout the day. If servers are not remotely hosted, offices need to move to an automated backup system that continuously transmits backup data to a remote location as a contingency plan. Despite continuous backup processes, however, testing of the backups is still vital. Be sure you require this as part of any contingency planning or disaster recovery service you acquire. Make sure also that the test results are transmitted to you in writing as part of your HIPAA compliance documentation. It is noted that one of the most common compliance issues found as part of the Office for Civil Rights (OCR) privacy and security audits is lack of contingency plans and evidence of their testing.

Facility Security Plan

The Facility Security Plan is what you use to secure your facility on an ongoing basis to re- duce the likelihood of disaster striking or emergencies occurring. This plan calls for you to "implement policies and procedures to safeguard the facility and the equipment therein from unauthorized physical access, tampering, and theft" (§164.310[a][2][ii]).

Plan Specifics

A facility security plan is needed even if you share office space with other tenants. If your office is co-located with other physician offices or other companies, your plan should com- plement the larger building's plan. Although it would be unusual for an office building not to have a facility security plan, check to ensure that one does exist, that it is current, and that it meets your needs. The building should also be responsible for regular maintenance of the plan and testing. Many building codes require at least annual fire marshal inspec- tions, and many also conduct annual disaster drills. Obtaining documentation of these ac- tivities should serve as your evidence of attention to facility security.

Facility security plans usually consist of environmental controls and access controls. These controls reduce the vulnerabilities that natural and environmental threats (identified in Chapter 5) pose to your facility. They can also thwart many of the human threats (also identified in Chapter 5) that relate to facility vulnerabilities.

As you create or review facility security plans, keep in mind the risk analysis factors of

- Size, complexity, and capabilities
- Technical infrastructure, hardware, and software
- Costs
- Probability and criticality of potential risks

Because everyone knows everyone in a small office, your staff is much less vulnerable to unknown persons who could enter your office to cause harm. This is also likely to be true in a stand-alone office building rather than in a building you share with others. Alter- natively, don't be inclined to automatically trust co-workers in a small office, especially those you don't know well. Although it was noted previously that you don't want to create an environment of suspicion, you do want to be careful about making assumptions.

Geographical location can be a significant issue with respect to selecting physical con- trols. You may face hurricanes in Florida, tornadoes in Oklahoma, and earthquakes in Cali- fornia; but don't be surprised by an earthquake in Illinois, flooding in Minnesota, or fires in New Mexico. In other words, do not make false assumptions. Differences also exist in terms of the size and type of community in which your practice is located. For example, college towns differ from bedroom communities, and high-tech corridors are different from depressed areas. In addition, proximity to major highways and industries may be an issue. Environments also change. Economic conditions worsen in many locations, causing in- creased theft or unhappiness in the workforce, which may become lax in security aware- ness. A run-down neighborhood might quickly turn upscale and offer different risks.

The services you offer and the populations you serve may also contribute to your physi- cal security considerations. For example, special precautions are necessary if you operate an abortion clinic, treat AIDS patients, or offer psychiatric services. Diagnostic imaging cen- ters have special physical requirements.

Facility Security Controls

Physical security controls cover all aspects of facility and information system protection. The intent of HIPAA's administrative simplification provisions is to promote use of information systems. As you continue to enhance your level of automation, greater physical controls must be applied. If only your billing system is automated, you can probably get by with one computer in a back office and secure backup files. As you become more reliant on a practice management system, more of your daily operations are impacted. For example, the network in your office may be small and you may not have a separate room in which to house your network equipment. As a result, other activities conducted in the same room may impact your systems.

CASE STUDY 8.1
The Multipurpose Room

A large specialty group office included a number of schedulers, coders, billers, and other administrative personnel. They initially did a moderate amount of electronic billing only, but recently expanded their information system use to scheduling, coding, and adoption of electronic remittance advice. As a result, their network grew, and many more devices were needed to manage their systems. Looking for secure space, they decided to use an internal, multipurpose lunch-mail-conference room. They thought that because there were no windows and virtually no access by visitors this was a secure environment. Their servers were located alongside their postage equipment, microwave oven, refrigerator, and heavy-duty copier. Pretty soon they started having problems. The room began to overheat, so they took the door off. That wasn't enough. They scheduled activities so that no one could do extensive copying and run the postage equipment at the same time. It was still a problem to use the space as a lunchroom. One day it got too crowded. Someone knocked over a chair that pulled out key cabling from the information system. At that point, they decided to get a data center and found space on another floor that someone else had just vacated. Their daily operations then returned to normal.

CASE STUDY 8.2
Uninvited Picnic Guests

A magnetic resonance imaging (MRI) center was located near a residential area. Its office hours included being open two evenings a week. A back room was used as the computer data center. The room had an unmarked, internal door that was generally kept closed, though not locked. In addition, this room had two large windows that were about one foot from the floor and a door that led to a yard in the back of the building where staff put a picnic table. On pleasant days, staff used the picnic table, keeping the back door of the computer data center room propped open in order to get back into the building without going around to the front. One day a raccoon entered the room unnoticed and found a hiding place in the computer data center. The next day, computer systems were down due to chewed cable. The savvy maintenance person who removed the raccoon suggested that the door be locked at all times and that window coverings be installed to hide the expensive computer equipment and not let the sun in to overheat the room.

Access Control and Validation Procedures

Access controls and validation procedures are not only considerations for security, they are also a requirement of the Privacy Rule.

Under facility access controls, you should "implement procedures to control and validate a person's access to facilities based on their role or function, including visitor control, and control of access to software programs for testing and revision" (§164.310[a][2][iii]). Physical access controls ensure that individuals with legitimate business needs obtain access to the facility and those without legitimate business needs are denied access. The type of physical access controls used is based on the types of people needing access and when access is needed.

What good is an expensive alarm system for your house if you leave the back door unlocked? Who would invite a stranger into their home without asking some basic questions, such as, Who are you and what do you want? Apply the same precautions you take at home at your office.

When performing your risk analysis, consider access by the following individuals or groups:

- You and your staff during normal business hours and after hours; consider whether these individuals may bring children or other relatives and friends to the office
- Your patients and those who may accompany them
- Visitors, including contractors, inspectors, and salespersons
- Cleaning crews who may work during off hours; consider whether they are supervised and/or bonded, whether you need a clean-desk policy with respect to PHI to ensure that nothing is inadvertently discarded or viewed and that there are no temptations to alter or steal information
- Trainees such as residents or student nurses who need temporary access
- Security guards, inspectors, and others who may need access as the result of an incident
- Volunteers, who may be relatives or friends who help you regularly or occasionally

Consider adopting the following access controls:

- Locked doors to facility and any restricted access areas that contain critical equipment, sensitive files, or other materials such as drugs or cash. A variety of locks are available, from simple keys and combination locks to swipe badges and proximity cards that require a reader and produce an audit log of accesses.
- Surveillance cameras, alarms, and motion detectors to deter and/or record unauthorized access to a facility. Ensure that cameras actually record and that photos or videos are of high enough resolution for facial recognition and are retained for an appropriate period of time. These can also be used internally to guard against removal of electronic devices, media, and software. This practice can also aid in documenting any other physical abuses or provide evidence of injury.
- Property controls such as property control tags or engraving the office's name on equipment to provide proof of ownership. These also help manage an office's inventory.
- Personnel controls such as requiring employees to wear identification badges. This can be extended to visitor badges and/or escorts for a large office or certain types of visitors. Such badges sometimes seem cold or impersonal, but can actually help ensure patient safety with positive patient identification and more customer-service orientation when patients can call staff by name.

- Panic buttons located under the front counter at patient check-in for calling security or the local police or fire department.

- Private security service to patrol facility. Depending on your risk analysis, you may find that police provide adequate patrols or that you need night watch or even around-the-clock surveillance.

- Signs warning of restricted access areas and the sounding of an alarm if an emergency exit door is opened.

- Locked file cabinets and enforcement of a clean-desk policy to prevent paper documents or removable media from being taken or misplaced (files should either be returned to the main file or be placed in a designated drawer with a master key lock). Safes that bolt to a wall or floor may be necessary. As offices become paperless, tablet computers can be secured to carts and laptops secured to furnishings with cut-proof cabling.

- Office layout to prevent unauthorized viewing of computer screens or overhearing confidential conversations. For instance, cubbyholes in hallways with desktop computers may be a convenience, but leaving a computer left on, unattended, and out of any staff person's line of sight not only is an invitation to access but creates a perception of lax practices.

- Media controls (covered in detail later in this chapter).

CASE STUDY 8.3
The Bored Child

An employee who worked in a data entry area at a university medical center brought her 13-year-old daughter to work. By "shoulder surfing" (surreptitiously watching someone enter a user name and password), the child gained access to the names and phone numbers of some patients who recently had lab tests performed. The child called the patients, pretending to be a nurse, and told them or their families they had AIDS or were pregnant. When one individual attempted suicide, the ensuing investigation led to discovery of the incident. (*Inside Healthcare Computing*, March 4, 1996.)

CASE STUDY 8.4
Florida Hospital's Husband and Wife Team

Although not the first incident of its kind, the case of a man, aided by his wife and at least one other person, accessing more than 760,000 patient records over a period of two years and selling data to a solicitor for chiropractors and lawyers hit the headlines in 2012.[1] In this case the man was arrested and two others were fired, including the wife. Public outcry called for more arrests. Based on news descriptions, the incidents occurred as a result of both weak physical and technical access controls as well as issues "outside of the control of the hospital," which essentially means collusion with a business associate that appeared to have been a shredding service.

1. iHealthBeat. Former hospital worker arrested for accessing, selling patient records. http://www.ihealthbeat.org/articles/2012/8/23/former-hospital-worker-arrestedfor-accessing-selling-patient-records.aspx?p=1. August 23, 2012.

Implementing Facility Access Controls

Facility access controls should afford security but not hinder safety. For example, a door that locks a person into a room, frequently used in a data center to deter thieves, should be on a spring return. When a person enters the room and finds a fire or other emergency situation, there will be time to leave through the door without activating the unlocking mechanism.

The facility security plan should be an integral part of daily operations. All employees must know their roles in facility security. This is necessary in a disaster or an emergency as well as in everyday operations, when employees must be aware of unusual activity. Review the plan periodically, especially when there are any significant changes in your environment or information systems.

If you are leasing office space, ensure that the plan includes collaboration between your office and building management. Building tenants often share a common access closet that houses telecommunications connections and distribution panels for building power. Verify that this closet is secure and accessible when needed. You may need a policy stating that two people are required to open such a closet, eg, a tenant and representative from the building management; or, at a minimum, access controls on the door should include an audit log of all who accessed the closet.

CASE STUDY 8.5
The Unauthorized Engineer

Someone claiming to be your new IT support technician shows up at your office. Do you ask for proof of identity or do you take the person's word that he really is who he says he is and permit him access to your server? Even if you asked this person to explain why you did not receive a call from the company regarding his arrival, would you believe the claim that the company was remotely receiving an error message from your server that needs to be fixed before it gets too serious and shuts down? Hopefully not, but there are many "social engineers" who make a living from these types of activities.

CASE STUDY 8.6
Black Market Equipment

There have been several reported cases in which thieves entered provider settings portraying themselves as technicians called to repair broken biomedical equipment. By looking and acting the part of service technicians, these imposters went unchallenged by staff. They were escorted to the equipment, where they pretended to work on it. Later they claimed that they did not have the parts they needed to repair the equipment and needed to take the equipment back to their shop for repair. Or they claimed the equipment needed to be recalibrated back at their shop. Whatever the story, the equipment left with the imposters to be sold on the black market.

Could this happen to your organization? September 11, 2001, changed our minds about what constitutes an unthinkable event. Although your odds of being exposed to such stunts are low, you still must address validation procedures. An axiom of security is, "Trust, but verify."

Your access control policy and validation procedures require validation of the identity and authority of any person you do not know and include instructions on how to perform such validation. It is perfectly acceptable to question a person's identity and ask for proof. There is nothing wrong with calling the person's company and asking for a description of the individual the company sent to your office.

Once you have verified identity and become familiar with the individual, it is probably not necessary to check identity every time the technician comes to the office, especially if you make a request and the company indicates they'll send that individual. But if the individual shows up without a request for service, be sure this individual still works for the company. Even if a different individual shows up and explains he or she is substituting for "Joe," your regular representative, verify.

Environmental Controls

Physical security controls that address vulnerabilities protect human lives and ensure continued operation of information systems by preventing or minimizing possible damage due to environmental threats. These controls include those listed in Figure 8.1:

FIGURE 8.1

Physical Security Controls Related to Environmental Threats

- Fire alarms and smoke detectors to give warnings and save lives
- Fire suppression equipment such as sprinklers or fire extinguishers as a first line of defense against fires
- Protective clothing and/or gear and kits for properly handling biohazards
- Water detection alarms to prevent equipment damage in the event of flooding or water leaks
- Power strips with surge protectors for protecting equipment against spikes caused by lightning
- Power conditioners to protect against power sags or surges
- Uninterruptible power supply for systematic and orderly shutdown of servers and other information systems in the event of a power outage
- Backup generators in the event of extended power failures due to downed power lines or high power demands that cause widespread overloads
- Heating, ventilation, and air conditioning (HVAC) systems to maintain a comfortable work environment and keep computer equipment operating in the correct temperature range
- Heat sensors to shut down overheated computer equipment before damage occurs
- Humidity controls to prevent static electricity or too much moisture in the air
- Air filtering systems to remove dust, dirt, and other contaminants that could harm sensitive computer equipment

Use a facility layout to check off the environmental controls that are already used in your facility. Then determine which needed safeguards are reasonable and appropriate and should be implemented to reduce risks to an acceptable level.

Maintenance Records

Part of facility access controls relates to maintenance and records of maintenance. The Security Rule requires you to "implement policies and procedures to document repairs and modifications to the physical components of a facility which are related to security (for example, hardware, walls, doors, and locks)" (§164.310[a][2][iv]).

You probably make many types of facility security repairs and modifications, including changing locks, making routine maintenance checks, and installing new security devices. Use a logbook to demonstrate that you have conducted appropriate maintenance, and note the date and reason for all repairs and modifications. Figure 8.2 is a sample maintenance record.

FIGURE 8.2

Sample Maintenance Record

Date	Change	Reason for Change	Authorization
5/5/13	Medical records room door, combination change	Medical records clerk, Susie Smith, resigned on Friday, 5/2/13	Debra Jones, Office Manager
7/23/13	Installed a new motion detector, sensor, and camera to monitor the back door to the clinic	Recommendation as a result of conducting a risk analysis of physical safeguards	Debra Jones, Office Manager
10/27/13	Installed new batteries in smoke detector	End of daylight savings time triggered reminder to replace batteries	Sam Smith, Building Maintenance

Locks and Keys

The most frequent physical security changes you are likely to make is rekeying door locks or changing the combination on a cipher lock door. These changes are made because a member of your workforce has been terminated or there is some other compromise to this access control.

Master key systems are commonly used in office buildings. In a master key system there are two keys that will open any given lock—the "normal" key and the master key. The "normal" key will only open your office. The master key opens all doors. Your office's physical security relies on controlling who has what keys to the doors of your practice. There should be a limited number of master keys, and the master key should also be a security key that prevents its duplication. However, be sure to have emergency procedures. There is a process for reproducing a master key available on the Internet, so guard against this by regularly rekeying your locks.

Cipher lock doors use a series of number buttons that are pushed in a certain combination to unlock a door. Your security policy should stipulate that this combination may never be shared with anyone; however, this is very difficult to enforce.

Change the door combination whenever a person who knows the combination terminates employment or services. Regularly change the combination as well. Many can recognize "worn" buttons as the buttons to the combination. Once narrowed to just four, it becomes much easier to guess the actual combination.

To overcome the problems associated with key and cipher lock systems, some facilities use door locks that rely on a card or badge reader. These systems are initially expensive to install but provide much greater security. They can be used to control a specific person's access to a room or facility based on day of the week and time of day. For example, an employee is granted access to the medical records room only on Monday through Friday, from 8 AM to 5 PM. If the person is in the office on a Saturday, access to this location is denied. Some systems include an emergency access mode, such as an extra password that generates an audit log.

Alternatively, someone in building maintenance may be called to provide access, which should be logged and reported to you. These systems are easy to use. You are able to add or delete access privileges using a computer; there is no need for a locksmith. Because the systems also maintain an audit log of who gained access and when, you can routinely check access and use these records as evidence if needed. If your office has a high turnover rate of employees, this system is likely to pay for itself in a short period of time.

WORKSTATION USE STANDARD

The Workstation Use standard requires you to "implement policies and procedures that specify the proper functions to be performed, the manner in which those functions are to be performed, and the physical attributes of the surroundings of a specific workstation or class of workstation that can access electronic protected health information" (§164.310[b]).

Workstation is a generic term that refers to any computer device that you use to create, receive, maintain, or transmit PHI. The term *workstation*, however, does not refer to a desk, workbench, or other physical place where you may perform work.

Inappropriate use of computer workstations exposes your office to risks such as virus attacks, compromise of your network and information systems, breaches of confidentiality, and legal issues. Create a policy that defines acceptable practices or rules of computer workstation use. Some practices to address include:

- Logging off before leaving a workstation unattended for any extended period of time such as lunch break and at the end of the day before going home.

- Avoiding food near workstations. Accidental spills will occur and can cause significant damage. This policy can be relaxed for locations where a standard PC and keyboard are kept; PC keyboards are much easier and cheaper to replace than an entire laptop.

- Complying with the terms and conditions of software licensing and copyright laws. (Although this is not included in HIPAA, violation of copyright and license agreements is a federal offense.) Note that the Business Software Alliance (http://www.bsa.org) and the Software and Information Industry Association (http:// www.siia.net) watch for software license violations.

- Using antivirus software. Antivirus software is the generic description of software that is designed to protect against viruses and other malicious software attacks. To be effective the software must be updated continuously with new virus definitions. Updates are generally supplied by connecting to the Internet. Computing devices that do not have Internet access are less prone to acquiring viruses, but should still have current antivirus software because a virus could be contained on a CD or flash drive. Such media should be scanned before opening or executing any files. Because there is no Internet access, there needs to be a procedure for manually applying updates.

Don't forget that the Security Rule extends to members of your workforce who work from home, such as transcriptionists or physicians using remote access. All safeguards required for office workstations must be applied to all computer workstations located off site.

WORKSTATION SECURITY STANDARD

Workstation security defines the physical security controls and practices used to restrict access to information stored on computer workstations and peripheral equipment such as printers and fax machines. The Security Rule specifies that you must "implement physical safeguards for all workstations that access PHI, to restrict access to authorized users" (§164.310[c]).

You can restrict access of PHI to authorized users in a variety of ways. One way is to minimize viewing by unauthorized persons. Consider these options:

■ Position workstations and other equipment from which PHI can be viewed so that the possibility of unauthorized access is minimized, particularly in publicly accessible areas. This may mean simply turning the monitor a certain way.

■ Install antiglare screens, privacy screens, covers, or another type of physical barrier to viewing. Be aware that many of these devices make it impossible for two or more people to view a screen simultaneously. This could be a problem if you want to discuss something with another caregiver or the patient. Also, be aware that some polarized screens are difficult to see through and can cause eyestrain.

■ Review the content of all displays. Often there is so much information displayed that it is difficult for anyone unfamiliar with the screen layout to discern who the patient is or to even see the specific words. However, remember that patients may still perceive this to be a violation of their privacy.

■ Install screen savers. Screen savers do not limit viewing while someone is working at the workstation, nor do they restrict access if someone touches the keyboard or mouse. However, they can be effective if there is a physical access barrier to the actual workstation and you only wish to prevent incidental disclosure when no one is at the computer. Some screen savers are password-protected. Because most people don't like to constantly reenter a password, the activation time is typically set for a relatively long period of disuse, which defeats the purpose of restricting access when the computer is not in use. Because screen savers can interfere with some types of software, consult with your IT vendor before installing them.

In addition to restricting viewing, additional security controls that restrict access include:

■ Equipment lock-down devices, such as a metal cable, to prevent theft of the device itself

■ Tokens to lock the workstation and work with a password to restrict access

■ Workstations without removable media drives to prevent copying and reduce risk of introducing a virus

■ Deactivation of USB (universal serial bus) and other ports to prevent attaching removable media devices

■ Software controls to prevent copying to a CD and/or printing to a printer to prevent copying

■ Power-on passwords for laptops and smart phones reduce the likelihood of access if these are lost or stolen; however, federal guidance on securing portable devices and media suggests that passwords are insufficient to protect such data and that encryption should be used. Increasingly providers are relying upon "thin clients" where their computing device does not retain any data but only accesses the server for data. This is also a good practice, but often it is not fully foolproof as local drives may still be used to store personal notes, schedules, small databases, temporary worksheets, and other files that may contain PHI.

Workstation security also relates to protection from fluctuations in electricity. Plug computer workstations into an electrical power strip that has a built-in surge protector. Do not use this same power strip for other electrical appliances that draw a lot of current (vacuum cleaner, toaster, coffeepot, microwave, space heater), because these devices can interfere with operation of a computer workstation.

CASE STUDY 8.7
Sacrifice the Surge Protector to Save Your Equipment

An office contained 13 computer workstations. The designated information security official (ISO) wanted each one to be plugged into its own surge-protected power strip. The office manager initially didn't want to invest in 13 power strips but finally gave the ISO permission to buy and install them. Many laughed at the ISO when she went looking under people's desks to check that the power strip was being used and that nothing else had been plugged in to the strip.

One day lightning struck nearby, causing a huge voltage spike on the power line. The 13 power strips and one computer monitor were destroyed, but all PCs and remaining monitors survived. The surge protectors had sacrificed themselves to save the rest of the office. It was agreed that it was much cheaper and quicker to replace 13 power strips than to replace 13 computer workstations. The incident finally made believers out of everyone in the office and the ISO a hero.

DEVICE AND MEDIA CONTROLS STANDARD

Mobile devices and media present a special physical security challenge. Because devices for storing PHI are getting smaller in size, large in capacity, and cheaper, they are becoming more prevalent in health care. However, they are much more difficult to track and easily lost. As a result, this standard on device and media controls is becoming ever more important. HIPAA requires you to "implement policies and procedures that govern the receipt and removal of hardware and electronic media that contain electronic protected health information into and out of a facility, and the movement of these items within the facility" (§164.310[d]).

Devices include any electronic equipment used to create, receive, store, and transmit PHI. Although devices technically include any computer equipment, of special concern are those that are small and can be concealed in a briefcase or pocket. Be aware that in a large office where everyone doesn't know everyone else and other vulnerabilities exist, it is possible for PCs on carts or virtually any other equipment to be wheeled out of the office under the guise of needing to use the equipment elsewhere by someone posing as a caregiver. A surprising number of servers have been stolen out of offices and other covered entity settings.

Media are the materials that hold information, including paper, CDs, magnetic tape, magnetic disks, hard drives, memory devices, and microfilm or microfiche.

In general, device and media controls policies and procedures should address the following important issues:

- Ownership of device. A practice that owns devices such as smart phones and laptop computers does have control over how they may be used and can determine that their use be audited and even that their use be terminated. However, your initial investment in these devices is high, and people using them may not take ownership and protect them in the same way as they might if they actually had to pay for them themselves.

- Access vs storage. Some devices can be configured with software that only serves to capture and retrieve data, not store it (this is referred to as a "thin client"). In this case, loss or theft of the device is less of a concern from a PHI perspective. Be aware that if this device is wireless, the device could still be used to gain access to PHI if the locations of the wireless access points are known. As noted above, however, many portable devices have ever larger storage capacity and sophisticated software applications. Even if used as a thin client with respect to the EHR, for instance, it can still be very tempting to store data locally for personal convenience.

■ Access controls and encryption. Although many newer mobile devices come with access controls and encryption as standard features, older devices may not have such features. Even when such features exist, they are not often used.

Train your workforce on how to properly handle, transfer, store, retain, and destroy devices and media containing PHI. When not in use, devices and media containing PHI should be stored in a way that protects the information from disclosure or damage. It may be necessary to lock the devices and media in a cabinet or desk drawer overnight. If used while traveling, they should be kept in a pocket, purse, or briefcase, not placed in luggage that will be out of your control. Encourage people to safeguard devices and media containing PHI as they would their wallets. This should be considered a personal safety factor as well, as people distracted by using a portable device can be a target for attack. Use high-quality electronic media as backups, and test them regularly to make sure data can be restored from them. Do not expose devices and media to extremes of temperature, spills, or magnetic fields.

APPLY PHYSICAL CONTROLS TO ALL PHI

Although the HIPAA Security Rule only refers to PHI held in electronic media and devices, remember that the "mini-security" rule in the Privacy Rule requires you to apply safeguards to PHI in oral, written, and electronic form. Apply appropriate physical safeguards to paper records as well as to your electronic records.

CASE STUDY 8.8

An office is located in a medical/dental building. The main door to the office is half glass. Medical record files are stored in open shelving behind an open reception area within the office. Although patients do not walk behind the reception area, the files appear accessible, not only to the patients in the waiting area but to anyone who may walk by the office and look into the window. This situation may not be a HIPAA violation if the reception area is continuously staffed during office hours, no unauthorized persons are permitted access to the medical record files, and the office door is locked during off-hours. However, perception is often stronger than reality; patients with heightened sensitivity to privacy may be concerned about the "openness" of the files. Furthermore, because the files are viewable from a public area during off-hours, the situation may tempt someone to act maliciously even without direct motivation. This office should consider any or several of the following measures: drawing a shade over the window in the outer door, replacing the window in the outer door with glass that cannot be seen through, erecting shutters or a sliding door around the open reception area, obtaining doors for the files, and moving the files to a back room. Such protections would not be a factor if the office had an EHR, although some offices continue to maintain paper as archives. In this case, however, the frequency of access is not as intense and so paper files could be moved to a back office.

HIPAA implementation specifications for the Device and Media Controls standard include disposal, media reuse, accountability, and data backup and storage. In April 2009, the US Department of Health and Human Services (HHS) issued Guidance to Render Unsecured Protected Health Information Unusable, Unreadable, or Indecipherable to Unauthorized Individuals (45 CFR Parts 160 and 164, available at http://www.hhs.gov/ocr/privacy/hipaa/understanding/coveredentities/federalregisterbreachrfi.pdf), which is consistent with and enhances HIPAA's Device and Media Controls standard.

Disposal

The Disposal implementation specification requires you to "implement policies and procedures to address the final disposition of PHI, and/or the hardware or electronic media on which it is stored" (§164.310[d][2][i]).

Dumpster diving is the act of going through other people's trash. This can be done to obtain sensitive information stored on paper or electronic media. Paper, including labels, containing PHI should be shredded or placed in secure storage bins for shredding or incineration by a company contracted to perform such secure disposal. Look in your trash cans to determine what PHI you may be providing to dumpster divers. The Security Rule only applies to PHI in electronic form; however, the Privacy Rule requires physical safeguards for all forms of PHI. You may also want to apply such safeguards to other confidential information, such as payroll data or credentialing information.

Render magnetic media such as hard drives, CDs, smart phones, and backup tapes or disks that are unusable or nonrepairable completely unusable prior to their disposal. Degaussing is a method whereby a strong magnetic field is applied to magnetic media to fully erase the data. If you don't have access to degaussing equipment, you can physically damage the media beyond repair, eg, drill a hole through it or cut it up with wire cutters or scissors. Optical disks must be physically damaged. Reformatting media is not sufficient to render the data totally inaccessible to people who know how to retrieve it.

Media Reuse

In addition to appropriate disposal, learn how to appropriately reuse any media you want to keep or donate. You need to "implement procedures for removal of electronic protected health information from electronic media before the media are made available for reuse" (§164.310[d][2][ii]).

To redeploy a PC or just reuse a CD or flash drive within your facility, take the following steps to ensure PHI is not accessible to someone who should not have access:

1. Check that all important files needed by someone else have been copied to another computing device or other media.
2. Use the "delete" command to remove files from the directory as an added measure.
3. Reformat the disk to render the files inaccessible to most users. Note that neither the "delete" nor "format" command ensures that the data could not be retrieved by using a special software utility program or some other sophisticated device. This process, however, is sufficient for reuse within your own office.

To donate or resell old devices or media or simply comply with local ordinances against throwing electronic devices in the trash, take the following steps:

1. Check that all important files needed by someone else have been copied to another computing device or other media.
2. Completely sanitize the media so they contain only files necessary to make them bootable and no file previously stored.
3. Consider removing the hard drive from the device and physically destroying it; then return it to the vendor or another reputable company that will properly dispose of what now has become toxic waste.

Accountability

If your hardware and media are frequently moved about your office or between locations, you need to "maintain a record of the movements of hardware and electronic media and any person responsible therefore."

For internal movement of hardware and electronic media, a software/hardware inventory can be used to maintain a record of the location of all devices and what is contained on them. If you have multiple devices of the same type, log their serial numbers on this inventory. Not only is this a good HIPAA security measure, it is also important for insurance purposes in the event of loss. Highly sophisticated offices may consider applying tracking devices. If devices or media are going to be removed from your office, consider maintaining a property-pass system, or a log in which persons sign these items out and in.

Establish a policy for where files are to be stored. If you have a network, require that all files be stored on the network drive, not on the computing system's hard drive. This way, files will be backed up when the network is backed up and no PHI will remain on the device. It may be necessary to acquire software that will scan computing devices when connected to the network to make sure no PHI resides on the local drive. Better yet, install encryption on every device and require its use. Although there are still risks that unscrupulous persons who have legitimate access to these encrypted devices could thwart this protection, you have at least complied with federal guidance. Your backup plan should assign responsibility for backing up the network, establish where backups are stored, and ensure that backups are encrypted. A Media Use and Control policy should hold persons accountable for appropriately storing files.

Accountability also involves knowing to whom PHI is disclosed outside of the office (vendor, billing company, etc), how it is disclosed (sent via express mail on a disk, sent via a courier on tape, mailed on a CD, e-faxed, etc), and when it is disclosed (date and time). (Note: This type of accountability is not the same as the Accounting for Disclosures Log maintained in compliance with the Privacy Rule, although it is complementary. The Privacy Rule only requires accounting for disclosures made for purposes other than treatment, payment, and operations; those pursuant to an authorization; and other exceptions [although this requirement may change under pending HITECH Privacy Rule modifications]. Security accountability ensures that all movement of media containing PHI can be accounted for as an internal security control.)

The proper handling of media—receipt, removal, backup, storage, reuse, disposal, and accountability—should be clearly defined by policy and enforced through periodic reviews and other security controls. A single Media Use and Control policy can address all of these controls.

Data Backup and Storage

Your contingency plans created under Administrative Safeguards called for a backup plan. This physical security implementation specification addresses how you will "create a retrievable, exact copy of PHI, when needed, before movement of equipment" (§164.310[d][2][iv]).

To simplify data backup and storage, have computer users store their files on the network. A way to accomplish this is to set controls in the operating system to prevent local saves. If equipment must be moved, backup the hard drive immediately prior to the move.

Storage of records (electronic or paper) should follow your backup plan. Retention of health information is generally determined by state statute. HIPAA does not address retention of PHI but does require six-year retention of your policies and procedures, documentation of communications required to be in writing by the Privacy Rule, and any actions, activities, designations, and assessments required by the Privacy Rule and Security Rule.

PHYSICAL SECURITY AND SAFETY

There are many types of environmental and human threats to a medical office facility, members of its workforce, and its information systems. Based on a risk analysis, physical safeguards are implemented to reduce the office's risks of security incidents to an acceptable level.

Physical access controls support information security by restricting physical access to a facility and its computers, devices, and media that process and store PHI (and other confidential information). Policies and procedures must be established to protect computer workstations from unauthorized viewing and provide direction regarding the proper use of computer workstations. Handling of media—their receipt, removal, backup, storage, reuse, disposal, and accountability—also requires physical controls to ensure their confidentiality, protect them from alteration, and ensure data are available from them.

As an added bonus, physical security measures taken to protect your information systems also contribute to the overall safety of the office.

CHECK YOUR UNDERSTANDING*

1. The biggest security threat to a small office is:
   a. Burglary
   b. Weather
   c. Power outage
   d. Depends on environment

2. An uninterruptible power supply:
   a. Allows power to be turned on when restored
   b. Provides power for several days
   c. Reduces the effects of spikes in power on computers
   d. Supplies power to shut down critical computer systems

3. The HIPAA workstation use standard requires you to consider which of the following controls:
   a. Antiglare screens
   b. Antivirus software
   c. Positioning workstations out of sight
   d. Screen savers

4. A best practice for the HIPAA workstation security standard is:
   a. Cloud computing
   b. Data encryption
   c. Disabling a USB port
   d. Heating, ventilation, and air conditioning (HVAC)

5. A "thin" client could eliminate the need for:
   a. Devices to store archived data
   b. Local data center
   c. Servers
   d. Storing data on the user input device

6. A means to fully remove PHI from magnetic media is:
   a. Copy over the data on the magnetic medium
   b. Degauss the medium
   c. Reformat the medium
   d. Wipe the medium clean

7. To limit loss of data in the event of a server crash:
   a. Backup data daily
   b. Have a contingency plan
   c. Store data on portable media
   d. Use a failover server

8. A good finding as a result of conducting a security risk analysis may be:
   a. An office with no information systems does not need physical security
   b. Contingency planning is too expensive at this time
   c. Small offices do not need facility security plans
   d. There is low probability of data loss when using an application service provider (ASP)

9. The best place for your new server is:
   a. Office manager's home
   b. Small closet
   c. Unused office
   d. Utility room

10. The best way to verify the identity of a computer repair person is:
   a. Match a government-issued photo identification with the name of the person expected to present to your office
   b. Call the number of the company that the repair person gives you to ask if the person is employed by the company
   c. Require person to sign a visitor's log and keep the log for a period of at least six years from date of signature
   d. Test the person's understanding of the security controls in your office by observing the person work on your computer systems

*For answers, refer to the Answer Key at the end of the book.

chapter 9

HIPAA Security Technical Safeguards

Technology can be a blessing and a curse. With each new technological innovation comes a new set of security challenges. Stories about hackers accessing "secure" Web sites and people's identity being stolen over the Internet are increasingly common.

Health care is not immune. Security incidents can harm patients, impact productivity, cost money to mitigate, and significantly impact your reputation. As you rely more on information technology to manage your office's critical business functions, implementing security controls becomes increasingly important to protect against both malicious acts of others and accidental incidents. Technical security controls are used to protect the confidentiality, integrity, and availability of your PHI and other important information, just as you use locked doors, safes, and burglar alarms to protect your physical assets.

To counter security threats, technical safeguards coupled with good security practices reduce the probability of threats exploiting the vulnerabilities inherent in your computer systems. Technical safeguards are the practices, products, tools, services, and system features that are used to implement and enforce an office's administrative policies and procedures.

HOW TO USE THIS CHAPTER

This chapter covers the required standards and implementation specifications that compose the Security Rule's Technical Safeguards. The chapter:

- Defines each technical security requirement
- Offers various methods for implementing controls to meet each requirement
- Provides examples of best practices for physician offices

HIPAA defines technical safeguards as "the technology and the policies and procedures for its use that protect PHI and control access to it" (§164.304). The Technical Safeguards standards and their implementation specifications (where they exist) are listed in Table 9.1.

It is likely that your office will work with your information systems application vendors to coordinate implementation of technical security controls, or even use an IT vendor to assist in implementing the controls. However, there are at least three reasons why you should understand the basic concepts behind the technical safeguards and not rely solely on your vendors:

1. Your security technology must fit your office. HIPAA calls for applying "reasonable and appropriate" safeguards to ensure the confidentiality, integrity, and availability of information. While the information security official (ISO) function can be outsourced, someone who is not an authority in your office cannot be delegated responsibility to determine what is right for your office. You must have some knowledge of information technology and security tools to effectively evaluate what would be considered "reasonable and appropriate" under HIPAA.

TABLE 9.1

Technical Safeguard Standards and Implementation Specifications

Security Standard	Code of Federal Regulations Section	Security Implementation Specifications (R) = Required, (A) = Addressable
Access Control	§164.312(a)	Unique User Identification (R) Emergency Access Procedure (R) Automatic Logoff (A) Encryption and Decryption (A)
Audit Controls	§164.312(b)	(R)
Integrity	§164.312(c)(1)	Mechanism to Authenticate PHI (A)
Person or Entity Authentication	§164.312(d)	(R)
Transmission Security	§164.312(e)(1)	Integrity Controls (A) Encryption (A)

2. Technical security tools, products, and solutions can be expensive. There are hundreds of vendors and thousands of solutions. You need to understand enough about the technology to make sound financial decisions on how best to apply your limited resources for security.
3. Security controls can be technically complex. You, or the ISO you appoint, need a basic reference source so that you can effectively communicate with IT support staff and/or vendors.

Do You Speak Geek?

Are there times when you struggle to understand your IT vendor or support staff, especially when they use technical jargon and acronyms? Check out TechWeb's TechEncyclopedia on the Web (http://www.techweb.com/encyclopedia). The site provides definitions and explanations of technical terms and acronyms. The next time you're unsure about a "techie" term, write it down and look it up later on this Web site, or set your browser to the word and surf the Internet for other descriptions and resources. You may not speak geek, but at least you'll have a better understanding of technical lingo.

The technical safeguards covered in this chapter apply to all computer workstations (see definition of workstation in Chapter 8), telecommunications and network devices, and all other components of information systems (hardware, software, and users). A multitude of security products are available for each type of electronic device. These security products are used for prevention (access controls, authentication, and transmission security), detection (audit controls and integrity), or both; and for data at rest, in use, or being transmitted.

ACCESS CONTROL STANDARD

The Access Control standard requires you to "implement technical policies and procedures for electronic information systems that maintain PHI to allow access only to those persons or software programs that have been granted access rights . . ."

Access Controls

Access controls give users of information systems the privileges to access, perform functions on, and transmit from information systems, applications, programs, or files based on a preestablished set of rules.

Access controls are managed at the operating system level and are associated with the unique user identification (user ID) you assign each person. For example, in a Windows environment, there is an Active Directory that carries out user access control functionality.

The HIPAA Privacy Rule Minimum Necessary Use standard requires you to identify the classes of persons who need access to PHI, the categories of PHI to which access is needed, and any conditions appropriate to such access except when the use of the information is for treatment purposes (§164.514[d]). The Security Rule Access Controls standard describes the means to carry out the Privacy Rule requirement.

Figure 6.5 (see Chapter 6) provides a sample set of access rules that identify classes of users, categories of information that may be accessed based on these rules, and the functions each class is privileged to perform.

If you are not clear about the categories of information you have, it may be helpful to perform an application and data criticality and sensitivity analysis. By knowing the criticality and sensitivity of each application and the data associated with it, you will be able to assign appropriate access controls. (Analyzing the criticality and sensitivity of data is also useful for establishing disaster recovery priorities.)

Criticality of an application refers to whether the application or data are absolutely required for an individual to perform his or her work. With respect to disaster recovery, criticality would be the application or data absolutely required for you to function in your office or whether you could get by for a short or long period of time without access to the information or system. Use a scale of high-medium-low to identify the criticality to a person's job function, or the number of hours you could manage without the information or system to determine criticality. For example, if a receptionist needs access to demographic information about your patients in order to schedule appointments, that information would have a high criticality for that individual. If you routinely print out your schedule of patients once each day, however, you could function for eight hours without your scheduling system, but you would probably have difficulty functioning beyond that (resulting in a medium criticality rating).

Sensitivity of an application refers to the nature of the data and the harm that could result from a breach of confidentiality or a security incident. Use a scale of high-medium-low for this determination as well. For example, if you were a pediatrician, immunization information that must be reported to the state and may even be posted on a public Web site is not sensitive information. Alternatively, if you were a "plastic surgeon to the stars," even your list of patients would be sensitive information.

Use Figure 9.1 to list your applications, major categories of data, and their criticality and sensitivity. Then list the classes of users and the functions they perform to determine to which categories of information each should be afforded access. To determine the criticality and sensitivity for disaster recovery purposes, it may be helpful to understand whether you create the data or receive them from someone else and whether you maintain and/or transmit the data. If you create and maintain the data yourself, it will be more critical to protect that data than data you receive from someone else or transmit to someone else, because those sources and users of data could supply the data again in the event of a disaster.

Access control functions are typically categorized by the ability to:

- Create (enter) data
- Read (view) information
- Write information to a file, printer, fax machine, or other transmission; this also means to receive information from an external source and place it into a file
- Delete information from active view while retaining the original information in an accessible archive file
- Administer system functions such as setting up access controls, assigning user names, etc

FIGURE 9.1

Application and Data Criticality and Sensitivity for Assigning Access Controls

Class of User	Function Performed: Create Read Write Delete SysAdmin	Application	Criticality: High Medium Low	Data	Function Performed: Create Receive Maintain Transmit	Sensitivity: High Medium Low

Reprinted with permission from Margret\A Consulting, LLC.

Case Study 9.1 provides an example of access control assignments. While many offices implement far less complex rules than those illustrated in this case study, it is important to note that most healthcare workers have significantly more access to PHI than they need to perform their jobs. There are two reasons for this:

1. The clinical applications or practice management software programs typically lack the ability to carry out the controls needed to restrict a user's access to only what is needed to perform the job.
2. Even where access control capabilities exist, the process to accommodate the needs of staff members who have multiple functions, especially those in smaller offices, is complex to administer.

CASE STUDY 9.1
Examples of Access Control Assignments

If an office has five people, Alan, Betty, Chuck, Diane, and Evelyn, each may have the same or different access controls based on their needs. Alan, whose user ID may be AlanA and who may be part time, may be a system administrator and needs system administration (SysAdmin) privileges. Betty (BettyB—following the schema for assigning user IDs) and Chuck (CharlesC) may be a nurse and a physician respectively and have "create" and "read" privileges in the electronic health record (EHR) and access only to those patients with whom they have a treatment relationship. (The treatment relationship in a small practice such as this may be all patients, but in a very large practice or a hospital, the treatment relationship may be defined by who the attending physician is [and associated nurses], on what nursing unit the patient is located, or other such schema.) Diane (DianeD) may be the office administrator/receptionist and have the need to create and read patient demographic and billing data (in the practice management system) and the need to write to and delete EHRs, but no need to create or read EHRs. (To wean people off paper and reduce inadvertent transmissions of PHI, many offices have restricted the ability for printing, faxing, and other transmissions to an office administrator.) Evelyn (EvelynE) may be a biller and have the need to read the EHR but not write to the EHR, and may have the need to read and write to the billing application for all patients who have open accounts. Note that in each case consideration is given to the class of person, functions needing to be performed, and the categories of PHI, which include not only the nature of the data (such as EHR data, demographic data, or billing data—and not necessarily all) but in some cases the relationship of the individual to the data (ie, as a treating professional, or as a biller) and in other cases the time frame or status of the data (ie, open or closed account).

Types of Access Controls

Access controls generally are described by types of models. HIPAA does not identify the type of model to use.

A common access control model is the use of access control lists (ACLs). When using ACLs, every type of data or application has a list of users associated with it who are allowed access. In this way, the system administrator can easily see which users have access to a given application. Changing access is straightforward if there is only one application and all users may have access to all data within the application in any context; the administrator simply adds or deletes a user from the ACL. ACLs are more difficult to use when there are a number of applications, many files and types of data are associated with each application, and contingencies exist on what data may be accessed when data may be accessed, or under what circumstances users may have access. The ACL for each application, file, data type, or circumstance must be updated whenever there is a change in user status (eg, job change or termination).

To streamline the process, especially for more complex computing environments, other technologies have been developed. One is discretionary access control (DAC), sometimes called user-based access control (UBAC). UBAC governs access to information based on the user's identity and rules that specify which users have access to what applications or data. When a user requests access to a particular application or data, the computer searches for a rule that specifies which users are allowed such access. If the rule is found, the user is given access; if not, the user is denied access. Mandatory Access Control (MAC) is similar to DAC but requires an administrator to manage the access controls, rather than having the user rely on prebuilt rules.

Another model for access control is role-based access control (RBAC), which is generally considered a best practice for health care today. RBAC is based on the worker's role rather than the user's identity. Users are assigned to predefined roles, which makes it easy for managers authorizing access to define more precisely what access a person performing a given job actually requires. If a member of the workforce performs multiple jobs, multiple roles can be assigned. Rule-based access control (also abbreviated RBAC) is an extension of role-based access control. This can accommodate not only roles predefined in accordance with job functions, but the context in which those functions may be performed. The context may be the physical location of the workstation, the time of day or day of week, or other parameters you establish. For most small office settings, this may be more control than you typically need, but you may increasingly find this in large offices and hospitals. You will need to work with your information systems vendors to determine what controls are available in their products and whether you need to supplement these with additional controls based on the risks you identify for your practice.

In reality, operating systems today use a combination of the described access control models. What is more important is for the rules to be defined and applied to individual users, not the other way around. Case Study 9.2 illustrates this.

CASE STUDY 9.2
Just Like Mary

A new employee, Sue, is hired to replace Mary. The office manager instructs the system administrator to assign Sue "the same access that Mary had." Mary had been an employee for 10 years. During that time, Mary's job changed three times. Each time Mary changed jobs, she was given access to additional information and applications, but her old access privileges were never taken away from her (just in case she needed to help her replacement). If Sue's access is set up just like Mary's, her access will exceed what she needs to do her job.

Access Control Policies

Regardless of the access controls you employ, be aware that the controls only work for the PHI that is maintained within the applications on which the controls have been placed. Users may create spreadsheets, databases, or word processing documents. These may be stored in separate files on the hard drive of a computer workstation, in a notebook computer, or on another computing device; they often are not stored in the original application from which the data were derived. Consequently, these files are not part of the access-controlled applications. Because most physician offices still maintain a significant amount of patient information on paper, access controls on electronic systems will be more strict than that possible for the paper files. In these cases, develop written policies that establish the most appropriate privileges, even though there are no technical controls to support the paper systems. An honor system must be used for access policies in the paper environment. Remember, these policies establish expectations. If someone violates the policies, sanctions can be applied in a manner consistent with the critical nature of the information, regardless of how it is stored. After all, an HIV-positive test result in a computer system is no different from an HIV-positive test result on paper.

Access Control Procedures

Access controls are established through privileged accounts known as system administrator accounts. These accounts represent a significant vulnerability to information systems. The rights and privileges afforded these accounts make them the "gods of the network," and the privileges permit the system administrator to add new user accounts, modify the privileges of existing user accounts, or delete accounts. System administrator accounts provide full access to the operating system, applications, critical system files, sensitive and confidential data files, and usually the system audit logs.

The individual assigned as the system administrator should obviously be a highly trustworthy individual. However, experts still recommend establishing a system of checks and balances. For example, never permit a system administrator to change a user's access privileges without written authorization from someone with supervisory authority. The office manager or an external auditor can audit such a procedure. Having in place a knowledgeable office manager and informed professional leadership who are conversant about technical security controls is another form of check and balance. The more you know, the less able someone is to fool you. It is also important to document all system administration activities, which can be compared with an internal audit log.

Because of their powerful system privileges, system administrator accounts are also the primary target of hackers and as such create a single point of failure or compromise to the security of information systems and networks. A hacker who obtains system administrator access can do just about anything. The hacker usually takes control of the audit logs to erase the digital evidence of the attack. For these reasons, system administrator accounts require tighter access controls and management procedures than the average system user account.

ACCESS CONTROL IMPLEMENTATION SPECIFICATIONS

In addition to access controls that comply with the HIPAA Access Controls standard, there are four implementation specifications to be considered: unique user identification, emergency access procedures, automatic logoff, and encryption and decryption.

Unique User Identification

Unique user identification means you must "assign a unique name and/or number for identifying and tracking user identity" (§164.312[a][2][i]).

User identification is a way to identify a computer user, typically using a user name or user ID. HIPAA's Security Rule requires unique user identification for tracking users' interactions with the computer systems and holding them accountable for their activities when logged into systems containing PHI.

You need to decide how to construct user IDs for your systems. The typical convention is to incorporate a person's name into the user ID, eg, first initial and last name or first name and last initial, and to apply a standard format for all users across the organization. If the user's name is Theresa Jones, Theresa's user ID might be tjones. An alternative that is less popular and more complex, but possibly affords greater security, is to assign a set of random numbers and characters to each individual user.

The problems with using any convention other than random assignment include that it is easier (for a hacker) to guess a user ID once the convention is discovered, and user IDs may get reused over time for persons with common names (eg, when Theresa Jones leaves and Tom Jones gets hired). A randomly assigned user ID overcomes these problems, but user IDs without meaning are sometimes more difficult for users to remember and for persons assigned audit responsibility to recognize.

Multiple information systems imply that users have multiple user IDs (and passwords). Because it's challenging to remember multiple user IDs and passwords, employees often write them down. Once you establish your system of user ID creation, consistently apply it to all information systems, if possible, so that users have only one user ID to remember for all systems.

The HIPAA standard requires not only user identification but unique user identification. This means that generic or shared user ID accounts should not be used to access PHI. If Theresa Jones and Tom Jones are both employed by the office, assign the first one tjones (or tjones1) and the second tjones2.

Many offices permit a generic user ID to access the network, and shared access to the network may be acceptable if each application has its own login. However, many offices also permit multiple users to share a login for access to the schedule or other practice management applications; some offices even permit a nurse to sign on in order to set up data retrieval or data entry functions for a physician. However, sharing logins for applications means that there is no accountability for who performed what function within an application and is not permitted under HIPAA's unique user identification standard. Although you may trust your staff to do the right thing, shared logins also typically do not have automatic logoffs. As a consequence, they become an open invitation for anyone to use the system, including patients, persons accompanying patients, or others left unattended in your office.

Emergency Access Procedures

HIPAA requires that you "establish (and implement as needed) procedures for obtaining necessary PHI during an emergency" (§164.312[a][ii]).

Emergency access control procedures are the documented instructions and operational practices for obtaining access to necessary information during a crisis. Any situation in which a delay in accessing vital information could create imminent medical danger to a patient requires an emergency access procedure. The formal access control procedures are bypassed in these situations. This should be a limited, one-time access and only used in real emergencies. To avoid abuse of emergency access, have strict "break-the-glass" procedures (from the concept of breaking a glass barrier to get access to a fire alarm) that justify when emergency access controls may be used, and use thorough audit logs to hold users accountable for their actions.

Determine the types of situations that would require emergency access to an information system or application by someone who does not have access privileges to that information. Work collaboratively with your IT vendor to establish emergency access procedures to accommodate those types of situations. Many current healthcare information systems do not have such controls but are being upgraded to support this HIPAA requirement. Emergency access could be as simple as creating a special user account with full access to all PHI; use of that particular account would trigger a special audit log. Some information systems permit use of a second password, rather than require an entirely separate account, to "break the glass." Some systems also require a brief description of the rationale for the access, and some can be set up to send an e-mail to the patient's primary care physician or other supervisory person to identify when emergency access was performed so it can be monitored.

Automatic Logoff

Automatic logoff implies that you will "implement electronic procedures that terminate an electronic session after a predetermined time of inactivity."

Healthcare workers frequently abandon their work area to react quickly to an urgent situation and often don't have the time to completely log off a computer system. Automatic logoff is an effective way to prevent unauthorized users from viewing PHI on computer monitors when they are left unattended for a period of time.

The preferred method for addressing this implementation specification is to have clinical applications sense when inactivity has lasted beyond the predetermined timeout period and then automatically log the user off. For applications without automatic logoff capability, the alternatives are to activate a password-protected screen saver or lock out the computer by pressing specific keys on the keyboard (eg, Ctrl/Alt/Delete pressed simultaneously will lock applications with newer Windows operating systems). In either case, the information that was displayed on the screen is no longer accessible, and the user is forced to enter a password to unlock and regain access to the computer.

It is necessary to determine the situations in which automatic logoff is appropriate and the appropriate amount of time before an automatic logoff activates. The time lag before automatic logoff occurs depends on the location of the computer workstation and the nature of the display. Computers that are located in high-traffic areas, such as a nurse station in an open hall, require a shorter period of time before logoff activates. Computers located in areas with limited access, such as a lab or an isolated file room, can have a longer period of time. The content of the information displayed may also be a factor in determining logoff time. Most experts believe that 10 minutes is the average wait time before logoff occurs for computer workstations located in open areas where they could be viewed by patients, family, or other nonauthorized personnel. Your risk analysis can be used to determine appropriate logoff times.

As a general rule, users should always log off their computer workstation when they leave it unattended for an extended period of time such as breaks, lunch, or before leaving at the end of the day.

Encryption and Decryption

The encryption and decryption specification means addressing how to "implement a mechanism to encrypt and decrypt electronic protected health information" (§164.312[a][2][iv]).

Encryption converts the contents of a file, document, or message from a readable format (known as plaintext) to an unreadable format (known as ciphertext). Decryption is the reverse. It permits an encrypted message to be decrypted back to a readable format. There are many different encryption methodologies, all with the same goal: to protect data from being read by unauthorized users.

Encryption/decryption is actually a part of a broader science known as cryptography. There are a variety of cryptographic technologies. Some solely address the confidentiality of data through encryption, and other technologies also ensure data integrity. Data integrity is accommodated because altered ciphertext cannot be decrypted. Failure of the decryption process to produce a readable document proves that the integrity of the data has been compromised.

Given enough time and computing power, any encryption method can be broken (ie, the mathematical formula that created the ciphertext can be determined in order to decrypt the message). The key to using encryption is to decide the extent of risk you are willing to assume.

Encryption must be strong enough to ensure either that the data it was protecting no longer have any value after the encryption is broken or that the costs of breaking the encryption are greater than the value of the information that was encrypted. Most encryption today is strong enough to meet the needs of health care. However, many in health care continue not to encrypt data, except perhaps when transmitting PHI through the Internet. As noted in Chapter 8, any PHI on portable devices (including those that can be adapted and made portable) and media should be encrypted as a precaution in the event of a loss or theft. If it can be proven that the device or media contained encrypted data, the loss or theft will not constitute a notifiable breach (see also the full discussion of breach notification in Chapter 10).

HIPAA does not identify the type of encryption required. However, the Guidance Specifying the Technologies and Methodologies That Render Protected Health Information Unusable, Unreadable, or Indecipherable to Unauthorized Individuals (published April 27, 2009) specifies that valid encryption process for data at rest are consistent with National Institute of Standards and Technology (NIST) Special Publication 800-111, *Guide to Storage Encryption Technologies for End User Devices*. This publication also provides good information on traveling with a laptop, guidelines for transferring files between computers, and other useful advice. When seeking to encrypt your devices and media, ask you vendor to demonstrate how the product addresses this specific guidance. The vendor should be able to provide specific assurances, instructions, and cryptographic key management for you.

AUDIT CONTROLS STANDARD

The Audit Controls standard requires you to "implement hardware, software, and/or procedural mechanisms that record and examine activity in information systems that contain or use PHI" (§164.312[b]).

Audit Controls Defined

Audit controls are the technical mechanisms that track and record computer activities. An audit log determines if a security violation occurred by providing a chronological series of logged computer events that relate to an operating system, an application, or user activities. Audit logs provide:

- Individual accountability for activities such as an unauthorized access of PHI (confidentiality)
- Reconstruction of an unusual occurrence of events such as an intrusion into the system to alter the results of a drug test (integrity)
- Problem analysis such as an investigation into a slowdown in a system's performance speed (availability)

Purpose of Audit Controls

Users' activities must be routinely audited. To avoid possible legal problems, conduct random audits of audit logs even if management does not suspect any wrongdoing by members of the workforce. If a manager does suspect wrongdoing, the performance of random audits may prevent an employee from claiming discrimination for being singled out for an audit. This doesn't mean you should not exercise your right to audit any time you suspect wrongdoing; awareness that auditing is actually being performed is often an effective deterrent.

Audit logs also serve numerous business functions, including:

- Monitoring employees' work efficiency
- Supporting the HIPAA privacy standard of "accounting for disclosures" by logging when certain types of files containing PHI are transmitted for purposes other than treatment, payment, and operations and when authorized by the patient
- Providing forensic evidence of an inappropriate access in a court

Audit Controls Policies and Procedures

The HIPAA Security Rule does not describe in detail the data that must be gathered in an audit log or the length of time the audit logs must be kept. It merely states that a covered entity must implement audit controls.

Activities to Audit

When determining activities to be audited, consider the following:

- Are users accessing information or performing tasks beyond the scope of their job? This would indicate that the user access authorization needs to be adjusted. The user access may have been initially established using weak rules that give access to PHI to all persons in the office.

- Are users sharing their user ID? Audit logs that reflect that the same user IDs was concurrently logged into two or more computers at the same time provide evidence of shared user IDs.

- Is the same user ID logged on continuously for days? This would indicate that the user fails to log off the system at the end of the day. (Note that if automatic logoff is implemented, this may not be an issue.)

- Are users violating patient confidentiality? An audit log that shows a user examining the PHI of someone who is a family member, friend, co-worker, or VIP may provide proof of a breach of confidentiality.

- Are employees wasting time? A review of Internet audit logs may be an eye-opener. Not only would it prove that users are wasting time, but it may also reveal the Web sites users are visiting. Viewing sexually explicit material using the office's equipment could result in an employee filing sexual harassment charges for a hostile workplace. While a staff member's seeking information about a drug or disease may or may not be legitimate, a staff member's searching for a used car is likely not to be related to the job. Visiting such sites using office equipment, even if performed on the worker's own time (such as during lunch or after hours), leaves a calling card—your Internet domain name! You probably would not want such access to become associated with the good name of your office.

- Are users downloading executable files from the Internet? These executable files often interfere with the proper performance of your applications. In addition, there has been a great deal of controversy about software piracy being conducted through the Internet. Downloading executable files may make your office liable for violating software license agreements. Remember, employers may be held liable for the actions of their workforce while those workforce members are using the Internet. Consistent auditing can reduce or prevent members of your workforce from wasting time or performing illegal activities.

- Are employees running program files that can impact the network's performance? Streaming videos, audio files, and other non–business-related programs eat up bandwidth and can slow your network to a crawl.

Audit Capabilities

After determining the types of audit activities you want to perform, verify with your IT vendor the capabilities and the overall impact on system performance. Verify that audit logs do not hinder performance. System performance and speed may become slower as a result of auditing. However, if auditing is set up correctly, the impact on system performance should be negligible to users. Compromises regarding what auditable activities are actually monitored or adding more computing power may have to be made in order to maintain acceptable levels of performance.

Notice of Auditing

You have probably called a business and heard a recorded message that states, "This call may be monitored for quality purposes." Do you really care about their quality process? Probably not. So why are they telling you this? Because businesses must notify you when you are being recorded, a rule that originates from old wiretapping laws.

The same principles apply to electronic "recording." To avoid legal troubles, notify members of your workforce that their activities are monitored and audited. Place this notification in a policy that covers all members of the workforce, even those who are not supposed to have access to information systems. However, simply having a policy regarding monitoring and auditing is not sufficient protection because your vendors or other non-employed users who access your information systems do not have prior knowledge of or access to your policies. A best practice is to add a notification of monitoring and auditing to the login screen, such as illustrated in Figure 9.2.

FIGURE 9.2

Sample Warning Banner

> **WARNING!** Use of this system constitutes consent to security monitoring and testing. All activity is logged by your user ID.

Reprinted with permission from Tom Walsh Consulting, LLC.

Using Audit Logs

Audit logs can be difficult to read, making review of them tedious. But no matter how tedious the task, audit logs must be analyzed in as close to real time as possible. What good is an audit log that indicates your network was hacked two weeks ago? In addition, audit logs should be reviewed periodically for patterns that may not initially reveal an issue. Case Study 9.3 provides an example of audit log use.

CASE STUDY 9.3
Use of Audit Logs

Your patient, Mary Smith, who was seen in your office on January 2, claims that her neighbor, a lab tech in your office (Tom Jones), must have accessed her data for an unauthorized purpose because Tom inquired of Mary's husband how she was doing on the medication you prescribed. Tom's user ID is 141555.

Sample Audit Report
Patient medical record number (MRN): 324290
Report of accesses of MRN 324290:
User ID Time Date DataCategory
142331 0915 1/2/12 Appointments
137999 1330 1/2/12 Visit Notes
142331 1345 1/2/12 Billing
124123 1015 1/4/12 Lab
141555 1110 1/5/12 Problem List

  This report shows that Tom did access Mary's data, and it was not lab data that were read but the problem list a few days after the visit. Further investigation would be needed to determine if Tom had a business need to access Mary's problem list as he did and if Mary had been given the opportunity to agree to disclosure of her PHI to her husband for involvement in her care (per the Privacy Rule's standard on Uses and Disclosures Requiring an Opportunity for the Individual to Agree or to Object [§164.510{b}]).

If you do not have the time or inclination to manually review audit logs for all of your systems, consider using one or more of the following techniques:

- Establish a policy stating that you will run audits continuously but will review them only randomly. If you establish such a policy, ensure that you, in fact, take random samples and actually review them.

- Establish a policy stating that you will run audits only randomly but will review all results. This is the reverse of the above and not quite as effective because it may not provide an archive, which may be necessary for future evidence.

- Work with your vendor to apply audit techniques to your most sensitive data, certain functions, or your most critical applications. Although this is not as comprehensive as the first option, it can be justified on the basis of your applications and data criticality analysis, which is part of your risk analysis.

- Work with your vendor to limit the granularity, or level of detail, that you get in your audit logs. You may not need all the data that are supplied with a system to perform an effective review of audit logs. If the additional information can be turned off or not shown, you may be more inclined to run the audit logs continuously and review all of them.

- Turn on audit controls only when requested by a manager because of suspect activity. This is the least desirable method because it has the potential to be discriminatory.

- Acquire software that analyzes audit log patterns. This may sound like the ideal solution, and it can be helpful; however, it takes training and analytical skill to set up the software to yield the desired results. If not set up properly, the software can generate many false positives, which can take considerable resources to investigate and can demoralize staff.

Confidentiality and Integrity of Audit Log Information

Audit logs should be stored on a separate computer system from your primary applications for two reasons: to minimize the impact auditing has on the primary system and to prevent access to the audit logs by those with system administrator privileges. This is done, not because you don't trust your system administrator, but to apply the security principle of separation of duties to protect the audit logs from hackers. If a hacker breaks into the network and obtains system administrator privileges, he or she would not be able to access the audit logs and therefore would not be able to cover up hacking activities by erasing or deleting them.

Audit Controls Risk

You may wonder why audit controls are needed if you have highly effective access controls. After all, the purpose of access controls is to prevent access, right? While audit controls only help you to identify inappropriate access after the fact, there are situations that even the most effective access controls cannot prevent. For example, a person with authority to access a certain record for certain functions may access the record, but not for the function intended. In those instances, you need audit logs as evidence of such access.

In addition, all established audit control policies and procedures must be followed. Your office could be considered negligent if audit logs were never reviewed in accordance with your policies. The rationale is that because you gathered the audit data, you had the capability of knowing what was occurring but failed to exercise your responsibility to take corrective action.

Audit Log Retention

A final consideration is whether to retain for the HIPAA-required six years the actual audit logs or only your analysis of them. Again, HIPAA is silent on this. If you do decide to retain only the audit log analysis, you must be sure you retain the audit logs with which to perform the analysis for a sufficient period of time to identify potential patterns that without it would otherwise not suggest an issue. This could be at least three months or longer. A best practice would be to retain the logs in an archive so they do not hinder performance or require extensive storage maintenance, but would be accessible for pattern analysis. Your risk analysis should also be helpful in determining how long to keep the logs. However, if you do decide to discard the logs, do so in the same manner in which you would discard any PHI, and make sure you have sufficient evidence of auditing the logs regularly.

INTEGRITY STANDARD

Integrity is the validity of data; data are valid if not altered or destroyed in any manner. HIPAA's Integrity standard means that you "implement policies and procedures to protect PHI from improper alteration or destruction" (§164.312[c]).

The accuracy of PHI is critical. In fact, inaccurate information could result in harm or even the potential death of a patient. Access controls and audit logs are intended to keep humans from breaching the confidentiality of PHI while limiting the introduction, accidental or intentional, of conditions that could harm the data.

However, it is possible for data or programs to become corrupt even without any human intervention. Data integrity can be compromised in a variety of ways, which are described in the following paragraphs.

Data Entry Errors

Humans make mistakes; it's a fact of life, but a mistake that costs a life is unacceptable. Data entry errors can be reduced by assigning a second person to periodically review work for accuracy. However, this is time consuming and not very efficient. A preferred method is to leverage technology by having error-checking built into the application or program. For example, edits in the practice management system would not allow a gynecological procedure to be scheduled for a male patient.

Hacking or Tampering

Intrusion-detection systems and other security mechanisms can be implemented to detect hacking attempts or data tampering. Audit logs can track when alterations are made to PHI and provide details as to when the data were changed and by whom.

Mechanical Errors With Data Retrieval

Technological advances have produced very small storage devices that are capable of storing huge quantities of data and performing data transfers at incredible speeds. Yet, hard disk drives, which are electromechanical devices with rapidly moving parts, will eventually fail, which is why portable backup devices are essential to data integrity. Recreating your database of patients from paper documents or the staff's recollection can be disastrous to your data integrity as well as your office's professional integrity.

Transmission Errors

Data integrity relies on the continuous quality of the signals transferred between computer system components. Error detection refers to the technical processes that automatically detect when a message may have been altered during its transmission. The simplest and most common technique is a checksum, which ensures data were written or read correctly from stored media such as a hard disk or CD. Data integrity may also be ensured through cryptography technology or digitally signing electronic documents. (These topics are covered in the section on transmission security.)

Poor Data Integration

Patient information is often stored on multiple information systems such as a lab system, a practice management system, and an EHR. Interfaces are programs that link these different information systems together so that common information can be synchronized, reconciled, and shared. Pulling patient information from multiple different systems without reconciling the data creates a potential integrity problem. Data integrity requires matching and accurately tracking the patient information on all clinical systems and notifying the user of possible duplications or errors. Many EHR systems today are built on data repositories that pull data from multiple sources into one centralized database that is then the source of all processing. This process of integrating the data reduces the risk of data integrity as there is then "one source of truth."

Programming Errors (Software Bugs)

Because of their size and complexity, computer programs may contain programming errors, often referred to as bugs. Software bugs can unintentionally alter data integrity. For example, large databases like the ones that drive clinical systems have relational tables that link associated data. If an error exists in the relational links, the wrong data could be pulled from the database.

Manufacturers try to eliminate as many programming errors as possible, but there will always be some programming bugs. This is why software products have version numbers associated with them. As software bugs are discovered, they are corrected in the next version or release of the product. This correction is usually indicated using a numbering system in which the number to the left of the decimal point indicates major programming changes that enhance the product's capabilities or functionality and the number to the right of the decimal point indicates minor changes. Thus, version 4.2 of a software program indicates the software had four major revisions and two minor revisions to the fourth revision. Technical support people often avoid purchasing a product that has "x.0" as its version number just to reduce the likelihood of serious bugs.

Computer Viruses and Other Types of Malicious Software

A computer virus or other form of malicious software (malware) can wreak havoc on your data. Most computer viruses embed themselves into an executable software program and literally rewrite code (ie, lines of instruction in the program). Antivirus software can be used to identify malicious software and therefore keep it from getting into your information systems.

This software is essentially a database of definitions of malicious code that are compared against incoming data files. If a match is made, the data file is flagged as containing a virus. Some antivirus software enables you to quarantine this file and either run software to remove the virus or destroy the file containing the virus. Other antivirus software performs this process for you. For small offices, it is probably best to acquire antivirus software that removes the malware rather than attempting to deal with it internally. Because malicious software is continuously being created, antivirus software must be updated continuously. Most newer antivirus software is sold as a subscription, and updates to the software are made automatically each time your computer system accesses the Internet or accesses your network, which is connected to the Internet. Even if a computer does not access the Internet directly or the network connected to the Internet, malicious software can still be introduced through portable media, so such computers must still have current antivirus software. Users should be trained on how to keep the software updated if the computers are not at least regularly connected to the Internet or your Internet-connected network. Antivirus software is one of the most cost-effective and important investments you can make.

Exposing Magnetic Media to a Magnetic Field

Magnetic media are sensitive to environmental threats such as heat and strong magnetic fields. Avoid leaving computers in trunks of cars where they could literally bake in summer, and don't keep magnetic media, such as CDs or (your backup) tapes or disks near scissors with magnetized tips, paper clips, or other metal objects or medical devices known to retain a magnetic field.

Human Error

The major cause of data integrity problems is human error. Users make data entry errors. Programmers make programming errors. People make decisions without considering risk. For example, if antivirus software is not updated automatically, most people are likely to at least occasionally forget to make an update, or make a decision to not take the few moments it takes to download an update. Even if the user is regularly on the Internet but not connected to your Internet-connected network, patches to operating system and application software may not be received. These patches supply updates that may be needed for the definitions of viruses from your antivirus software to work (as well as to fix bugs in software and add functionality). Patch management is becoming increasingly important and sophisticated. (Microsoft refers to patches as hotfixes and often bundles them into service packs, but they are all patches just the same.) Since most offices use a networked environment if there is more than one computer, a system administrator should take on the task of patch management and monitoring all devices for current applications of all software. In managing patches, it is very important to:

- Evaluate software patches in a test environment before implementation
- Ensure that patches have been applied
- Document which security patches are implemented

Another important area concerning data integrity is in backup systems. If you have a practice management system that experiences unplanned downtime, you probably have some backup paperwork that can be used to backfill the system with data once it returns to its operational state. However, if you have an EHR and do not use paper source documents, a decision not to acquire and use a fully redundant backup system, which is costly, could result in an even more costly situation if data are lost during unplanned downtime, because now you have no paper to fall back on for the period of time since your last backup and must rely on human memory. Integrity controls represent important investments and should be as automated as possible. Policies and procedures for integrity must include independent checks for error situations.

Mechanism to Authenticate PHI

The Integrity standard includes an implementation specification for a mechanism to authenticate PHI. This means that you must address how you "implement electronic mechanisms to corroborate that electronic protected health information has not been altered or destroyed in an unauthorized manner" (§164.312[d]).

There are mechanisms to ensure data accuracy when data are transferred between computers or read from electronic media. Figure 9.3 summarizes guidance for implementing policies and procedures to authenticate PHI.

FIGURE 9.3

Threats to Integrity and Mechanisms to Preserve Integrity

- Clerical errors when data are entered (unintentional human errors); use programs with built-in intelligence that automatically checks for human errors.
- Hacking and tampering; implement intrusion detection systems that warn of potential hacking and audit trails.
- Mechanical errors or other types of hardware malfunctions while data are being retrieved; backup your information systems; regularly test the backups of media such as hard disks.
- Transmission errors; consider using encryption to preserve the integrity of data as they pass between computer systems. This is primarily for data passing through open networks, such as the Internet.
- Poor data integration between two different applications; check for possible duplication of data, especially between two systems.
- Programming or software bugs; test your information systems before you start using them for accuracy as well as functionality; update your systems when IT vendors release fixes to address known bugs or problems.
- Computer viruses or other types of malicious code; use antivirus software to detect and prevent malicious code from altering or destroying your data.
- Exposing magnetic media to a strong magnetic fields; keep magnetic media away from strong magnetic fields and from heat.

Reprinted with permission from Tom Walsh Consulting, LLC.

PERSON OR ENTITY AUTHENTICATION STANDARD

The Person or Entity Authentication standard requires you to "implement procedures to verify that a person or entity seeking access to PHI is the one claimed" (§164.312[d]).

Access controls and authentication go hand in hand. Access controls establish who (via the unique user identification) can do what on specific applications. Authentication ensures that the right person is who he or she claims to be and can have access to the right amount of information. This is usually accomplished by providing some proof of identity, either locally within your organization or with your trading partner where someone vouches for you and assigns you a user ID and a form of authentication. There are several types of authentication, some stronger than others. The strength of the authentication mechanism determines how likely it can be thwarted (eg, guessed, cracked).

For most workers in the healthcare field, the credentials used for access and authentication are a user ID in combination with a password. If credentials entered into a computer match those stored in the computer system, the user is authenticated. Once properly authenticated, the user is granted the authorized access privileges.

There are three components of authentication with various mechanisms available to support each (see box).

Authentication Components and Their Mechanisms

- Something you know: password, personal identification number [PIN], mother's maiden name, pass phrase, challenge question
- Something you have on your person or on your computer: ATM card, smart card, token, key, swipe card, badge
- Something you are: biometric, such as fingerprint, voice scan, iris scan, retina scan

Any single-factor authentication mechanism can be made stronger by using two or even three mechanisms in combination. The combination of any two of these methods is considered two-factor authentication. Two-factor authentication is considered strong authentication because it greatly reduces the opportunity for an imposter to falsify identity. It is important to point out that a user ID combined with a password is *not* two-factor authentication because the user ID is a means to provide access, not an authentication mechanism.

Passwords: The Problems

Although the password is the most common way to obtain authentication and the easiest to establish, it is usually the weakest method of authentication. Exploitation of user accounts through weak passwords is one of the most troublesome issues in network security. Other problems stemming from passwords include the following:

- There is no absolute certainty that the person who enters a user ID and password is the rightful owner of those credentials or if the person is entering another person's credentials. This is why the password is the weakest form of authentication and why biometric devices, such as those that read fingerprints, are becoming more popular.
- Initially, passwords are inexpensive to set up. However, in the long run, they can be expensive to support because of the problems associated with them, including the labor costs of resetting forgotten or compromised passwords. Teaching users to select strong passwords and then not changing them frequently is one way to get around the management cost.
- Users who select their own passwords need training on selecting strong passwords. You've probably seen a pop-up window that notifies you that it's time to change your password. This usually occurs at an inconvenient time, and you probably don't spend time planning your new password. Instead, you create a new password on the fly. A poor practice (that many people follow) is to take the current password and increment

it by one, eg, if your password was Salami, subsequent password changes would result in Salami1, Salami2, etc. Another problem occurs when a newly created password is not memorized. Because strong passwords should not spell a word and should include a combination of alpha, numeric, and special characters, but the only thing that is displayed on the screen when the new password is entered is a string of asterisks or other marks, one for each character typed, the user cannot be sure of the exact string of characters actually entered. It is no wonder that the most common call to a help desk is to get a password reset.

■ Information systems usually come with default user accounts and passwords that are often not changed, even after the systems have been in operation for years. It is critical to change these to strong passwords of your own. A hacker formerly employed by your information system's vendor could know the default passwords.

■ Even when encrypted, passwords can be easily broken or compromised. Password cracking refers to the use of tools to guess passwords that are stored on an information system. There are several password-cracking tools; many are freeware tools, available for download from the Internet. These tools are used to guess encrypted passwords stored on a computer server by attempting every alphanumeric combination possible. Given enough time, any password can be broken. The stronger the password, the longer it takes to break it. Some of these tools are now sold commercially to monitor for weak passwords.

■ Some programs and operating systems allow users to store their passwords in their computer's memory. The downside to this practice is that anyone who has access to the computer can gain unauthorized access.

Users with numerous user IDs and passwords are more likely to write them down and keep them near their computers. In a larger office, individuals may have and may share multiple passwords. The paper on which these passwords are written becomes especially sensitive information. The practice can and must be avoided.

Similarly, users in organizations with many different applications but without sophisticated access controls frequently find they have to share passwords in order to conduct their work because access controls have not been set up to enable a person to have access to applications under the circumstances specified. Even temporary passwords that are assigned for occasional staff, and kept in a sealed envelope or locked in a drawer or file cabinet with only the office manager or system administrator having the key, are better than sharing passwords. Another alternative is simply to have the occasional user "break the glass" on your emergency mode access. Document that this was approved so that later review of the audit log will not raise questions.

Some users store passwords on a smart phone or other portable device. This may not be a bad idea if proper security safeguards are in place to protect the device, but if it does not have encrypted password protection, the device becomes a gold mine.

The best practice is to synchronize your user IDs and strong passwords so they are all the same for every information system used and ensure that access controls, including emergency access procedures, are constructed to afford access when needed.

Hackers often gain access to information systems through social engineering (ie, tricking people into disclosing information that is supposed to be kept confidential). For example, a hacker may claim to be with your IT vendor. His line to you might be: "Hi. This is Bob with XYZ. We noticed you might be having some network problems with your current configuration. I am going to fix that for you. To do that, I'm going to need your user ID and password." Train all members of your workforce never to reveal their user ID and password. Even if there is a legitimate computer problem and you personally know the system administrator or vendor, they should not need your user ID and password to fix the system. It may necessitate that they blindly erase the existing password and require you (not them) to change your password after the system has been fixed.

Passwords: The Rules

Password rules were created in response to attacks that easily broke users' passwords. In his article "The Strong Password Dilemma" (*Computer Security Journal*, November 2002), Richard E. Smith, PhD, CISSP, notes three basic rules for passwords:

1. Each password you choose must be new and different.
2. Passwords must be at least six characters long, probably longer.
3. Passwords must be replaced periodically.

Smith also notes that "the rules must be applied in the light of practical human behavior and peoples' motivations."

Remind your workforce members that the stronger the password, the less frequently the password will have to be changed. A strong password (see Figure 6.7 in Chapter 6) only needs to be changed about every six months or whenever you know it has been compromised. To ensure use of strong passwords, ensure that there are parameters to control the types of password users may select. Password-checking software is readily available to check that a password has not been reused, is of appropriate length and composition, and so on.

Advanced Technology Methods of Authentication

Other methods of authentication such as biometrics and tokens, though more expensive to implement, are coming down in price and are cheaper in the long run to maintain than passwords. These methods do not require the technical support and money needed to frequently reset passwords. As previously noted, the Drug Enforcement Administration (DEA) has issued a ruling that allows controlled substances to be e-prescribed so long as the user has two-factor authentication and is set up with a certified e-prescribing gateway that provides a digital certificate (discussed in the section on electronic signature in this chapter). (This regulation was issued on March 21, 2010. It has taken some time for e-prescribing gateways to establish the requirements necessary to support the ruling. In addition, some state laws and regulations will require changes before controlled substance e-prescribing will be fully legal in those states. The AMA and collaborating organizations in April 2011 issued an updated version of *Clinician's Guide to e-Prescribing* that addresses e-prescribing of controlled substances and the authentication requirements required.)

Biometrics

Biometrics provide authentication by verifying a unique, personal attribute via fingerprint scan (most widely used), hand geometry, iris scan, retina scan, voice recognition, and face recognition. The strength of biometrics is that "everywhere you go, there you are." Biometrics eliminates the need to remember a password or carry a token, and the user being identified must be physically present at the point of identification. The price of biometric systems has dropped over the last few years while the technology has improved.

As with any authentication process, there are downsides to biometrics:

■ The authentication process can be slow if the user tries to authenticate on a different computer workstation from what is normally used. Biometric technology is based on pattern recognition, and this recognition process must be acquired by each computer.

- There are issues surrounding personal privacy. Digital images of a person's fingerprint could be intercepted. Because there is increased concern today about identity theft, users may oppose having an image of their finger(s) stored on a computer file in your office. In addition, some persons have religious preferences that preclude taking images of their body. This may possibly be addressed by educating people that the image is not stored, but that a limited number of characteristics taken from the biometric print are stored in digital form. So a fingerprint ends up being stored only as a long string of numbers.

- Because the technology is still fairly new, not all vendors have adopted the Federal Bureau of Investigation (FBI) standards for interoperability between different makes of biometric devices.[1,2]

- Fingerprint technology is the most common and most inexpensive, but also the most problematical to use. It has been demonstrated that very cold fingers are difficult to read (in which case, you can't activate your computer right after you come inside on a cold day). The FBI has found that the skin of Asian people is very thin and may not have sufficient ridges to establish a pattern. Also, continuous use of a fingerprint scanner may leave bacteria, causing the spread of colds or worse. And, a finger within a sterile glove can generally not be scanned. Retinal scanners are still more expensive but probably more convenient for some healthcare uses.[3]

Tokens

Token devices, which use hard tokens, include an employee badge with a bar code or magnetic strip or a small electronic device such as a smart card or memory stick that can generate a one-time password. The user must enter a PIN (something they know) to activate the device (something they have). Some tokens attach to a keychain or can be worn around your neck, making them easily accessible.

There are also software tokens (soft tokens) that can be stored on your computing device. There are two primary types. A shared-secret token requires an administrator to generate for each user a configuration file that contains a user ID, a PIN, and a secret known only to the user. The shared-secret architecture is potentially vulnerable to theft and can be difficult to distribute. A newer type of software token uses public-key cryptography or asymmetric cryptography. The PIN can be stored on a remote authentication server, making a stolen software token unusable unless the PIN is also known. If there are attempts made to guess the PIN, it can be detected and logged on the authentication server, which can disable the token. Software tokens, especially shared secrets, can be more susceptible to viruses than hard tokens, but benefits include that there is no physical token to carry or lose, they do not contain batteries that will run out, and they are physically cheaper than hardware tokens.

1. Lepley M, Marques J, Nill N, Orlans N, Rivers R, White R. State of the art biometrics excellence roadmap. http://www.biometriccoe.gov/_doc/CPL%2020%20Nov.pdf. MITRE Technical Report. Updated October 2008.

2. New NIST protocol enables secure biometric data access. InfoSecurity Web site. http://www.infosecurity-magazine.com/view/25576/new-nist-protocol-enables-secure-biometricdata-access/. Published May 3, 2012.

3. Park M. At Bronx clinic, the eyes are windows to medical records. CNN Web site. March 15, 2010. http://articles.cnn.com/2010-03-15/health/bronx.clinic.iris.scan_1_medical-clinic-medicalerrors-iris-identification?_s=PM:HEALTH.

Electronic Signature

Electronic signature was not included in the HIPAA Security Rule because at the time of the regulation's adoption, electronic signatures were not widely used, none of the HIPAA financial and administrative transactions required a signature, and electronic signature technology was still somewhat immature. Despite the fact that electronic signature is not required by HIPAA yet today, there is increasing interest in using an electronic signature, a form of digital signature is required for transmitting electronic prescriptions for controlled substances, and a number of healthcare settings are adopting at least two-factor authentication if not public-key infrastructure for remote access to health information. A few things to know about electronic signature are described here.

Electronic signature is a somewhat generic term that is often misused. Forty-seven states, the District of Columbia, Puerto Rico, and the Virgin Islands have adopted the Uniform Electronic Transactions Act (UETA), legislation that provides a legal framework for electronic signatures (http://www.ncsl.org/issues-research/telecom/uniform-electronic-transactions-acts.aspx). Technically, an electronic signature should be distinguished from an authentication mechanism as described above (ie, password, token, or biometric), a digitized signature, and a digital certificate used with a digital signature.

A digitized signature is one in which a person writes his or her signature on a signature pad and the image is retained with the information system. As most of you have experienced at the grocery store or other location that uses digitized signatures, this form of electronic signature is weak as most cannot be read very well. However, for retail and other purposes where only the intent to sign is needed, the digitized signature is sufficient. This draws from the Electronic Signatures in Global and National Commerce (ESIGN) Act of 2000, where any evidence of intent to sign is deemed legally sufficient to bind the user to an agreement (such as to pay the credit card company). Digitized signatures may be useful in health care for patients to electronically sign authorization forms, consents, etc. Some provider settings like to use the digitized signature on forms physicians have to fill out for patients, such as return to work, camp physicals, etc, as it provides some reassurance to the unknown recipient that the physician actually completed the form and signed it.

Authentication mechanisms as described above are generally considered stronger than a digitized signature. However, there are new forms of digitized signature technology called signature dynamics that verify signature attributes (such as how hard the signer presses, how rapidly the signer writes, when "i's" are dotted and "t's" crossed, etc) against a known signature. The Internal Revenue Service is said to use such technology. For most provider settings, passwords, tokens, and biometrics continue to be the norm. As previously noted, these can be strengthened by using a strong password and when passwords, tokens, and/or biometrics are used in combination. One problem with use of such authentication mechanisms is that the authentication may not be visible to others who may need to know who signed certain content or documents in a computer system. This is especially true in health care, where the name, credentials, and date/time of signature are vitally important. It is not sufficient to know that just because an entry appears in an EHR, for instance, that it was made by the person authorized to make the entry because the system would have rejected access if the authentication process was not legitimate. Because of this, many healthcare application systems provide evidence of the person logging on. In addition, some applications require additional verification processes. For instance, if a physician has dictated a note, the first authentication process was that to access the dictation system. To review the transcription, the physician must log on again. But some systems account for the fact that by merely logging on, the physician may not have reviewed the entire document. These systems are then designed to require the user to scroll down to the end of the document and either click a box indicating the content was reviewed (or agreed to) or (less frequently in health care) reenter an authentication mechanism.

Digital signature is also a class of signatures, all of which are stronger than either the digitized signature or the authentication mechanisms described above. In general, digital signatures use encryption that can result in both authentication and nonrepudiation (the process that positively identifies the sender so that the sender cannot deny sending the message). Digital signatures can also afford integrity of the message (see the section on transmission security in this chapter).

Public-key infrastructure (PKI) is a digital signature framework that enables digital signatures to be exchanged across different networks and the Internet. It is probably the most widely used form of digital signature today. PKI consists of programs, data formats, procedures, communication protocols, security policies, and public-key cryptography. In PKI, a digital certificate is an electronic document that uses a digital signature (mathematical scheme for demonstrating the authenticity of a digital message or document) to bind together a public key with an identity. If a digital signature is used to authenticate a user in health care, just as with the password, token, or biometric form of authentication, evidence of who performed the digital signature process can be displayed in association with the data, document, or other form of entry into the system (see Figure 9.4).

FIGURE 9.4

Public Key Infrastructure

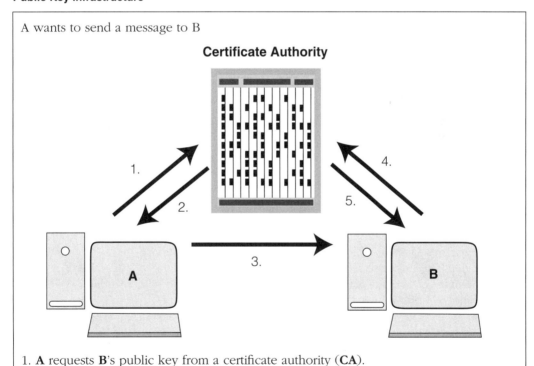

A wants to send a message to B

Certificate Authority

1. **A** requests **B**'s public key from a certificate authority (**CA**).
2. The **CA** sends **B**'s public key to **A**.
3. **A** sends a session key encrypted with **B**'s public key and **A**'s own public key to **B**.
4. B validates **A**'s public key with the **CA**.
5. If the **CA** responds that **A**'s public key is still valid, **B** decrypts the session key with **B**'s private key. Now **A** and **B** can communicate in a secure manner.

Entity Authentication

The discussion thus far has focused on person authentication. Entities such as computer devices also need access to data stored in another computer. These entities must also be authenticated, usually through exchange of serial numbers or other mechanisms. Entity authentication is generally established through the device manufacturer or computer program.

TRANSMISSION SECURITY STANDARD

HIPAA's Transmission Security standard means you need to "implement technical security measures to guard against unauthorized access to PHI that is being transmitted over an electronic communications network" (§164.312[e]).

It is easier to protect tangible paper documents than to protect the unseen bits and bytes of information that are transmitted among and between computers and devices. If someone steals paper, there is physical evidence that it is missing. In contrast, information stolen in electronic format as it passes over a network or the Internet may go undetected because the original file still exists and there is no reason to suspect anything might have been taken.

Effective application of transmission security controls requires an IT professional with a thorough understanding of networks, comprehensive knowledge of the potential threats to your network, access to options for protecting the various components of the network, and methods for monitoring network traffic for potential problems. Although your application vendors are aware of the importance of security and attempt to build in appropriate controls, these controls are generally not at the network level because they have not installed your network. This places the responsibility for securing the network with the owner. Thus most small practices will hire an IT professional—at least part time or contracted. Due to the rapidly changing environment of threats to networks, if you contract for these services you should contract for routine maintenance, not occasional use for only when something disastrous happens. This will keep your network running optimally and reduce the risk of a disaster happening.

The two implementation specifications in the Transmission Security standard, Integrity Controls and Encryption, are discussed in the following sections.

Integrity Controls

To address the implementation specification for integrity controls, you need to "implement security measures to ensure that electronically transmitted PHI is not improperly modified without detection until disposed of" (§164.312[e][2][i]).

The principles of integrity as they relate to data maintained in your computer systems were explained earlier in this chapter.

Integrity as it relates to the Transmission Security standard addresses assurance that files or messages are not modified during transmission. The primary method for controlling the integrity of data as they are transmitted is through the use of standard network protocols or rules for making sure that the data that are transmitted are the same data that are received.

In addition to standard network protocols, a digital signature may also be used to ensure integrity. As noted in the section on authentication, a digital signature is a special code that when used for data integrity can be computed based on the contents of a message. This is often then called a hash. If the digital signature has been altered, it cannot be verified, indicating an integrity problem. Because digital signatures can be somewhat difficult to use and are not required by HIPAA, you need to decide what form of integrity you will use in your data transmission. This decision will be based on whether you are transmitting through an entirely open network (ie, the Internet) or you are using a private telephone connection, virtual private network (VPN), or other form of transmission.

When transmitting over the Internet, the most commonly used security protocols include the Secure Sockets Layer (SSL) protocol and the newer Transport Layer Security (TLS) protocol. These are cryptographic protocols that provide communication security over the Internet. They use asymmetric cryptography (public and private keys) for key exchange, symmetric encryption (using only private keys) for confidentiality, and message authentication codes (hash) for message integrity. The protocols signal a Web browser to trust a transmission based on the digital certificate authority that is part of the software, enabling encrypted communication and secure identification of a network Web server.

Encryption

To address the implementation specification for encryption, you need to "implement a mechanism to encrypt PHI whenever deemed appropriate" (§164.312[e][2][ii]).

As previously described, encryption is a mathematical process that makes data unreadable unless someone has the key to decrypt the data. Encryption and associated cryptographic technology (such as PKI) protect information from being viewed or altered by unauthorized users while it is in transit from one computer system to another, and ensure that only the intended recipient can read the transmitted message and no one can change the message while it is in transit without being detected.

For encryption and other cryptographic technologies to work properly, both the sender and the receiver must be using the same or compatible technology. The fact that two different systems can use compatible technology is referred to as interoperability and is generally achieved through the use of standards. Some standards do exist for PKI, and increasingly vendors are adopting these standards. However, full interoperability still remains elusive and subject to trading partner agreement. Outside of using a private TCP/IP connection or non-TCP/IP protocols (eg, X.25, SNA, and Frame Relay), perhaps the most secure structure today is the Nationwide Health Information Network. Although the network is still somewhat in limited production mode and not yet fully available to all providers, its broader use is being enabled by CONNECT, which is an open-source software and community that promotes interoperability. It is anticipated that governance of the Nationwide Health Information Network will move to the private sector in 2013 and then will be ready to aid individual providers in secure exchange of data.

While encryption is an addressable implementation specification under the Security Rule, HITECH breach notification, use of the e-prescribing gateway, and participation in the Nationwide Health Information Network are all by default encouraging broader use of encryption. HHS guidance for breach notification describes valid encryption processes for data during transmission as those that comply with the requirements of Federal Information Processing Standards (FIPS) 140-2. These include, as appropriate, standards described in NIST Special Publications 800-52, *Guidelines for the Selection and Use of Transport Layer Security (TLS) Implementations*; 800-77, *Guide to IPsec VPNs*; or 800-113, *Guide to SSL VPNs*, and may include others that are FIPS 140-2 validated.

Work with your IT vendors and business associates to identify an encryption methodology that works well for all parties exchanging data. Certainly secure portals for exchanging data are increasingly available. If you choose not to encrypt messages or files containing PHI, you must fully understand the risks associated with your decision.

NETWORK SECURITY

Although not addressed as a separate standard within HIPAA, understanding basic network security architecture can assist you in assuring that all aspects of your network are secure. Technical considerations with respect to a network are listed in Figure 9.5.

F I G U R E   9.5

Technical Considerations to Ensure Confidentiality, Integrity, and Availability of Your Network

- ■ *Bandwidth:* Capacity of a network to carry data.
- ■ *Latency:* Time required for data to be transmitted between communicating entities. (Also response time, ie, time required for a message to be transferred and acknowledged.)
- ■ *Availability:* The likelihood the network can provide service and is functioning properly.
- ■ *Security:* The capability of a network to ensure the confidentiality and integrity of information transmitted across it. (An important part of confidentiality is authentication of participants in the transaction.)
- ■ *Ubiquity:* The degree of access to a network. (The "digital divide" separates those with access from those without access.)

Adapted from National Research Council. *Networking Health: Prescriptions for the Internet.* Washington, DC: National Academy Press; 2000.

Typically, network security is best constructed in a layered approach, as illustrated in Figure 9.6.

F I G U R E   9.6

Layered Approach to Network Security

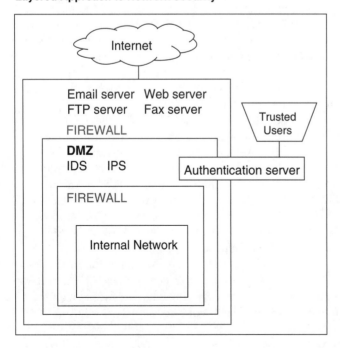

Layered Approach to Network Security

Multiple layers to any network (local wired or wireless, wide-area, etc) provide additional protection in the event that any one part of the network security is compromised. Starting from the outside in, the idea is to provide servers that capture whatever data you want to receive, but firewall them from your internal network until their contents have been checked. Typically intrusion detection systems, and possibly intrusion prevention systems, are applied in what is referred to as a demilitarized zone (DMZ). This is neutral territory where dangerous things can be rejected and acceptable things kept. Once this process is completed, another firewall performs additional checks.

Firewalls are hardware appliances and/or software devices that examine traffic entering and leaving a network and prevent some types of traffic from passing through based on a set of rules. Firewalls serve as gatekeepers when positioned between an untrusted network, such as the Internet, and a trusted network, such as an organization's internal network. As increasing use of the Internet is made, it may be important for at least two firewall levels to be constructed. Configure firewalls and other network equipment to deny rather than allow as their default policy. Close any unused firewall ports unless there is documentation as to why they need to remain open, the time frame for which they will remain open, and the person who approved keeping them open. Firewalls must be properly maintained and updated because new threats and vulnerabilities are being discovered every day. It is important to examine firewall audit logs daily and to reevaluate the security configuration of the firewall periodically.

Just as firewalls are the gatekeeper to the network, intrusion detection systems (IDSs) are the burglar alarms for networks. They warn of possible inappropriate attempts to access networks, hosts, programs, or data by examining (or sniffing) network traffic as it passes by. An IDS requires considerable setup and tuning to avoid false alarms. An activated alarm is one that indicates that the system has been compromised. Intrusion prevention systems (IPSs) are more sophisticated and do not just warn of a problem but will automatically block traffic that appears to be troublesome. While these can be useful, they require a tremendous amount of overhead to manage and probably are more work than any small practice really needs.

An authentication server may be used to manage remote access. On the layered security diagram in Figure 9.6 it is partially located within the DMZ, not requiring the first firewall pass but requiring the second firewall pass. An authentication server is a special type of server where authentication of trusted parties is verified before they may access the internal network.

Wireless Network Security

Wireless networking technology allows computing devices equipped with wireless devices to access a network from anywhere within the range of a wireless transmitter (access point) without having to plug the device into a cable. Once authenticated, users have the same access privileges to browse the Web, send and receive e-mail, transfer files, enter and retrieve data, etc, as if they were wired to the network. Transmitters send radio frequency waves through the air that allow wireless devices access to the network. Some operate locally, from up to several hundred feet away. Wide-area wireless networks allow a user with a computing device and a wireless wide area network (WWAN) card to surf the Web, check e-mail, or connect to a virtual private network (VPN) from anywhere within the regional boundaries of cellular service. Most wireless networks are based on the Institute of Electrical and Electronics Engineers (IEEE) 802.11x family of standards (also known as Wi-Fi or wireless ethernet) that transmits signals over radio frequencies. This family of standards provides both transmission and security. Two common encryption tools used to protect wireless transmissions are:

- Wired equivalent privacy (WEP) is the native encryption protocol for Wi-Fi (802.11). WEP uses static encryption keys (ie, keys that never change). If a hacker is monitoring the transmission, the WEP encryption key can eventually be cracked. WEP will keep out many casual hackers because there are so many other wide-open wireless networks that are easier targets. However, it will not keep out someone determined to get at your data.

- Wi-Fi Protected Access (WPA) is a wireless security protocol and security certification program developed by the Wi-Fi Alliance to secure wireless computer networks. It is now in the second version (WPA2), which requires testing and certification by the Wi-Fi Alliance and implements the mandatory elements of IEEE 802.11i with stronger encryption protocols.

In addition to sniffing data from wireless devices, another security issue with wireless networks is the creation of unauthorized rogue access points. Because access points are easy to set up, they can be created by virtually anyone, including well-intentioned employees, consultants, or contractors who wish to use their own wireless devices in your environment. (Hospitals are reporting that physicians are creating their own wireless access points within the hospital, effectively creating a rogue access point.) Rogue deployments are especially vulnerable to hackers because they are often set up casually with little attention to keeping security protocols up-to-date.

Although wireless access points can be established easily, a fully robust wireless network can be difficult to manage. In addition to securing the data during transmission and preventing rogue deployments, there are performance and interoperability issues as well. A sufficient number of access points must be used or connectivity will be broken in building stairwells and elevators. Signals can bounce off of stainless steel food carts in hospitals. Older buildings built of brick to last forever are particularly troublesome in which to install a wireless network.

Virtual Private Network

The most commonly used method for transmitting data outside of a local area network today, whether wired or wireless, is a virtual private network (VPN). A VPN uses a secure tunnel reserved for a particular pair of senders and receivers in a public network such as the Internet or a public telephone network. VPNs typically use some combination of encryption, digital certificates, strong user authentication, and access control to provide security to the traffic they carry. They usually provide connectivity to the internal network or information systems behind a firewall. VPN products fall into three broad categories: hardware-based systems, firewall-based systems, and stand-alone application packages.

The key feature of VPNs is that they take advantage of the economies of scale of public networks like the Internet rather than rely on expensive, privately leased lines. They can also reduce costs by eliminating the need for long-distance telephone charges for remote access users. The user merely calls into the service provider's nearest local access point. In addition to their low operating cost, VPNs are scalable, making it easy to add new users to the system.

Secure Portal

A secure portal is a very similar alternative to a VPN for secure remote connection. Portal technology, however, is more accommodating to different types of operating systems and provides a greater degree of control for creating special types of workflows and policy-managed content publication. (In this case, publication refers to provision of information to view by an authorized user.) In health care, a provider portal refers to provision of secure access to all or parts of specific applications, especially the EHR. It may enable a physician to view lab results from a hospital or enter orders into its computerized provider order entry system. Increasingly, these portals require a user ID and a token for authentication. A patient portal serves as an entranceway to different functions to which you wish patients to have secure access. You set them up with a user ID and typically a password. Frequently you begin by offering secure e-mail communications through this portal, perhaps to request an appointment, obtain lab results, or pay bills. By policy and often with special redesign of certain functions in your information systems, you may also provide access through this patient portal to your scheduling system, which patients can use to directly schedule appointments or even to access a personal health record (PHR), which is partially data supplied from your EHR and partially data supplied directly by the patient.

E-mail

A secure portal may overcome the issue of exchanging e-mail in the clear. Many offices have restricted e-mail use to only that not containing PHI, or have attempted to set up encryption for e-mail with PHI. Neither of these approaches has been very successful. A better solution is to establish a secure portal through which you can notify patients or others that they have mail waiting behind a user ID and password-secured page on your Web site.

Be aware that even when e-mail is encrypted, the sender cannot control what happens to a sent message. The legitimate receiver of the e-mail message could decrypt it and forward it to others. The receiver could print it out on a network printer and forget to pick it up, making it available to an unintended recipient. If e-mail is sent to a person at a company account, the message may become the property of the company. Because the sender loses control of e-mail once it is sent, the information in an e-mail should be considered public. If the information is sensitive, consider another more secure means of communication. E-mail may also be used to deliver files. Files containing PHI can be encrypted and then attached to an e-mail. When e-mail is used to carry an encrypted file, make sure that the key to decrypt the file is not sent along with the e-mail. Instead, send encryption keys using another communication method, preferably by phone or postal service.

In all cases of e-mail use, apply caution in opening the e-mail. It is still a common practice for hackers to attempt entry or to deliver malware by spoofing someone's identity, ie, hiding the true identity of the sender by masquerading as someone else, typically someone you know. This may not happen often, but it serves as a reminder to people to exercise caution when receiving e-mail messages that may be from someone with whom you have not communicated in a long time, where the subject and/or content is missing or unusual, and where there is a request to reply with sensitive information.

Cell Phones

Mobile phones, which are getting smarter every day, present security challenges. Although newer phones no longer are viewed as an interference threat to sensitive medical equipment, many provider organizations continue to ban cell phone use primarily as a courtesy to others. In addition to special antenna systems that lower the amount of electromagnetic energy transmitted by older cell phones, the US Food and Drug Administration (FDA) requires medical equipment and device makers to shield devices from electromagnetic energy.

There are, however, other privacy and security concerns surrounding use of cell phones. NIST Special Publication 800-124, *Guidelines on Cell Phone and PDA Security*, provides the following list of threats:

- Loss, theft, or disposal
- Unauthorized access
- Malware
- Spam
- Electronic eavesdropping
- Electronic tracking
- Cloning

Server-Resident Data

Cell phone threats also vary by type of operating system, with the Android operating system most vulnerable to malware. All cell phones, however, are subject to loss. Even without any PHI or other confidential information on the cell phone, losing one's phone is a nuisance. However, most people do retain passwords and other confidential information on their phones, which can be used to gain access to information systems where much more harm can be done.

Some of the best safeguards surround user orientation, maintaining physical control, enabling user authentication with all of the same precautions as described for authentication of computer systems, backing up data, being aware of suspicious messages, adding prevention and detection software, and limiting functionality. Android users especially should be careful to avoid excessive permission requests embedded in apps they download (mobile security tools are available to scan for malicious software and are well worth the investment).

Organizational measures recommended by NIST include establishing a mobile device security policy, including defining ownership and acceptable use. Offices should treat cell phones as any other computer and prepare deployment and operational plans, perform a risk analysis, train users, and perform configuration management to ensure that security controls are up-to-date and documented.

SECURITY SUPPORTS CONFIDENTIALITY, INTEGRITY, AND AVAILABILITY

Clearly, errors happen and exploitation occurs for any number of reasons. The Security Rule gives you great flexibility in applying technical safeguards based on your office's size, complexity, and technology. To some extent these are being tightened up by other pieces of legislation, including the HITECH breach notification regulations and associated guidance for use of encryption as well as the DEA's regulation permitting e-prescribing of controlled substances with much stronger security controls that many are adopting for other purposes as well.

But appropriate security safeguards are not only a regulatory requirement; they are good business practice. Safeguards minimize your risk of embarrassing breaches of confidentiality and harm to your patients, and they also ensure that users are not wasting time or placing the office in a legal predicament.

Of course, providing patient information to the right people at the right time is worthless if the information is wrong. Data integrity ensures that you have accurate information about your patients.

Applying appropriate access controls and audit logs, authenticating users, and using encryption or other transmission controls as necessary ensures that users are accessing the minimum necessary information to do their jobs in compliance with the Privacy Rule. These steps also minimize the risk of an attack on your information systems, which would render information unavailable to you when you need it.

CHECK YOUR UNDERSTANDING*

1. Which of the following directs the information system to provide access to a user?
   a. Electronic signature
   b. Password
   c. Personal identification number (PIN)
   d. User ID

2. Which is the strongest form of authentication?
   a. Biometric
   b. Digital signature
   c. Password
   d. Token

3. Which of the following is true?
   a. Access controls should follow the Privacy Rule minimum necessary standard
   b. Audit logs are not necessary if there are strong access controls
   c. Automatic logoff should be set to eight hours to accommodate a full day of work
   d. Emergency access procedures are not required in a physician office

4. A best practice for audit logging is:
   a. Perform ad hoc analysis of audit logs only when there has been a breach
   b. Analyze audit logs for potential patterns of risk
   c. Keep all audit logs for 10 years
   d. Require each user to review his or her own audit logs

5. State law permitting e-prescribing of controlled substances is permitted by the Drug Enforcement Administration (DEA) if the information system incorporates:
   a. Audit logging
   b. Digital certificate
   c. Password protection
   d. Positive patient identification

6. A hard token is:
   a. Hardware used for authentication
   b. Signature keypad for handwriting a signature
   c. Software used for authentication
   d. Strongest form of authentication available

7. Which of the following is a method used to assure the integrity of the data being transmitted?
   a. Firewall
   b. Hash
   c. Secure Sockets Layer (SSL)
   d. Virtual private network (VPN)

8. The security risk associated with most cell phone use today is primarily:
   a. Exposure to hacking
   b. Lack of password protection
   c. Loss of unencrypted PHI
   d. Medical device interference

9. A more secure alternative for electronic communication with your patients is:
   a. Anonymous social media
   b. Patient portal
   c. Public-key encryption
   d. Telephone call

10. If you have been assigned access to read a file, you have the ability to:
    a. Enter data into the computer
    b. Make changes to data in the computer
    c. Only view data
    d. Transmit data to a printer or other computer

*For answers, refer to the Answer Key at the end of the book.

Practical Tips for Applying Security Controls

Information security is layered like an onion. The outer layer represents the administrative safeguards: policies, procedures, plans, and practices. The next layer represents physical security: door locks, environmental controls, and media controls. The final layer, which surrounds PHI, represents the technical safeguards: access and audit controls, authentication, integrity, and transmission security. It is the combination of the layers that provides full security coverage. This chapter describes how the layers work together and identifies best practices relative to applying security controls. (Note that best does not necessarily mean most expensive, but the practice that is most effective and efficient.)

Use this chapter in conjunction with Chapter 5 on risk analysis to identify, implement, maintain, and periodically reevaluate security controls as your office adopts more information technology. As you learn more about your office's current threats and vulnerabilities, and have a better understanding of what is required for each of the HIPAA administrative, physical, and technical security standards categories, this chapter offers suggestions on various ways to mitigate the risks you've identified and also to address the HITECH breach notification requirements

The target audience for this chapter is the person(s) responsible for selecting and applying security controls. Your information security official (ISO) should understand the Security Rule requirements and best practices being used in health care and other industries. If your IT support person is different than your ISO, this chapter will help your IT person understand how the security controls should work. If you use an IT vendor for support, you and your ISO must at least know what controls are needed in order to establish appropriate policies and procedures and provide oversight of the controls that support these policies and procedures. Responsibility for physical controls may fall to the person responsible for the physical security of your office, such as your office manager, or another member of your workforce, your building landlord, a protective services company you employ.

Irrespective of who will actually carry out the implementation of the security controls, remember that it is ultimately the physician practice that has responsibility and authority for what controls you implement and how well others comply with them.

HOW TO USE THIS CHAPTER

Use this chapter as a final checklist to assure that you have the controls you need to mitigate your risks. It:

- Helps you budget for your security controls
- Discusses options for managing security services and their implementation
- Stresses the importance of policies and procedures, training, documentation, and change control

- Helps you respond to an Office for Civil Rights (OCR) complaint or audit
- Provides tools to use in breach notification

Previous chapters provided information specific to the HIPAA Security Rule (and "mini-security rule" in the Privacy Rule). Reference has been made to the HITECH breach notification that will be discussed in detail here. Reference has also been made to modifications to the Privacy Rule called for in HITECH and for which there is a proposed regulation. At the time of this writing, the modification has not been finalized. There is nothing in the proposed modifications to the Privacy Rule that would alter your information security plans except for a change in the status of business associates with respect to enforcement of the rules that may require revision of business associate contracts (see Chapter 4).

BUDGETING FOR SECURITY CONTROLS

The investment to comply with the Security Rule and afford peace of mind may be large or small. If you have security mechanisms in place already and are only upgrading your security plans for additional automation you have acquired, the marginal cost of adding security features to stay in compliance with the Security Rule can be relatively small. If you must apply many new controls, especially as you are acquiring an electronic health record for the first time, the cost will be greater.

Table 10.1 lists budget items to consider for your information security program. The budget template provides for expenditure estimates by calendar year. It is helpful to understand when the expenditure for these items is most likely to occur. Some items only have an initial expenditure; others have a large initial expenditure with small ongoing expenditures, and still others are only ongoing expenditures.

Some ongoing expenditures include education, training, books, and subscriptions. More money is likely to be spent during the first three to six months after implementing any new or modified security controls. Similarly, hiring staff will have an initial expenditure associated with your search and training, as well as ongoing costs. Many software security controls will have an initial setup cost and ongoing subscription/maintenance fees. Most software security requires human intervention to be effective. Although this may be your ISO or IT staff, some of these may require skills that are different than what an IT staff member or even an ISO has. Any remote contingency planning services will also have an initial startup and then ongoing expenditures.

Your IT staff, ISO, and senior management can conduct a risk analysis. You may wish to seek advice from a consultant for the types of controls that best meet your risk analysis findings. In addition, you may want to consider a neutral, third party to perform the risk analysis with you so that it accurately reflects risk and mitigation strategies. While a risk analysis does not have to be performed on a regular basis, it does need to be performed anytime there are significant changes in your environment, including automation and other changes. The cost of an external risk analysis may not need to be incurred every time if an initial analysis or analysis after a significant change has taken place and there is a template to follow. Similarly, clearance checks for your workforce will be a large expenditure the first time you perform the checks on the entire workforce (if you have not already conducted these checks in the past), but the ongoing expense will be lower because you will incur these expenses only for new employees and potentially for those changing roles in your practice.

It may be appropriate to consider including a contingency budget as well. There continue to be increasing complaints filed with the OCR and increasing numbers of audits, including those that are proactive rather than reactive. Consider what these might cost.

T A B L E 10.1

Budget Considerations

Item	2010	2011	2012	Annual Ongoing
Staff time (salary and benefits): ■ To implement security ■ For ongoing security	$	$	$	
Resource material, books, and subscriptions	$	$	$	
Risk analysis, evaluation, testing (if contracted or outsourced)	$	$	$	
Policy and procedure (template purchase, consultation, legal review)	$	$	$	
Business associate contract (review and negotiation)	$	$	$	
Clearance checks	$	$	$	
Software licenses (if not up to date)				
Physical facility changes (eg, locks, security storage)	$	$	$	
Media destruction services	$	$	$	
Technology expenses (hardware, software, consultation, technical support) ■ E-mail and data transmission (protection) ■ Network protection ■ Replacement applications ■ Backup technology ■ Badges, tokens, readers ■ Incident tracking and reporting	$	$	$	
Training ■ Training programs ■ Release time ■ Reminders	$	$	$	
Telecommunications (increased expenses for increased bandwidth, Internet Service Provider [ISP], or other services if applicable)	$	$	$	
Disaster recovery plan and resources	$	$	$	
Legal services (in addition to above for security incident management, if applicable)	$	$	$	
Changes to liability insurance (if applicable)	$	$	$	
Total	$	$	$	

Reprinted with permission from Boundary Information Group.

The largest budget considerations for security for many physician practices are likely to be in the area of technology. Even here, the expenses may not be significant. Some hospitals offer a security link that connects hospitals, physician practices, and patients so participating parties can securely share electronic communications. Because the infrastructure costs are shared, the expense to your practice may be nominal. On the other hand, if your practice implements its own security methodology for communicating data to other physicians, hospitals, and patients, the cost to your practice could be significant. It can also be expensive to implement contingency planning and disaster recovery. Many organizations do not make a sufficient investment in the backup process and equipment. Many physician practices have lost significant revenue when their billing system crashed and there was no backup. This loss far exceeds the cost of a good backup system. Hard drive crashes, viruses, and other technology-related incidents occur frequently enough in all businesses that it is prudent to invest in highly reliable systems.

Many organizations skimp when it comes to other forms of contingency planning, emergency mode operations, and disaster recovery, simply because they have not yet had a disaster. Such an event would quickly change your mind. Do you want to put yourself at risk for a regulatory compliance issue? What about all of your business records? The HIPAA Security Rule is focused on PHI, but adding security controls to protect all your important information is a good business practice.

OPTIONS FOR MANAGING SECURITY SERVICES

Throughout this book there has been description of how to do it yourself, or whether to consider hiring a contractor to perform some or all of your information security work. This is not an all-or-nothing decision. Some offices decide to get initial help and then do much of the security management with their own staff. Others decide to outsource as much as possible. It may be that you find it best to use your risk analysis to help direct you to what options for managing security services are best for you. You should also be aware of what types of services may be available to you.

Risk Analysis

Previously mentioned is the option to have a consultant perform a risk analysis for you. At least initially or when there is a significant change in your environment, this can be both cost effective and educational. On an ongoing basis, you may want to follow the lead of the consultant to do your own risk analysis until such time as another major change is being undertaken, or when you find yourself the subject of a complaint or audit.

Policies, Procedures, and Documentation

Security controls implement your office's policies and procedures. This implies that policies, at least, should come before selection of controls. For example, if you have not established a policy that you will use two-factor authentication for remote access to your EHR, how will you know what controls to put into place?

However, many offices find that even where they have decent security controls in place, they often are missing *documented* policies and procedures. Some offices find that buying a set of policy and procedure templates can kick-start the process of documentation. Be forewarned, however, that any good auditor can easily spot a template that has not been modified for your precise environment. Review any such templates thoroughly and make sure they reflect your risk analysis and needs. Previous chapters provided insight into establishing those policies. With the understanding you gained regarding the goals you want to accomplish with security, write these goals down in policy statements to guide selection of other security controls. Such policy direction ensures that you address every vulnerability in a way that leaves no gaps nor results in overlaps. Gaps contribute to noncompliance with law. Overlaps can frustrate your ability to use your information systems.

Acquiring templates for documentation of actions, activities, or assessments also required by the Security Rule is generally not as feasible as acquiring templates for policies and procedures. However, an external consultant conducting a risk analysis can advise you whether you have adequate documentation and make recommendations for what more needs to be documented and how to go about doing so.

Training and Awareness

Many large offices consider acquiring training tools and awareness materials from an external source. These can often be purchased as booklets with self-study tips and "check your understanding" components that can help you track that your staff have been trained and understand the content. Webinars are another cost-effective option. Just including information security periodically in office meetings helps build awareness—perhaps even more than catchy posters you have purchased but that get tiresome and ignored quickly.

Don't forget that the ISO will need to keep up-to-date on current security issues and mitigation strategies. This may require a subscription to services that help the ISO keep current. Alternatively, it may be that the ISO can keep current by regularly scanning the Internet for new information. Web sites that are especially useful to identify new security issues include CERT (http://www.cert.org), FIRST (http://www.first.org), and SANS (http://www.sans.org). Finally, the OCR maintains a Web site with frequently asked questions (FAQs). Use this site frequently: http://www.hhs.gov/ocr/privacy/hipaa/faq/index.html.

Some exposure to salespersons or even free seminars held locally by security service companies can be very insightful, so long as the ISO does not return with a long shopping list of the latest gadgets that may not be necessary. However, it is very important to appreciate that some part of the ISO's time must be spent in keeping current in order to know what new risks there may be to your security program.

A best practice to ensure ongoing information security awareness is to periodically conduct a walkthrough of your office. While this primarily serves as a means to assess physical security, practices associated with not adhering to administrative safeguards and some technical safeguards can often be identified as well. Consider doing the following:

- Play thief: Walk around your office both internally and externally and examine it the way a thief might. Many local police departments offer courtesy inspections. Investigate how door locks are keyed, changed, and controlled. Depending on your office's size, location, and risk analysis, you might consider use of surveillance cameras, alarms, and motion detectors to deter and/or record unauthorized access. Other property controls can be used, including property control tags or engraving the office's name on equipment (or the IT vendor's name if the equipment is leased) to provide proof of ownership in the event your physical controls fail against theft. Additionally, property tags are an efficient way to track and maintain your inventory.

- Pretend you're a patient: Look at your office from a privacy perspective, the way a patient or a patient's family member might view things. Make sure that your office layout prevents unauthorized viewing of computer screens. Reposition monitors or install anti-glare screens, privacy screens, covers, or other types of physical barrier to viewing. Lock file cabinets that store PHI. Enforce a clean-desk policy to prevent paper documents or removable media from being taken or misplaced.

- Use a checklist to validate that documentation of your security practices is in order, such as illustrated in Figure 10.1.

F I G U R E   10.1
Documentation Checklist

- Do you have documentation that you validated the authorization of contractors or vendors before granting them physical access to areas where PHI is processed and stored?
- Do you have a documented process for collecting devices used to obtain physical access to the building and restricted access areas when an employee leaves the organization (keys, badges, and proximity cards collected, and door combinations changed)?
- Do you maintain records for work performed on door lock systems or changes to door combinations or keys?
- Do you follow proper destruction and disposal methods for sensitive information and paper documents containing PHI, including shredding or locking up documents while waiting for destruction or disposal? Ensure there is a manifest of destruction that you can keep with your documentation.
- Do you have business associate contracts signed by each business associate who works for you?
- Do you have an inventory of organization-owned equipment, including that which may be in an employee's home (eg, transcriptionist or coder working from home)?
- For larger organizations, do contractors receive visitor badges and are they escorted or supervised while performing maintenance on information systems?
- Look at your office's computer workstations to verify that workstations located in publicly accessible areas are not vulnerable to view from unauthorized personnel and that passwords are not stuck to monitors, under keyboards, or in other places where they may be compromised.
- Protect workstations against environmental threats. Check documented policies that computer workstations must be connected to power strips that contain surge protectors to protect against surges on power lines caused by lightning strikes.
- Ensure that hand-held computing devices such as PDAs and laptop computers have power-on passwords or data encryption.
- Maintain an inventory of all software, including license numbers. Verify that if any unlicensed software has been installed on a computer workstation, it can be detected. Conduct random desktop audits to ensure that workstations have properly licensed software.
- Verify and document your review that unattended workstations automatically log off in accordance with the time you establish.

Business Associate Contracts

Business associate contracts can be written and managed completely within the office, although many seek legal counsel to at least draft an initial business associate contract for the office to use. It should not be necessary to hire legal counsel to negotiate every business associate contract, but if a business associate offers a contract to you and you have any concerns about language that is not in your standard draft or in the HIPAA Security Rule itself, you should definitely seek outside help.

Contingency Planning and Implementation

This may be one of the more likely processes you will want to acquire external help to manage. With the importance of backup and disaster recovery becoming an increasing concern with heightened automation, this is an area you do not want to risk doing poorly. Contingency planning and implementation take both initial time to set up and considerable time to manage on an ongoing basis. If you are using an application service provider (ASP), software as a service (Saas), or other hosted arrangement for your major information systems, the contingency planning should be a part of that service. However, do not forget the other information you have in your office that needs both protection and backup/disaster recovery.

TECHNICAL SECURITY CONTROLS SELECTION, IMPLEMENTATION, AND MAINTENANCE

While your information systems vendors will implement some of the technical security controls you will need as part of the information systems package of applications, there are numerous technical security controls you will need to decide upon and acquire for yourself. These definitely include network security controls, but may also include controls over and beyond what your information system application vendor supplies. A best practice is to consider what others with whom you anticipate exchanging data are using. This will help any interoperability issues that may arise. Certainly if you participate in a health information exchange organization (HIO), it may direct you to certain types of controls, and may also be able to help you with specific product recommendations. If you do not yet participate in an HIO, the hospital with which you exchange data may be very happy to help you.

Be aware that many of the technical security controls that you acquire beyond what is available in your information system applications will require some configuration during implementation and some ongoing maintenance. These may require a specialist to implement or to use. For instance, if you decide to periodically conduct a penetration test, you may want a specialist to do this. A penetration test is a method of evaluating the security of your information systems and network by simulating an attack from malicious outsiders and insiders (who have some level of authorized access). It can involve active exploitation of security vulnerabilities.

While you can conduct such network testing yourself, even using freeware from the Internet, you may want to be sure that the test is legitimate, have someone who really understands the results advise you on the findings, and assure that you have not created a vulnerability through the process of simulating the attack. Penetration tests can identify vulnerabilities that may be difficult or impossible to detect with only network or application vulnerability scanning software and provide evidence that such a test was performed. Figure 10.2 identifies security land mines that are often found through a penetration test. Figure 10.3 describes the components of penetration testing, and Figure 10.4 provides a comparison of vulnerability scanning and penetration testing. Penetration tests are a component of a full security audit. In fact, they may be required if you are required to comply with the Payment Card Industry Data Security Standard (PCI DSS).

FIGURE 10.2

Security Land Mines

- Authorized computer users misusing their privileges
- Failure to fix newly identified problems
- Poor password policies, especially failing to change or eliminate default passwords when installing new operating systems
- Failure to disable unnecessary services
- Poorly designed networks, allowing disparate systems to communicate directly with one another
- Allowing transmission of unencrypted data over the Internet
- Failure to deactivate remote dial-up access points

Reprinted with permission from Margret\A Consulting, LLC.

FIGURE 10.3

Penetration Testing Components

Network Security

- Network surveying
- Port scanning
- System identification
- Services identification
- Vulnerability research and verification
- Application testing and code review
- Router testing
- Firewall testing
- Intrusion detection system testing
- Trusted systems testing
- Password cracking
- Denial-of-service testing
- Containment measures testing

Wireless Security

- Wireless networks testing
- Cordless communications
- Privacy review testing
- Infrared systems testing

Communications Security

- PBX testing
- Voice mail testing
- Fax review
- Modem testing

Physical Security

- Access controls
- Perimeter review
- Alarm response testing
- Location review
- Environment review

Administrative Security

- Social engineering
- Request testing
- Guided suggestion testing
- Trust testing
- Training and awareness
- Policies and procedures

Reprinted with permission from Margret\A Consulting, LLC.

F I G U R E   10.4

Vulnerability Scanning vs Penetration Testing

Vulnerability Scanning	Penetration Testing
Passive assessment of network and server configurations	Active testing to the point where the security of network and server are attempted to be breached
Checks against known vulnerabilities	Attempts to exploit vulnerabilities
Can be well managed internally	Can be self-conducted but better performed by neutral third party
Must use reliable scanning tools to avoid incorrect results	Must use trusted third party to prevent creation of vulnerabilities

Reprinted with permission from Margret\A Consulting, LLC.

Change Control

Also called information systems configuration, change control is the process of receiving requests for changes, evaluating the potential impact of the requested changes (such as on security functionality), obtaining approval for appropriate changes, installing and testing changes, documenting the changes, and then releasing the changed software into production. The original proposed Security Rule included a separate requirement for configuration management. In the final Security Rule, however, configuration management was assumed to be a normal part of every information system practice. But assumptions are not always correct, so it is strongly recommended that configuration management procedures be adopted for both changes relating to security and all other changes.

Changes are very common in information systems. Some are made to implement an update or to add functionality. Others are made to improve utilization of the system. While most changes do not present issues, some changes should only be made after careful review. For instance, if clinicians are complaining about certain data elements being required in the EHR that have not been collected in the past, they may want the data elements eliminated or changed to being optional for entry. Upon inspection, however, it may be found that some or all of these data elements are required for a clinical decision support rule to work properly—perhaps reminding a clinician of a best practice or alerting a clinician about a potential drug contraindication. The decision then needs to be made whether to risk the fact that the clinical decision support may not work, perhaps delete the clinical decision support rule, move the location of where the data elements are to be entered to better fit the office's workflow, or not make any change. This is not an IT decision. Changes made to clinical systems should be approved by whatever group in the office makes critical clinical decisions. All changes should be documented.

Formal change control procedures are also related to security functions because it is often necessary to turn off certain security controls in order to upgrade a system. Such change control procedures should have you double-check that you returned your security controls to their normal state after any change to the system.

Critical information systems, servers, and network devices also need to be hardened by verifying they are properly configured and managed to ensure security. Applying security controls after systems are in place is costly and may lead to trade-offs in security. It's far more cost effective to start off secure and manage the existing security.

Configuration management includes establishing a test environment. When you install or upgrade a system, it should be tested and users may need to be trained on new functions. It is good practice to test and train in a special test environment, rather than your live or production environment, because if something goes wrong, it does not impact your current operations.

Many organizations have two computing environments: one is for conducting normal business, referred to as the production environment, and the other is the test environment. The test environment simulates the work environment and can be used for training or testing changes or upgrades to software in an environment that will not hinder the normal business of the office.

The federal government has indicated that any disclosure of PHI made during an information systems test is generally an incidental disclosure and not a violation under the HIPAA Privacy Rule. But why risk such a disclosure and your entire production system as well? It is a good business practice to use a test environment if at all possible.

RESPONDING TO AN OCR COMPLAINT OR REQUEST FOR AUDIT

The Office for Civil Rights (OCR) has the authority to receive, investigate, and determine resolution of complaints about violations of the HIPAA Privacy Rule and Security Rule (since enforcement of the Security Rule was transferred to OCR from the CMS on July 27, 2009). The OCR Web site (http://www.hhs.gov/ocr/privacy/hipaa/enforcement/index.html) provides a description of the complaint process (as illustrated in Figure 10.5); enforcement highlights summarizing the number of cases in which corrective action was obtained, no violation was found, or other resolutions were achieved; and enforcement data, including case examples and resolution agreements. It can be very helpful to periodically review the data presented on this Web site as a means to keep current on the major concerns of those who file complaints. The case studies and resolution agreements might be used as a source of a scenario to bring to an office meeting that may help build awareness, especially if you are experiencing problems with a similar situation. It is important to recognize that both complaints and audits are equal opportunity actions—where small providers are just as likely to be involved as large providers and often more likely to be involved in HIPAA action than other types of HIPAA covered entities (ie, health plans and clearinghouses).

Should you be the subject of a complaint, generally you will receive a letter outlining a request for books and records. Everyone advises that your first step should be not to panic. While not to belittle the process, it is known that many complaints result in no violation being found or the requirement for you to prepare a corrective action plan (CAP). In addition, most complaints surround the Privacy Rule, and there can be security implications to a privacy complaint. Whether the initial focus is on privacy or security, there are extremely few cases where the OCR would show up at your door unannounced. Whatever complaint would trigger such an action would have to be an extremely egregious situation.

You should be prepared with a plan to respond to a written complaint. This plan should include engaging your attorney, executive management, the IPO and ISO, your general compliance officer, and your health information management department/custodian of records to review the complaint and the request for books and records.

If you have followed the advice in this book, you will have your policies, procedures, and documentation from which to select the requested information to send to OCR. Make sure you respond within the deadlines specified. Most attorneys will want to review what you plan to send before you do so. They will also very likely advise you to send only what is requested and not more. If you are uncertain whether to send something that appears unrelated to the request, it is probably best not to send it. OCR can request additional information if needed. However, not sending information you have that is pertinent to the request only because it appears to implicate you, could make matters worse. If you truly

FIGURE 10.5

OCR Complaint Process

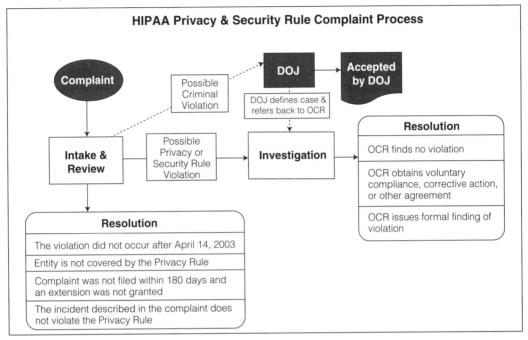

From US Department of Health and Human Services (HHS). Health Information Privacy: Enforcement Process. http://www.hhs.gov/ocr/privacy/hipaa/enforcement/process/index.html.

do not have information you know you should have, you might consider responding explicitly that you do not have the information. Obviously, if a violation is found, improving your documentation will be included in your CAP.

If you are found in violation and are given a CAP, you will want to make sure you address the specifics in the plan. You may be required to provide specific information on an ongoing basis for a specified period of time. As of this writing, HHS has entered into nine resolution agreements and issued civil monetary penalties (CMPs) to one covered entity. A resolution agreement is a contract signed by HHS and a covered entity in which the covered entity agrees to perform certain corrective steps or obligations (eg, staff training) and make reports to HHS, generally for a period of three years. During the period, HHS monitors the covered entity's compliance with its obligations. A resolution agreement likely would include the payment of a resolution amount. These agreements are reserved to settle investigations with more serious outcomes. When HHS has not been able to reach a satisfactory resolution through the covered entity's demonstrated compliance or corrective action through other informal means, CMPs may be imposed for noncompliance against a covered entity. There have been no criminal actions taken by HHS as of this writing.

The HITECH Act also gave state attorneys general (SAGs) the authority to bring civil actions on behalf of state residents for violations of the HIPAA Privacy Rule and Security Rule. The HITECH Act permits SAGs to obtain damages on behalf of state residents or to enjoin further violations of the HIPAA Privacy Rule and Security Rule. As of this writing, the only known SAG action is that in Minnesota, where the SAG filed a lawsuit in 2012 against a business associate (a debt collection agency) of a healthcare provider for failing to adequately safeguard patients' PHI.

Despite the limited civil and criminal penalties, as of December 31, 2011, there had been nearly 67,000 complaints investigated by OCR. With the exception of one year, the number of complaints has increased each year. HITECH also increased the amount of the civil monetary penalty that can be levied, and clarified that (civil and criminal) penalties could be levied on individuals as well as organizations. In addition, there have been arrests and lawsuits filed for other actions related to PHI where HHS has not been involved. The most recent instance as of this writing was the case, previously cited in Chapter 8, of a Florida hospital staff member who was arrested for allegedly inappropriately accessing more than 760,000 EHRs with the intent to disclose, transfer, or sell certain information for personal gain. News reports indicated the sale was to an agent of chiropractors and attorneys.

Finally, the HITECH Act of 2009 requires HHS to provide for periodic audits to ensure that covered entities and business associates are complying with the HIPAA Privacy Rule and Security Rule and Breach Notification standards. To implement this mandate, OCR piloted a program to perform 115 audits of covered entities to assess privacy and security compliance. Audits conducted during the pilot phase began in November 2011 and concluded in December 2012. Additional information about the audit program, including the audit protocol, is available from http://www.hhs.gov/ocr/privacy/hipaa/enforcement/audit/protocol.html. Once the pilot has been evaluated and any modifications made in the process, auditing will become an ongoing activity of the OCR.

If you are identified for an audit, you will want to prepare similarly to how you would prepare to respond to a complaint, but the audit will entail a visit (usually scheduled in advance) to your office. You will be sent a request for documents to be submitted within 10 days of the request. (It is recommended that you prepare and keep an extra copy of what is sent for any further inspection once the auditors arrive.) There will be a pre-audit conference call with the auditors. The audit itself could last from 6 to 10 days, although for a very small office the time period would be less. Once on site, as with others who request access to your books and records, you should verify the identity of the auditors against the notice of audit. It is advised that you do not leave them alone. Although the audit will include interviews with employees, it is appropriate to assign a staff member to assist each auditor and to learn from the process. This will also assure that the auditors do not extend the scope of the audit beyond privacy and security—perhaps to claim audits, etc. Do not be solicitous; do not offer food. Do not initiate any conversation with them—even though this is only an audit, anything that you say can be held against you. Because this is not a search of your premises, auditors should not seize original documents. To date, copies of patient records have not been requested. Consult with your attorney as to the extent to which you should supply copies of any patient records requested. In general, the audit approach is "show me your written policy, and show me you follow it."

There are four possible outcomes of the HIPAA/HITECH audits: (1) The report may yield no major compliance gaps and only a simple CAP. (2) Significant issues could be found so that the report will present concerns along with a proposed remediation plan. The majority of the pilot audits have fallen into one of these two outcomes. (3) The auditors could identify a serious deficiency warranting escalation to OCR for further review. (4) The audit could uncover willful neglect, which would lead to OCR notification and potential fines and other charges. In general, findings to date have identified the following issues:

- Policies and procedures are lacking
- HIPAA compliance programs are not a high priority
- Small providers have the most problems
- Larger entities face the most security challenges
- Risk analysis is missing, incomplete, or not well managed

- Third-party risks are not managed well
- Privacy challenges are widely dispersed throughout the rule with no clear trends by entity type or size
- Security issues are focused heavily on user activity monitoring and contingency planning, with physical access controls of least concern

Every recommendation that has come forth from the audits, complaint process, or general compliance guidelines is to ensure documentation is adequate and kept up-to-date. Many experts recommend conducting periodic mock audits yourself (which would essentially be a risk analysis). Integrate HIPAA compliance with usual business operations. Be transparent with employees. They are essentially your first line of defense. As suggested in Chapter 1, a culture of privacy and security goes a long way toward ensuring compliance with the details.

BREACH NOTIFICATION

Federal breach notification is a separate regulation that has come out of the HITECH Act of 2009. Prior to 2009, 44 states had enacted breach notification laws. Most addressed both health information as well as other personal information (eg, social security numbers, credit cards), and are still in effect and require reporting in addition to federal reporting. The federal government adopted a universal breach notification requirement in 2009 specifically for protected health information (PHI). Required is immediate reporting of large breaches (500 or more persons impacted) and annual reporting of small breaches (fewer than 500 persons impacted). There has been considerable action in a relatively short period of time. Results of the 2010 report (last available) to Congress are illustrated in Figure 10.6.

FIGURE 10.6

Federal Breach Notifications as of December 2010

Cause of Breaches Impacting 500 or More Persons	Number of Incidents
1. Theft of electronic devices/media or paper	252
2. Loss of electronic devices/media or paper	37
3. Intentional unauthorized access, use, or disclosure	35
4. Human error	29
5. Improper disposal (all paper)	11
Total	364
Individuals impacted	7,800,000 individuals
Cause of Breaches Impacting Less Than 500 Persons	
Misdirected communications	30,521
Individuals impacted	62,000 individuals

The process one must undertake to identify a reportable breach and conduct the notification is provided in Figure 10.7. Breach notification is a significant process, is costly, and can potentially result in irreparable reputational harm. Many breaches could be prevented if federal guidance was followed to secure PHI (by encryption, destruction, or de-identification). See Chapter 8 and the CD-ROM for the full text of the guidance.

FIGURE 10.7

Workflow for Breach Notification

1. Discovery of (paper-based or electronic) security incident
   a. Acquisition, access, use, or disclosure of protected health information (PHI) compromises the security or privacy of the PHI
      i. Poses a significant risk of financial, reputational, or other harm to the individual
      ii. De-identified data are excluded
   b. Discovery of breach (or date when entity should have known of breach) starts 60-day clock for notification
2. Determine if PHI was:
   a. Secured (ie, encrypted, destroyed, or de-identified): breach notification may not be required
   b. Unsecured PHI: determine if exception applies
3. If unsecured, notification not required if:
   a. Unintentional access by member of covered entity (CE) or business associate (BA) workforce
   b. Inadvertent disclosure to person at same CE or BA and no further use or disclosure in violation of Privacy Rule
   c. Disclosure where CE or BA believes unauthorized recipient would be unable to retain PHI
4. Delay notification if law enforcement agencies have requested delay where notification may hinder investigation
5. Determine if breach may result in imminent misuse of unsecured PHI, in which case CE should notify individuals by telephone or other means in addition to written notice
6. Send notification letters via first-class mail within 60 days of breach discovery
   a. Record breach in a log. If fewer than 500 individuals affected, report breach annually
   b. If 500 or more individuals affected, notify HHS: http://transparency.cit.nih.gov/breach/index.cfm
   c. If 500 or more live within one state, send a press release to major media outlets
   d. If 10 or more letters returned due to out-of-date or insufficient contact information, provide substitute notice (eg, e-mail, Web site notice, major print or broadcast media)
7. Notice must be in plain language and include:
   a. Description of breach, date of breach, and date of discovery
   b. Description of types of information breached
   c. Steps individuals should take to protect themselves
   d. Description of what CE is doing to mitigate harm and protect against further breaches
   e. Contact procedures for individuals to ask questions, including toll-free number, e-mail address, Web site, or postal address

Reprinted with permission from Margret\A Consulting, LLC.

Also in HITECH, the Federal Trade Commission (FTC) was called upon to assure that health information in PHR vendors' control could also be protected, as such vendors did not fall under HHS jurisdiction. On August 25, 2009, the FTC issued the Health Breach Notification Rule.[1] The wording in this rule duplicates almost verbatim the HHS Breach Notification for Unsecured Protected Health Information, issued the day prior,[2] with the

1. Federal Trade Commission. 16 CFR Part 318, Health Breach Notification Rule; Final Rule, Federal Register. (August 25, 2009.) Available at: http://www.ftc.gov/os/2009/08/R911002hbn.pdf.
2. Health and Human Services. 45 CFR Parts 160 and 164. Breach Notification for Unsecured Protected Health Information; Interim Final Rule. Federal Register. (August 24, 2009.) Available at: http://www.gpo.gov/fdsys/pkg/FR-2009-08-24/pdf/E9-20169.pdf.

exception of the target audience (PHR vendors) and to which agency notification must be made (FTC). PHRs that fall under this rule include those offered by commercial vendors that individuals use as stand-alone products. This rule does not pertain to PHRs offered by a provider as part of its EHR system—breaches from that PHR would fall under the HHS Breach Notification Rule, which makes physician practices subject to such reporting if there were a breach.

YOUR CHOICE

This chapter has offered you a variety of things to consider as you budget for your security controls and plan for any untoward consequences of being out of compliance. Often at this point, small offices wonder "Why didn't the government just tell us what to do?" Remember, the intent of the Security Rule is to be comprehensive, scalable, and technology neutral. One size does not fit all in security. This chapter has demonstrated that there is no one right way, nor a way that will last forever. You must decide what is right for you based on the threats in your environment and your level of risk tolerance.

CHECK YOUR UNDERSTANDING*

1. True or False: Once security controls are in place, they do not need updating.

2. True or False: Change control means that no or very few changes should ever be made to information systems.

3. True or False: The best way to keep on top of needed security changes is to monitor reliable Web sites.

4. True or False: Small providers are generally not at as great a risk for complaints as are large providers.

5. True or False: Most OCR complaints have led to civil monetary penalties.

6. True or False: Individuals are not subject to HIPAA criminal penalties.

7. True or False: Many breaches can be prevented by encrypting data on portable devices and media.

8. True or False: Breach notification only applies to breaches of electronic protected health information.

9. True or False: Patients must be notified when their protected health information is breached.

10. True or False: Entities that have a breach of PHI must take steps to mitigate harm to those individuals whose information has been breached.

*For answers, refer to the Answer Key at the end of the book.

HIPAA Security Rule

The HIPAA Security Rule is reproduced for you in full on the CD-ROM. Appendix A to Subpart C of Part 164 (reproduced beginning on page 207) supplies the actual regulatory language in the Rule, along with a handy Security Standards Matrix that summarizes the standards and implementation specifications.

After glancing at the Rule, you may wonder:

- Why should I read the Rule?
- How do I read the Rule?

These are legitimate questions. After all, you have just read comprehensive guidance written in plain language! To understand *why* you should read the Rule, you must first understand *how* to read the rule.

READING THE RULE

Two government documents relate to the security provisions of HIPAA: a Preamble, and the Final Rule itself.

Preamble

When the federal government issues a final regulation, such as the HIPAA Security Rule, it includes introductory information, commonly known as the Preamble. The Preamble to the Security Rule is typical of most regulations and includes:

- *General information*, including title, name of government agency issuing the regulation, summary statement of what law the regulation pertains to (ie, HIPAA Administrative Simplification), effective date (when you must start implementing the rule) and compliance date (when you must comply with the rule's requirements), and information about who to contact for questions and how to obtain copies of the regulation.
- A *Background section* that describes more fully the context in which the regulation is being issued. In this case, it provides a summary of HIPAA.
- A *General Overview of the Provisions of the Proposed Rule* that references when the notice of proposed rulemaking (NPRM) was issued and briefly describes what is included.
- *Analysis of, and Responses to, Public Comments on the Proposed Rule* is a fairly lengthy but highly insightful section. It begins with general information and then provides specific information on each provision in the Proposed Rule. A summary of the comments received from the public in response to its NPRM is provided as is the government's response and rationale for the way they constructed the Final Rule with respect to each topic in the notice. This information is not the official statement of the Rule but provides valuable insight into why the Rule is stated the way it is.

- *A Regulatory Impact Analysis* is a required section of regulations that has a significant economic impact. Essentially this is a cost–benefit analysis. Review this section to understand who is impacted by the Rule and to learn the government's estimates of time and expenditures for compliance. Remember that the covered entities under HIPAA range from solo practitioner offices to large, multistate integrated delivery networks and huge health insurance companies. Also covered are major corporations whose primary business focus is not health care but have components of health care (eg, self-insured health plans, employee clinics, or retail pharmacies).

- The *Federalism* section describes the federal government's efforts to reach out to states and local governments as well as industry leadership groups.

The Rule

The Preamble is followed by the Rule itself. Recall from Chapter 1 that the Security Rule is being added to the Code of Federal Regulations (CFR), title 45, subtitle A.

- Part 160 contains definitions of terms that relate to both the Privacy Rule and the Security Rule. Because the final Privacy Rule was issued before the final Security Rule, reference to Part 162 is actually the removal of a definition. The government is moving some definitions so that there is a single, common set of definitions that applies to both the Privacy Rule and the Security Rule.

- Part 164 is labeled "Security and Privacy" because both the Privacy Rule and Security Rule are folded into this part of the CFR. This material includes content relating to the Privacy and Security Rules, as well as content that relates only to Security. Sections 164.103, 164.104, and 164.105 relate to both the Privacy Rule and Security Rule and include:

  - Definitions of terms (164.103)
  - Applicability of the Rules to covered entities (164.104)
  - Organizational requirements with respect to how covered entities may be organized (164.105)

- Subpart C (of Part 164) is the Security Rule itself. This includes definitions (164.304) and the standards and implementation specifications for:

  - General rules (164.306)
  - Administrative safeguards (164.308)
  - Physical safeguards (164.310)
  - Technical safeguards (164.312)
  - Organizational requirements (164.314)
  - Policies and procedures and documentation requirements (164.316)

   Note that reference is made throughout the Security Rule to Subpart E, which is the Privacy Rule (including sections 164.500 to 164.534).

UNDERSTANDING THE RULE

Now that you know what the Rule contains, you can see why you should read it. It contains valuable information from the government on why the Rule is written the way it is. The Preamble provides the government's rationale and interpretation. The Rule itself contains the exact wording to which your office must comply and serves as a handy reference without the interpretive information supplied in this book.

Appendix A to Subpart C of Part 164—Security Standards: Matrix

Authority: 42 U.S.C. 1320d–2 and 1320d–4.

§ 164.302   Applicability.

A covered entity must comply with the applicable standards, implementation specifications, and requirements of this subpart with respect to electronic protected health information.

§ 164.304   Definitions.

As used in this subpart, the following terms have the following meanings:

Access means the ability or the means necessary to read, write, modify, or communicate data/information or otherwise use any system resource. (This definition applies to "access" as used in this subpart, not as used in subpart E of this part.)

Administrative safeguards are administrative actions, and policies and procedures, to manage the selection, development, implementation, and maintenance of security measures to protect electronic protected health information and to manage the conduct of the covered entity's workforce in relation to the protection of that information.

Authentication means the corroboration that a person is the one claimed.

Availability means the property that data or information is accessible and useable upon demand by an authorized person.

Confidentiality means the property that data or information is not made available or disclosed to unauthorized persons or processes.

Encryption means the use of an algorithmic process to transform data into a form in which there is a low probability of assigning meaning without use of a confidential process or key.

Facility means the physical premises and the interior and exterior of a building(s).

Information system means an interconnected set of information resources under the same direct management control that shares common functionality. A system normally includes hardware, software, information, data, applications, communications, and people.

Integrity means the property that data or information have not been altered or destroyed in an unauthorized manner.

Malicious software means software, for example, a virus, designed to damage or disrupt a system.

Password means confidential authentication information composed of a string of characters.

Physical safeguards are physical measures, policies, and procedures to protect a covered entity's electronic information systems and related buildings and equipment, from natural and environmental hazards, and unauthorized intrusion.

Security or Security measures encompass all of the administrative, physical, and technical safeguards in an information system.

Security incident means the attempted or successful unauthorized access, use, disclosure, modification, or destruction of information or interference with system operations in an information system.

Technical safeguards means the technology and the policy and procedures for its use that protect electronic protected health information and control access to it.

User means a person or entity with authorized access.

Workstation means an electronic computing device, for example, a laptop or desktop computer, or any other device that performs similar functions, and electronic media stored in its immediate environment.

§ 164.306   Security standards: General rules.

(a) *General requirements.* Covered entities must do the following:

(1) Ensure the confidentiality, integrity, and availability of all electronic protected health information the covered entity creates, receives, maintains, or transmits.

(2) Protect against any reasonably anticipated threats or hazards to the security or integrity of such information.

(3) Protect against any reasonably anticipated uses or disclosures of such information that are not permitted or required under subpart E of this part.

(4) Ensure compliance with this subpart by its workforce.

(b) *Flexibility of approach.*

(1) Covered entities may use any security measures that allow the covered entity to reasonably and appropriately implement the standards and implementation specifications as specified in this subpart.

(2) In deciding which security measures to use, a covered entity must take into account the following factors:

(i) The size, complexity, and capabilities of the covered entity.

Federal Register / Vol. 68, No. 34 / Thursday, February 20, 2003 / Rules and Regulations   **8377**

(ii) The covered entity's technical infrastructure, hardware, and software security capabilities.

(iii) The costs of security measures.

(iv) The probability and criticality of potential risks to electronic protected health information.

(c) *Standards.* A covered entity must comply with the standards as provided in this section and in § 164.308, § 164.310, § 164.312, § 164.314, and § 164.316 with respect to all electronic protected health information.

(d) *Implementation specifications.* In this subpart:

(1) Implementation specifications are required or addressable. If an implementation specification is required, the word "Required" appears in parentheses after the title of the implementation specification. If an implementation specification is addressable, the word "Addressable" appears in parentheses after the title of the implementation specification.

(2) When a standard adopted in § 164.308, § 164.310, § 164.312, § 164.314, or § 164.316 includes required implementation specifications, a covered entity must implement the implementation specifications.

(1) When a standard adopted in § 164.308, § 164.310, § 164.312, § 164.314, or § 164.316 includes addressable implementation specifications, a covered entity must—

(i) Assess whether each implementation specification is a reasonable and appropriate safeguard in its environment, when analyzed with reference to the likely contribution to protecting the entity's electronic protected health information; and

(ii) As applicable to the entity—

(A) Implement the implementation specification if reasonable and appropriate; or

(B) If implementing the implementation specification is not reasonable and appropriate—

(1) Document why it would not be reasonable and appropriate to implement the implementation specification; and

(2) Implement an equivalent alternative measure if reasonable and appropriate.

(e) *Maintenance.* Security measures implemented to comply with standards and implementation specifications adopted under § 164.105 and this subpart must be reviewed and modified as needed to continue provision of reasonable and appropriate protection of electronic protected health information as described at § 164.316.

§ 164.308 Administrative safeguards.

(a) A covered entity must, in accordance with § 164.306:

(1)(i) *Standard: Security management process.* Implement policies and procedures to prevent, detect, contain, and correct security violations.

(ii) *Implementation specifications:*

(A) *Risk analysis* (Required). Conduct an accurate and thorough assessment of the potential risks and vulnerabilities to the confidentiality, integrity, and availability of electronic protected health information held by the covered entity.

(B) *Risk management* (Required). Implement security measures sufficient to reduce risks and vulnerabilities to a reasonable and appropriate level to comply with § 164.306(a).

(C) *Sanction policy* (Required). Apply appropriate sanctions against workforce members who fail to comply with the security policies and procedures of the covered entity.

(D) *Information system activity review* (Required). Implement procedures to regularly review records of information system activity, such as audit logs, access reports, and security incident tracking reports.

(2) *Standard: Assigned security responsibility.* Identify the security official who is responsible for the development and implementation of the policies and procedures required by this subpart for the entity.

(3)(i) *Standard: Workforce security.* Implement policies and procedures to ensure that all members of its workforce have appropriate access to electronic protected health information, as provided under paragraph (a)(4) of this section, and to prevent those workforce members who do not have access under paragraph (a)(4) of this section from obtaining access to electronic protected health information.

(ii) *Implementation specifications:*

(A) *Authorization and/or supervision* (Addressable). Implement procedures for the authorization and/or supervision of workforce members who work with electronic protected health information or in locations where it might be accessed.

(B) *Workforce clearance procedure* (Addressable). Implement procedures to determine that the access of a workforce member to electronic protected health information is appropriate.

(C) *Termination procedures* (Addressable). Implement procedures for terminating access to electronic protected health information when the employment of a workforce member ends or as required by determinations made as specified in paragraph (a)(3)(ii)(B) of this section.

(4)(i) *Standard: Information access management.* Implement policies and procedures for authorizing access to electronic protected health information that are consistent with the applicable requirements of subpart E of this part.

(ii) *Implementation specifications*:

(A) *Isolating health care clearinghouse functions* (Required). If a health care clearinghouse is part of a larger organization, the clearinghouse must implement policies and procedures that protect the electronic protected health information of the clearinghouse from unauthorized access by the larger organization.

(B) *Access authorization* (Addressable). Implement policies and procedures for granting access to electronic protected health information, for example, through access to a workstation, transaction, program, process, or other mechanism.

(C) *Access establishment and modification* (Addressable). Implement policies and procedures that, based upon the entity's access authorization policies, establish, document, review, and modify a user's right of access to a workstation, transaction, program, or process.

(5)(i) *Standard: Security awareness and training.* Implement a security awareness and training program for all members of its workforce (including management).

(ii) *Implementation specifications.* Implement:

(A) *Security reminders* (Addressable). Periodic security updates.

(B) *Protection from malicious software* (Addressable). Procedures for guarding against, detecting, and reporting malicious software.

(C) *Log-in monitoring* (Addressable). Procedures for monitoring log-in attempts and reporting discrepancies.

(D) *Password management* (Addressable). Procedures for creating, changing, and safeguarding passwords.

(6)(i) *Standard: Security incident procedures.* Implement policies and procedures to address security incidents.

(ii) *Implementation specification: Response and Reporting* (Required). Identify and respond to suspected or known security incidents; mitigate, to the extent practicable, harmful effects of security incidents that are known to the covered entity; and document security incidents and their outcomes.

(7)(i) *Standard: Contingency plan.* Establish (and implement as needed) policies and procedures for responding to an emergency or other occurrence (for example, fire, vandalism, system failure, and natural disaster) that damages systems that contain electronic protected health information.

(ii) *Implementation specifications:*

(A) *Data backup plan* (Required). Establish and implement procedures to create and maintain retrievable exact copies of electronic protected health information.

(B) *Disaster recovery plan* (Required). Establish (and implement as needed) procedures to restore any loss of data.

(C) *Emergency mode operation plan* (Required). Establish (and implement as needed) procedures to enable continuation of critical business processes for protection of the security of electronic protected health information while operating in emergency mode.

(D) *Testing and revision procedures* (Addressable). Implement procedures for periodic testing and revision of contingency plans.

(E) *Applications and data criticality analysis* (Addressable). Assess the relative criticality of specific applications and data in support of other contingency plan components.

(8) *Standard: Evaluation.* Perform a periodic technical and nontechnical evaluation, based initially upon the standards implemented under this rule and subsequently, in response to environmental or operational changes affecting the security of electronic protected health information, that establishes the extent to which an entity's security policies and procedures meet the requirements of this subpart.

(b)(1) *Standard: Business associate contracts and other arrangements.* A covered entity, in accordance with § 164.306, may permit a business associate to create, receive, maintain, or transmit electronic protected health information on the covered entity's behalf only if the covered entity obtains satisfactory assurances, in accordance with § 164.314(a) that the business associate will appropriately safeguard the information.

(2) This standard does not apply with respect to—

(i) The transmission by a covered entity of electronic protected health information to a health care provider concerning the treatment of an individual.

(ii) The transmission of electronic protected health information by a group health plan or an HMO or health insurance issuer on behalf of a group health plan to a plan sponsor, to the extent that the requirements of § 164.314(b) and § 164.504(f) apply and are met; or

(iii) The transmission of electronic protected health information from or to other agencies providing the services at § 164.502(e)(1)(ii)(C), when the covered entity is a health plan that is a government program providing public

benefits, if the requirements of § 164.502(e)(1)(ii)(C) are met.

(3) A covered entity that violates the satisfactory assurances it provided as a business associate of another covered entity will be in noncompliance with the standards, implementation specifications, and requirements of this paragraph and § 164.314(a).

(4) *Implementation specifications: Written contract or other arrangement* (Required). Document the satisfactory assurances required by paragraph (b)(1) of this section through a written contract or other arrangement with the business associate that meets the applicable requirements of § 164.314(a).

§ 164.310   Physical safeguards.

A covered entity must, in accordance with § 164.306:

(a)(1) *Standard: Facility access controls.* Implement policies and procedures to limit physical access to its electronic information systems and the facility or facilities in which they are housed, while ensuring that properly authorized access is allowed.

(2) *Implementation specifications:*

(i) *Contingency operations* (Addressable). Establish (and implement as needed) procedures that allow facility access in support of restoration of lost data under the disaster recovery plan and emergency mode operations plan in the event of an emergency.

(ii) *Facility security plan* (Addressable). Implement policies and procedures to safeguard the facility and the equipment therein from unauthorized physical access, tampering, and theft.

(iii) *Access control and validation procedures* (Addressable). Implement procedures to control and validate a person's access to facilities based on their role or function, including visitor control, and control of access to software programs for testing and revision.

(iv) *Maintenance records* (Addressable). Implement policies and procedures to document repairs and modifications to the physical components of a facility which are related to security (for example, hardware, walls, doors, and locks).

(b) *Standard: Workstation use.* Implement policies and procedures that specify the proper functions to be performed, the manner in which those functions are to be performed, and the physical attributes of the surroundings of a specific workstation or class of workstation that can access electronic protected health information.

(c) *Standard: Workstation security.* Implement physical safeguards for all workstations that access electronic

protected health information, to restrict access to authorized users.

(d)(1) *Standard: Device and media controls.* Implement policies and procedures that govern the receipt and removal of hardware and electronic media that contain electronic protected health information into and out of a facility, and the movement of these items within the facility.

(2) *Implementation specifications:*

(i) *Disposal* (Required). Implement policies and procedures to address the final disposition of electronic protected health information, and/or the hardware or electronic media on which it is stored.

(ii) *Media re-use* (Required). Implement procedures for removal of electronic protected health information from electronic media before the media are made available for re-use.

(iii) *Accountability* (Addressable). Maintain a record of the movements of hardware and electronic media and any person responsible therefore.

(iv) *Data backup and storage* (Addressable). Create a retrievable, exact copy of electronic protected health information, when needed, before movement of equipment.

§ 164.312   Technical safeguards.

A covered entity must, in accordance with § 164.306:

(a)(1) *Standard: Access control.* Implement technical policies and procedures for electronic information systems that maintain electronic protected health information to allow access only to those persons or software programs that have been granted access rights as specified in § 164.308(a)(4).

(2) *Implementation specifications:*

(i) *Unique user identification* (Required). Assign a unique name and/or number for identifying and tracking user identity.

(ii) *Emergency access procedure* (Required). Establish (and implement as needed) procedures for obtaining necessary electronic protected health information during an emergency.

(iii) *Automatic logoff* (Addressable). Implement electronic procedures that terminate an electronic session after a predetermined time of inactivity.

(iv) *Encryption and decryption* (Addressable). Implement a mechanism to encrypt and decrypt electronic protected health information.

(b) *Standard: Audit controls.* Implement hardware, software, and/or procedural mechanisms that record and examine activity in information systems that contain or use electronic protected health information.

(c)(1) *Standard: Integrity.* Implement policies and procedures to protect electronic protected health information from improper alteration or destruction.

(2) *Implementation specification: Mechanism to authenticate electronic protected health information* (Addressable). Implement electronic mechanisms to corroborate that electronic protected health information has not been altered or destroyed in an unauthorized manner.

(d) *Standard: Person or entity authentication.* Implement procedures to verify that a person or entity seeking access to electronic protected health information is the one claimed.

(e)(1) *Standard: Transmission security.* Implement technical security measures to guard against unauthorized access to electronic protected health information that is being transmitted over an electronic communications network.

(2) *Implementation specifications:*
(i) *Integrity controls* (Addressable). Implement security measures to ensure that electronically transmitted electronic protected health information is not improperly modified without detection until disposed of.

(ii) *Encryption* (Addressable). Implement a mechanism to encrypt electronic protected health information whenever deemed appropriate.

§ 164.314   Organizational requirements.

(a)(1) *Standard: Business associate contracts or other arrangements.*

(i) The contract or other arrangement between the covered entity and its business associate required by § 164.308(b) must meet the requirements of paragraph (a)(2)(i) or (a)(2)(ii) of this section, as applicable.

(ii) A covered entity is not in compliance with the standards in § 164.502(e) and paragraph (a) of this section if the covered entity knew of a pattern of an activity or practice of the business associate that constituted a material breach or violation of the business associate's obligation under the contract or other arrangement, unless the covered entity took reasonable steps to cure the breach or end the violation, as applicable, and, if such steps were unsuccessful—

(A) Terminated the contract or arrangement, if feasible; or

(B) If termination is not feasible, reported the problem to the Secretary.

(2) *Implementation specifications* (Required).

(i) *Business associate contracts.* The contract between a covered entity and a business associate must provide that the business associate will—

(A) Implement administrative, physical, and technical safeguards that reasonably and appropriately protect the confidentiality, integrity, and availability of the electronic protected health information that it creates, receives, maintains, or transmits on behalf of the covered entity as required by this subpart;

(B) Ensure that any agent, including a subcontractor, to whom it provides such information agrees to implement reasonable and appropriate safeguards to protect it;

(C) Report to the covered entity any security incident of which it becomes aware;

(D) Authorize termination of the contract by the covered entity, if the covered entity determines that the business associate has violated a material term of the contract.

(ii) *Other arrangements.*
(A) When a covered entity and its business associate are both governmental entities, the covered entity is in compliance with paragraph (a)(1) of this section, if—

(*1*) It enters into a memorandum of understanding with the business associate that contains terms that accomplish the objectives of paragraph (a)(2)(i) of this section; or

(*2*) Other law (including regulations adopted by the covered entity or its business associate) contains requirements applicable to the business associate that accomplish the objectives of paragraph (a)(2)(i) of this section.

(B) If a business associate is required by law to perform a function or activity on behalf of a covered entity or to provide a service described in the definition of business associate as specified in § 160.103 of this subchapter to a covered entity, the covered entity may permit the business associate to create, receive, maintain, or transmit electronic protected health information on its behalf to the extent necessary to comply with the legal mandate without meeting the requirements of paragraph (a)(2)(i) of this section, provided that the covered entity attempts in good faith to obtain satisfactory assurances as required by paragraph (a)(2)(ii)(A) of this section, and documents the attempt and the reasons that these assurances cannot be obtained.

(C) The covered entity may omit from its other arrangements authorization of the termination of the contract by the covered entity, as required by paragraph (a)(2)(i)(D) of this section if such authorization is inconsistent with the statutory obligations of the covered entity or its business associate.

(b)(1) *Standard: Requirements for group health plans.* Except when the only electronic protected health information disclosed to a plan sponsor is disclosed pursuant to

§ 164.504(f)(1)(ii) or (iii), or as authorized under § 164.508, a group health plan must ensure that its plan documents provide that the plan sponsor will reasonably and appropriately safeguard electronic protected health information created, received, maintained, or transmitted to or by the plan sponsor on behalf of the group health plan.

(2) *Implementation specifications* (Required). The plan documents of the group health plan must be amended to incorporate provisions to require the plan sponsor to—

(i) Implement administrative, physical, and technical safeguards that reasonably and appropriately protect the confidentiality, integrity, and availability of the electronic protected health information that it creates, receives, maintains, or transmits on behalf of the group health plan;

(ii) Ensure that the adequate separation required by § 164.504(f)(2)(iii) is supported by reasonable and appropriate security measures;

(iii) Ensure that any agent, including a subcontractor, to whom it provides this information agrees to implement reasonable and appropriate security measures to protect the information; and

(iv) Report to the group health plan any security incident of which it becomes aware.

§ 164.316   Policies and procedures and documentation requirements.

A covered entity must, in accordance with § 164.306:

(a) *Standard: Policies and procedures.* Implement reasonable and appropriate policies and procedures to comply with the standards, implementation specifications, or other requirements of this subpart, taking into account those factors specified in § 164.306(b)(2)(i), (ii), (iii), and (iv). This standard is not to be construed to permit or excuse an action that violates any other standard, implementation specification, or other requirements of this subpart. A covered entity may change its policies and procedures at any time, provided that the changes are documented and are implemented in accordance with this subpart.

(b)(1) *Standard: Documentation.*
(i) Maintain the policies and procedures implemented to comply with this subpart in written (which may be electronic) form; and

(ii) If an action, activity or assessment is required by this subpart to be documented, maintain a written (which may be electronic) record of the action, activity, or assessment.

(2) *Implementation specifications:*

(i) *Time limit* (Required). Retain the documentation required by paragraph (b)(1) of this section for 6 years from the date of its creation or the date when it last was in effect, whichever is later.

(ii) *Availability* (Required). Make documentation available to those persons responsible for implementing the procedures to which the documentation pertains.

(iii) *Updates* (Required). Review documentation periodically, and update as needed, in response to environmental or operational changes affecting the security of the electronic protected health information.

§ 164.318   Compliance dates for the initial implementation of the security standards.

(a) *Health plan.*

(1) A health plan that is not a small health plan must comply with the applicable requirements of this subpart no later than April 20, 2005.

(2) A small health plan must comply with the applicable requirements of this subpart no later than April 20, 2006.

(b) *Health care clearinghouse.* A health care clearinghouse must comply with the applicable requirements of this subpart no later than April 20, 2005.

(c) *Health care provider.* A covered health care provider must comply with the applicable requirements of this subpart no later than April 20, 2005.

Appendix A to Subpart C of Part 164—Security Standards: Matrix

Standards	Sections	Implementation Specifications (R)=Required, (A)=Addressable
Administrative Safeguards		
Security Management Process	164.308(a)(1)	Risk Analysis (R) Risk Management (R) Sanction Policy (R) Information System Activity Review (R)
Assigned Security Responsibility	164.308(a)(2)	(R)
Workforce Security	164.308(a)(3)	Authorization and/or Supervision (A) Workforce Clearance Procedure Termination Procedures (A)
Information Access Management	164.308(a)(4)	Isolating Health care Clearinghouse Function (R) Access Authorization (A) Access Establishment and Modification (A)
Security Awareness and Training	164.308(a)(5)	Security Reminders (A) Protection from Malicious Software (A) Log-in Monitoring (A) Password Management (A)
Security Incident Procedures	164.308(a)(6)	Response and Reporting (R)
Contingency Plan	164.308(a)(7)	Data Backup Plan (R) Disaster Recovery Plan (R) Emergency Mode Operation Plan (R) Testing and Revision Procedure (A) Applications and Data Criticality Analysis (A)
Evaluation	164.308(a)(8)	(R)
Business Associate Contracts and Other Arrangement.	164.308(b)(1)	Written Contract or Other Arrangement (R)
Physical Safeguards		
Facility Access Controls	164.310(a)(1)	Contingency Operations (A) Facility Security Plan (A) Access Control and Validation Procedures (A) Maintenance Records (A)
Workstation Use	164.310(b)	(R)
Workstation Security	164.310(c)	(R)
Device and Media Controls	164.310(d)(1)	Disposal (R) Media Re-use (R) Accountability (A) Data Backup and Storage (A)
Technical Safeguards (see § 164.312)		
Access Control	164.312(a)(1)	Unique User Identification (R) Emergency Access Procedure (R) Automatic Logoff (A) Encryption and Decryption (A)
Audit Controls	164.312(b)	(R)
Integrity	164.312(c)(1)	Mechanism to Authenticate Electronic Protected Health Information (A)
Person or Entity Authentication	164.312(d)	(R)
Transmission Security	164.312(e)(1)	Integrity Controls (A) Encryption (A)

The definitions in this glossary have been simplified for clarity and understanding. They are not intended to be used in a court of law. For legal definitions pertaining to HIPAA's Security Rule, consult the Office for Civil Rights at www. hhs.gov/ocr/hipaa.

Acceptance Verification that performance and security requirements have been met.

Access Controls Mechanisms and methods of providing access to authorized users while restricting access to all others.

Access Control List (ACL) List of users or entities that are authorized to access a particular system or program with assigned access privileges.

Access Privileges Types of actions an authorized user or entity is permitted; these may include create, read, update, delete, and system administration.

Administrative Simplification Title II, Subtitle F, of the Health Insurance Portability and Accountability Act of 1996 (Public Law 104-191) is intended to gain efficiencies through standards for financial and administrative transactions and code sets; establish national identifiers for providers, health plans, and employers; and provide for privacy and security of individually identifiable healthcare information that would promote adoption of information systems.

Alarm Provides real-time notification that a possible event is occurring (eg, intrusion detection system may notify a computer system administrator of a potential hacker attack).

Algorithm (Cryptographic) Mathematical rules or formulae used to convert plain text to ciphertext and back with the use of an encryption key.

American National Standards Institute (ANSI) Organization that accredits standards-setting organizations.

Anti-Virus Software (A/V Software) Software that helps prevent, detect, and remove viruses and other malware, usually by recognizing patterns against a database of virus signatures, or profiles.

Applications and Data Criticality Analysis The process of identifying the importance of an organization's applications and data in the event that systems have to be restored after being unavailable and the priority for restoring the applications and data. The analysis may also include the potential impact of the unavailability of applications and data on key business functions and critical business operations.

ASC X12N (Accredited Standards Committee X12) Standards-setting organization that has created standards for electronic data interchange, several of which are adopted under HIPAA for administrative and financial transactions.

ASP (Application Service Provider) An organization that hosts software applications for other organizations, providing use of the applications via a secure Internet or private network connection.. ASP clients pay monthly fees for the use of applications.

Asymmetric Cryptography   A form of public key encryption in which two keys are used, one of which is secret and the other of which is public. They are mathematically linked so that the secret key encrypts data and the public key (given to the recipient of the data) decrypts data.

Attack   An attempt to bypass security controls to gain access to a system for the purpose of exploiting a vulnerability.

Audit Log   Record of events or actions in an information system; used as forensic evidence after an incident has occurred.

Authentication   Verification of the identity of a user or entity as a prerequisite to allowing access to information systems.

Authorization   Permission given to a user to access the computing resources, programs, processes, and/or data of an entity.

Availability   Verification that information or data is accessible and attainable to authorized users or entities when needed.

Back Doors (aka Trap Doors)   A hidden entry point into a system or application triggered by certain commands or keystrokes, usually inserted by software developers to allow easy entry at a later time; a vulnerability that can be exploited by a hacker.

Backup   The process of copying and moving data to another medium so that the data may be restored if the original medium is corrupted or destroyed.

Biometric Identification Systems (aka Biometrics)   A means of identifying a human being using a measurement of a physical feature or repeatable action of the individual, referred to as something you are. Examples of biometric measures are hand geometry, retinal or iris scan, fingerprint patterns, facial characteristics, DNA sequence characteristics, voiceprints, and written signatures.

Broadband   A telecommunications signal that has a great capacity for traffic, improving the speed and capacity with which one can use the Internet.

Breach   As defined under the HITECH Act, an impermissible use or disclosure under the HIPAA Privacy Rule that compromises the security or privacy of the protected health information such that the use or disclosure poses a significant risk of financial, reputational, or other harm to the affected individual.

Break-the-Glass   A form of emergency access procedure in which access is provided an otherwise unauthorized individual based upon a specific, second action identifying the need for such access, such as selecting a reason from a drop-down menu. This access is then logged for subsequent review. This access procedure is named after the ability to pull a fire alarm after breaking its glass enclosure which protects the alarm from being used indiscriminately.

Browser   A software application that helps locate, retrieve, and display content from the Web. Browser-based technology which may be used in an EHR uses software and techniques similar to a Web browser to help browse any database for data.

Brute Force Attack   An exhaustive attempt to break the security of an information system, such as attempting all possible combinations of characters to guess a user's password.

Business Associate   Under HIPAA Privacy and Security rules, a person who is not a member of a covered entity's workforce (see Workforce) and who performs any function or activity involving the use or disclosure of individually identifiable health information or who provides services to a covered entity that involves the disclosure of individually identifiable health information, such as legal, accounting, consulting, data aggregation, management, accreditation, etc.

Business Associate Contract   Under HIPAA Privacy and Security rules, a legally binding agreement entered into by a covered entity and business associate that establishes permitted and required uses and disclosures of protected health information (PHI), provides obligations for the business associate to safeguard the information and to report any uses or disclosures not provided for in the contract, and requires the termination of the contract if there is a material violation.

Business Continuity   Ensures that critical business functions will continue to be performed and to provide rapid recovery, thus reducing the overall impact of a disaster or disruption and minimizing the potential risk of loss. See also Disaster Recovery.

Business Resumption   The process of restoring business operations following a disaster or interruption of services.

Callback (or Dialback)   A procedure for identifying a person or system that requests access to PHI.

CCTV (Closed-Circuit Television)   Mounted cameras positioned at key points within a facility that send pictures back to a security command center or a recording device such as a VCR.

CERT (Computer Emergency Response Team)   An organization that is responsible for monitoring security incidents on the Internet and providing security advisories or bulletins to the user community to reduce risks.

Chain of Custody (aka Chain of Evidence)   The process of labeling (date, time ,initials of collector, etc), sealing, and storing evidence so that it will be admissible in court.

Challenge-Response   An authentication process that verifies an identity by requiring correct authentication information to be provided in response to a challenge.

Cipherlock   A programmable lock that requires a password, swipe card, or proximity card to control access into an area.

Ciphertext   Data that has been rendered unreadable as a result of an encryption process.

Classification   Identification of the sensitivity of information, which ensures that sensitive and confidential data (including PHI) is properly controlled and secured.

Clearinghouse   A third party that performs services that aid in the exchange of information. A healthcare clearinghouse is a covered entity under HIPAA because its purpose is to convert financial and administrative transactions from standard to nonstandard or nonstandard to standard. A healthcare clearinghouse is frequently needed because the information systems of a payer or a provider may not be capable of generating or receiving a standard transaction.

Cleartext (or Plaintext)   Data that is not encrypted.

Cloud Computing   Computing resources (including applications and servers) offered as a service over the Internet.

Code   A representation of something. In computer programming, it is the representation of instructions that process data.

Cold Site   A facility that is available for use in an emergency that provides basic utilities and empty floor space but does not provide information system infrastructure or any computer or network equipment.

Compromise   A violation of the security policy of a system or organization that permits unauthorized disclosure or modification of information.

Computer Security Incident   An unusual occurrence or adverse event that occurs on any part of an information system and network. Some examples of security incidents include compromise of system integrity, denial of system resources, unauthorized access to a system or data (either internal or external), malicious code, or any kind of damage to an information system.

Computing Environment   The description of an information system consisting of hardware, application software, data, and procedures in which it is operated. Computing environments may also be physical surroundings or a description of the facilities where information systems reside.

Confidentiality   Assurance that private information that is shared will not be disclosed to unauthorized persons.

Configuration Management (aka Change Control)   The documented control of changes to an information system's hardware, software, policies, and documentation.

Contingency Plan   A document containing the operational procedures and instructions for business functions when information systems are unavailable, such as in a temporary outage or in the event of a disaster.

COTS (Commercial off the Shelf)   Computer software that is available for purchase by the general public.

Countermeasure   A method or procedure to prevent a threat from exploiting a vulnerability; used to mitigate or reduce risks. See also Safeguards.

Covered Entity   The specific types of organizations to which HIPAA applies, including health plans, clearinghouses, and providers who conduct electronic transactions.

Criticality   The importance of a data, applications, and information systems to the mission of the organization.

Cryptography   The science of creating a message that enables storage and transmission of data in a form that is available only to authorized users who have the means to decrypt the message.

Custodian   An individual who is responsible for the protection of specific information in support of business activities.

Data Center   Room where the organization's computing resources reside (generally a restricted access area).

Data Owner   An individual who is responsible for making and communicating judgments and decisions with regard to use, identification, classification, and protection of information systems.

Data Stewardship   Responsibility, guided by principles and practices, to ensure the knowledgeable and appropriate use of data derived from individuals' PHI.

Degauss   Using a magnetic field to erase (neutralize) the data bits stored on magnetic media.

De-identification   The process of removing individual identifiers from PHI so that it may be used or disclosed without compromising patient privacy.

Denial of Services (DOS) Attacks   A planned series of actions to shut down a system or to prevent the system from functioning properly by flooding the network with requests. This causes regular network traffic to slow significantly or it completely interrupts network services.

Digital Certificate   The mechanism used to authenticate the owner of a digital signature. See also PKI.

Digital Signature   A means to provide the authentication of the sender of a message, verifying the origin and identity of the sender. See also PKI.

Disaster Recovery Plan (DRP)   A plan for continued business and computer operations after a catastrophic event occurs.

Disclosure   The release, transfer, provision of access to, or divulging in any other manner of information outside the entity holding the information.

Discretionary Access Control (DAC)   An access control method whereby the data owner has the discretion of allowing or denying access to the resources (objects) they own based on the identity and/or group membership of the subject.

DMZ (Demilitarized Zone)   A network segment external to the internal network that has some security controls in place that are not as restrictive as the internal network.

Domain   The set of objects (eg, data, software instructions) that share a common security policy that a person or entity is allowed to access.

DNS (Domain Name Service)   Protocol that allows users to locate computer systems on a transmission control protocol/internet protocol (TCP/IP) network by translating domain names into numeric IP addresses.

Downstream Liability   Liability resulting from network connectivity to another organization. For example, an entity that has its information systems exploited by hackers may have downstream liability resulting from the damage to other organizations' systems caused by the hacked systems.

DRS (Designated Record Set)   According to the HIPAA Privacy Rule, the group of records that are used, in whole or in part, by or for a covered entity to make decisions about individuals.

Due Care   Minimum and customary practice of responsible protection of assets.

Due Diligence   The prudent management and execution of due care on a continual basis.

Dumpster Diving   Rummaging through another person's garbage. Trash is not protected by federal law, although some states have enacted dumpster diving laws that afford limited protections.

EDI (Electronic Data Interchange)   Specific way of sending data from computer to computer between two organizations, or trading partners.

EHR (Electronic Health Record)   An electronic record of health-related information on an individual that conforms to nationally recognized interoperability standards and that can be drawn from multiple sources while being managed, shared, and controlled by the individual.

Electronic Signature   A process used to authenticate a user in electronic form. An electronic signature usually refers to the application of a password for authentication. In contrast, a digitized signature is merely an image of an actual signature. A digital signature is a form of authentication that incorporates nonrepudiation that digitized and electronic signatures do not.

Emergency Access Procedure (aka Break-the-Glass)   Procedure for granting emergency access to information systems on a temporary basis that circumvents the standard access processes due to the urgency of the access need.

EMR (Electronic Medical Record)   An electronic record of health-related information on an individual that conforms to nationally recognized interoperability standards and that can be created, managed, and consulted by authorized clinicians and staff across more than one health care organization.

Encryption   A method for securing data stored (temporarily or permanently) or during transmission by transforming plain text into ciphertext, which cannot be accessed without the proper encryption keys.

ESIGN (Electronic Signatures in Global and National Commerce Act of 2000)   A federal law that facilitates the use of electronic signatures in interstate and foreign commerce by ensuring the validity and legal effect of contracts entered into electronically.

Failover   A backup operation that automatically switches to a standby system if the primary system fails or is taken offline.

Firewall   A device that examines traffic entering and leaving a network and keeps some types of traffic from passing from one network (such as the Internet) to another network (such as the internal network) based on a set of rules.

Freeware   Software that is distributed and licensed without a charge (although the source code in which the software is written may not be accessible to the acquirer). (Contrast this with shareware, for which there is a small fee for use, but no access to source code; and open source software which may require payment to acquire but which provides the source code to the acquirer.)

FTP (File Transfer Protocol)   A network protocol used to transfer files over a Transmission Control Protocol/Internet Protocol (TCP/IP) network such as the Internet.

Granularity   The property with which something can be broken down into parts.

Hacker   A commonly used term to describe an individual who attempts or succeeds in achieving unauthorized access, regardless of motivation.

Hash   A form of digital signature used for data integrity that is computed based on the contents of a message to determine if the message has been altered.

HHS   US Department of Health and Human Services.

HITECH Act (Health Information Technology for Economic and Clinical Health Act of 2009)   This law is part of the American Recovery and Reinvestment Act (ARRA), or stimulus legislation that provides significant funding for health information technology, including workforce training, incentives for making meaningful use of certified EHR technology, modifications to the Privacy Rule, and breach notification requirements.

HL7 (Health Level Seven)   A standards-setting organization that has primarily created message format standards to address interoperability of information systems within and across health care organizations.

Hot Key   The key or key combination that has been programmed to perform some function such as logging off or locking the computer keyboard, taking priority over any other program that is currently running.

Hot Site   A facility that is available for use in an emergency that has all of the necessary computer hardware and infrastructure (power, environmental controls, network connectivity, etc) to allow the recovery of operations within a few hours by restoring the information systems from backup media.

HTTP (Hypertext Transfer Protocol)   A protocol used to connect servers on the World Wide Web (www).

HTTPS (Hypertext Transfer Protocol Secure)   Hypertext Transfer Protocol (HTTP) wrapped in an encrypted secure sockets layer (SSL) or transport layer security (TLS) tunnel.

Incident   An unusual occurrence. See also Computer Security Incident.

Incidental Disclosure of PHI   Inadvertent access to PHI without intent, business need, or authorization to use such information but which, according to the HIPAA Privacy Rule, does not constitute wrongful access or disclosure.

Individually Identifiable Health Information (IIHI)   Information, in any form or medium, created or received by certain participants in health care, relating to the health of an individual or payment for health services, that either identifies the individual or provides a reasonable basis to believe the information can identify the individual. IIHI includes PHI, but may also include information outside of the protection of HIPAA, such as that maintained by an individual in a personal health record.

Information Systems   Computer workstations connected by network equipment to servers or mainframe computers that process and store information.

Integrity   One of the three main functions of security (confidentiality and availability being the other two) that verifies that information has not been altered, manipulated, or destroyed in an unauthorized manner.

Integrity Controls   Security mechanisms and methods that are employed to ensure the validity of information that is electronically transmitted or stored.

Intrusion Detection System (IDS)   Security alarms that warn of possible inappropriate attempts to access networks, hosts, programs, or data by examining (also referred to as sniffing) network traffic.

ISO (Information Security Official or Officer)   The individual assigned responsibility for developing and implementing information security policies and procedures.

LDAP (Lightweight Directory Access Protocol)   A protocol used to access directories (databases) of information, eg, user names and passwords.

Least Privilege   The principle of granting users only the access they need to perform their official assigned duties. (Privileges should be the most restrictive possible without hindering health care operations.)

Malicious Code (aka Malware)   Computer programs (viruses, Trojan horses, worms, etc) intentionally written to cause data integrity or availability problems to information systems.

Media   Any physical places that store or have the capacity to store information. Examples include, but are not limited to, CDs, tapes, hard drives, flash drives, microfiche, microfilm, and paper documents.

Message Authentication Code (MAC)   A value that is calculated during an encryption process and appended to data to protect against tampering during transmission. (A form of integrity control.)

Minimum Necessary   Limiting use, disclosure of, or requests for PHI to the least possible amount that is necessary to accomplish the purpose. Access controls afford the means to achieve minimum necessary use in information systems.

NCVHS (National Committee on Vital and Health Statistics)   Statutory advisory committee to the Secretary of the Department of Health and Human Services. Has been tasked under HIPAA to monitor implementation and develop recommendations for additional standards.

Need-to-Know   Access to information or systems based on a user's role and current responsibilities or business need. See also Least Privilege.

NIST (National Institute of Standards and Technology)   An agency of the US Department of Commerce that is responsible for standards setting; NIST's special publications series of guidelines are referenced in the Security Rule.

Nonrepudiation   A process that positively identifies the sender, so that the sender cannot deny sending a message.

NPRM (Notice of Proposed Rule-making)   The publication, in the Federal Register, of proposed federal regulations for public comment.

OS (also O/S)   Operating system that causes the computer to process instructions (eg, Windows, MacOS X, Linux, Unix).

Password   A character string used to authenticate a user to an information system.

Patch   A temporary program used to fix a vulnerability or other type of problem in a computer program.

PCMCIA (Personal Computer Memory Card International Association)   A standard for connecting peripherals to portable computers created by an international standards body and trade association.

PDA (Personal Digital Assistant)   Handheld computer, primarily used as an organizer, but becoming a powerful computing device.

Penetration Testing   A probe of a network or component of a network to identify and exploit potential security exposures and weaknesses. Penetration testing is intrusive and can be destructive and/or disruptive in nature.

Piggybacking   An unauthorized access into a restricted area achieved by closely following behind another person when the door is opened.

PKI (Public Key Infrastructure)   A secure method for exchanging information through the use of public and private keys for encrypting and decrypting data and information.

Plaintext   Original data prior to it being encrypted.

Platform   A systemic environment capable of hosting and storing applications, files, directories, and electronic data.

Portable Computer (PC)   Easy-to-carry electronic device that is capable of storing PHI in its memory. Examples include, but are not limited to, laptops, notebooks, and/or personal digital assistants (PDA).

Portal A type of software used to create a single access point to specific files or applications for which an organization wants its employees, physicians, patients, vendors, or others so authorized to have secure access. Portal software can provide view only, can construct a user-friendly version of an existing program, or provide direct access to specified functionality based on the organization's specifications.

POTS (Plain Old Telephone Service) Dialing a telephone and using a modem to convert analog and digital signals as a way to connect to a network for remote access.

Privacy Information belonging to or concerning a person that is not widely known.

Private Network A network established and operated by an organization for users within that organization.

Probability Chance or likelihood that an event will occur.

PHI (Protected Health Information) Any information in any form or medium that is created or received and that relates to the past, present, or future physical or mental health or condition of an individual or can be used to identify an individual.

Protocol A standard set of rules that determines how computers communicate with each other across networks.

Prudent Person Rule Duties that prudent people would exercise in similar circumstances. Often used as a test of reasonableness in a court of law.

Public Network A network established and operated by a telecommunication administration or by a recognized private operating agency (RPOA) for the specific purpose of providing circuit-switched, packet-switched, and leased-circuit services to the public.

Read-Only Access Read-only access allows a user to view data or information but does not allow any form of modification to the original data; however, data could potentially be copied to another location and modified.

Residual Risk The risk that remains after security controls are applied.

Restricted Access Area An area where confidential information is processed and/or stored and only individuals with a legitimate need to know are allowed to work unescorted. These areas require physical access authorization beyond that needed to gain access to the facility.

Reuse Reissuing magnetic media or a computer workstation to another user.

Risk Probability of a threat exploiting a vulnerability and exposing an asset to a loss.

Risk Analysis Identification of vulnerabilities in resources and the threats to those resources to determine appropriate safeguards or controls.

Role-Based Access Controls (RBAC) A preapproved set of access levels that grants access to information systems and is established based on an individual's roles or job functions and legitimate business need-to-know.

Sanitization The procedures and mechanisms used for removing confidential information from magnetic media such that data recovery is prevented, thus making the media acceptable for reuse or disposal. This is typically performed by overwriting the media with random patterns of ones and zeros or degaussing the media.

Safeguards Risk-reducing measures that act to detect, prevent, or minimize loss associated with the occurrence of a specified threat or category of threats. See also Countermeasure.

SSL (Secure Sockets Layer)   A protocol that manages the security of messages transmitted over the Internet. SSL has recently been succeeded by a more advanced protocol, Transport Layer Security (TLS). SSL uses public-and-private key encryption, including the use of a digital certificate.

Sensitivity   In information security, the degree to which a loss or compromise of data would have a negative effect.

Separation of Duties   Dividing roles and responsibilities so that a single individual cannot subvert a critical process.

Service Pack   A software patch (typically provided by the vendor) to fix a vulnerability, improve performance, and/or correct a programming error to an application or computer program, such as the operating system.

Shareware   Software that is distributed on a trial basis. Continued use requires the payment of a fee. See also Freeware.

Shoulder Surfing   Situation in which a person looks over the shoulder of another person while working, typically used to obtain unauthorized information such as a user's password.

Significant Changes   Any major addition of software or configuration change to the system's hardware or operating system or a modification of the environment.

SMTP (Simple Mail Transfer Protocol)   A protocol used by many e-mail applications to send and receive e-mail.

Sniffer   A software program or device that examines network traffic.

Social Engineering   The art of tricking a person into telling confidential information. Typically, social engineers portray themselves as being entitled to the information.

Spam   Unsolicited, usually commercial or objectionable, form of communication sent to a large number of recipients.

System Administrator (SysAdmin) or Super User   A person with full, unrestricted access to an information system that allows that person to view, modify, replace, create, or delete data, files, programs, services, and other user's access.

TCP/IP (Transmission Control Protocol/Internet Protocol)   The core Internet communications protocol, often used to refer to the entire set of protocols used on the Internet for communications of all types defined, accepted, and implemented by the request for comments (RFC) process.

Threat   An event representing potential danger to a computer, network, or data, the occurrence of which could have an undesired impact.

Token   A physical item that contains the identity of the holder. It is one means of authentication. Examples of tokens include an ATM bankcard and smart cards.

TPO (Treatment, Payment, and Healthcare Operations)   Used in HIPAA regulations to describe the conditions under which authorization is not required before disclosing PHI.

TLS (Transport Layer Security)   See SSL.

Trojan Horse   A program that has an apparent or actual purpose (can be benign or beneficial) that also contains malicious code designed to exploit a vulnerability and/or provide unauthorized access into a system.

Tunneling   Wrapping one connection or protocol inside another so it can be sent across a network.

UPS (Uninterruptible Power Supply)   A battery that provides power to a system in the event of a power failure; usually includes an alerting mechanism to signal the system to shut down "gracefully" to preserve the integrity of programs and data.

Use   With respect to individually identifiable health information, the sharing, employment, application, utilization, examination, or analysis of such information within an entity that maintains such information. See Disclosure.

User   An individual authorized to access information systems and services.

User Data   Data created, used, maintained, or backed up by individuals.

User ID (User Identity)   A character string that identifies a person or other entity that accesses information systems or applications. User IDs are accompanied by a password or other form of authentication, known to or possessed by the individual associated with the ID.

User-Based Access Controls (UBAC)   A form of access control that governs access to information based on a user's identity as authorized by the user's manager or supervisor.

Virus   A small application or string of code that can infect other programs that usually gets buried within an existing program. Once the virus program is executed, it attempts to copy itself to other programs in the system.

Visitor   A visitor is any person who is not a member of the workforce and who physically accesses the facility, including but not limited to, patients and their families, former members of the workforce, workforce family members, information technology vendors, pharmaceutical representatives, etc.

VPN (Virtual Private Network)   A method for providing secure remote access to the internal network or information systems behind a firewall by establishing a secure tunnel in a public network such as the Internet. VPNs typically employ some combination of encryption, digital certificates, strong user authentication, and access control to provide security to the traffic they carry.

Vulnerability   An inherent weakness or absence of a safeguard that could be exploited by a threat that produces risk in a system.

Vulnerability Assessment (VA)   A probe of a network or component of a network such as a server to identify potential security exposures and weaknesses. Vulnerability assessment does not attempt to exploit such vulnerabilities. See also Penetration Testing.

War Dialing   A systematic program that automatically dials the 10,000 telephone numbers of a telephone number prefix (xxx0000 through xxx-9999) in random order searching for phone lines that respond with a tone, which indicates a modem connection. These programs are readily available on the Internet and are often used by hackers to gain unauthorized access into information systems. May also be used to identify all modem connections in a large organization.

War Driving   Driving around an area with a laptop computer and wireless network adapter in order to find unsecured wireless networks.

Warm Site   A facility that is available for use in an emergency that has the infrastructure but not the all of the computer and network equipment needed for full operations.

Web (aka World Wide Web)   A system of interconnected documents, images, videos, and other media accessed using a special application called a browser. Web-based applications utilize browser technology to search for, retrieve, and present information. Web-based applications are often accessed through the Internet, but the technology can also be applied locally.

WEDI (Workgroup on Electronic Data Interchange)   Organization formed in 1992 to promote use of electronic data interchange in health care. One of four organizations named in HIPAA as advisory to the Department of Health and Human Services.

Workforce   As defined in HIPAA, employees, volunteers, trainees, contractors, and other persons under the direct control of a covered entity, whether or not paid by the covered entity, who have access to PHI.

Workstation (also Computer Workstation)   Any computer device used to create, receive, update, or delete information.

Workstation Peripherals   Workstation peripheral devices include, but are not limited to, printers, copiers, fax machines, flat screen monitors, and any other mechanisms that can transmit, store, or display information.

Worm   A destructive program that replicates itself throughout disk and memory, using up the computer's resources and eventually bringing the system down.

Zero-day Threat   A potential attack by a virus for which there are as yet no known signatures that can be incorporated into existing anti-virus software. To thwart such threats, software using generic signatures can potentially identify new viruses or variants of existing viruses by looking for slight variations of known viruses. Some antivirus software can analyze an unknown file in a "sandbox" to see if it performs any malicious actions.

CHAPTER 1

1. I
2. C
3. A
4. I
5. C
6. Information access management
7. Access controls
8. Awareness and training
9. Device and media controls
10. Incidents
11. Theft
12. Unauthorized access
13. Loss
14. Laptops
15. Paper

CHAPTER 2

1. a
2. b
3. e
4. c
5. d
6. I
7. W
8. I
9. W
10. I

CHAPTER 3

1. d
2. a
3. d
4. a
5. d
6. Threat
7. Vulnerability
8. Vulnerability
9. Threat
10. Threat

CHAPTER 4

1. d
2. a
3. b
4. a
5. c
6. e
7. c
8. d
9. a
10. b

CHAPTER 5

1. Understand your information security management practices
2. Identify threats in your environment
3. Identify your office's vulnerabilities
4. Determine the probability a threat could attack a vulnerability
5. Implement security measures
6. Document your risk analysis
7. L
8. M
9. H
10. H

CHAPTER 6

1. d
2. h
3. a
4. f
5. b
6. i
7. c
8. e
9. g
10. j

CHAPTER 7

1. No
2. No
3. Yes
4. Yes
5. Yes
6. No
7. Yes
8. No
9. No
10. Yes
11. Process of combining PHI of one covered entity with PHI from another covered entity to analyze data relating to the health care operations of the respective covered entities
12. PHI that excludes certain direct identifiers of the individual, or of relatives, employers, or household members of the individual
13. A financial strategy where software is paid for as a subscription rather than a large upfront license fee; as well as an acquisition strategy where servers are hosted at the ASP location. ASP does not imply that the software services are supplied over the Web, or that a Web services architecture (WSA) is used to design the software
14. A financial strategy where software is delivered from a hosted location and paid for on demand. SaaS takes advantage of virtualization and more frequently, but not necessarily, has a WSA
15. A company that hosts servers and often supplies IT contractors but does not sell or service software

CHAPTER 8

1. d
2. d
3. b
4. c
5. d
6. b
7. d
8. d
9. c
10. a

CHAPTER 9

1. d
2. b
3. a
4. b
5. b
6. a
7. b
8. c
9. b
10. c

CHAPTER 10

1. False
2. False
3. True
4. False
5. False
6. False
7. True
8. False
9. True
10. True

Some of the tables and checklists featured on this CD-ROM are included in the *Handbook for HIPAA-HITECH Security*, Second Edition, and some are exclusive to the CD-ROM for your convenience and documentation. Use these tools as described in the book and modify them as suitable to your office environment. Retain these and other documents as evidence of your compliance activities.

The following is a list of what is included in each folder on the *Handbook for HIPAA-HITECH Security* CD-ROM:

Timeline and Budget Folder

- Checklist of Tasks, Timeline, and Resources (Microsoft Word file)
- Budget Considerations (Microsoft Word file)

Risk Analysis Folder

- Hardware/Software Inventory (Microsoft Word file)
- Information System Security Controls (Microsoft Word file)
- Application and Data Criticality and Sensitivity (Microsoft Word file)
- Common Sources of Threats (Microsoft Word file)
- Risk Analysis and Risk Management (CD only; Microsoft Excel file)

Administrative Controls Folder

- Workforce Security Functions (Microsoft Word file)
- Steps to Take at Termination or Job Change (Microsoft Word file)
- Access Rules (Microsoft Word file)
- Information Access Review Form (Microsoft Word file)
- Backup Inventory Log (Microsoft Word file)
- HIPAA Security Training (CD only; Microsoft PowerPoint file)

Physical Controls Folder

- Environmental Controls Checklist (CD only; Microsoft Word file)
- Workforce Access Controls Checklist (CD only; Microsoft Word file)
- Physical Facility Controls Checklist (CD only; Microsoft Word file)
- Workstation Controls Checklist (CD only; Microsoft Word file)
- Device and Media Controls Checklist (CD only; Microsoft Word file)

Technical Controls Folder

- Technical Controls Checklist (CD only; Microsoft Word file)
- Vendor Checklist (Microsoft Word file)

Also included are:

- Final Security Rule [Federal Register] (PDF)
- Federal Register Breach for Unsecured PHI (PDF)
- Federal Register IFR for Enforcement (PDF)

CD-ROM INSTRUCTIONS

The *Handbook for HIPAA-HITECH Security* CD-ROM is a cross-platform CD-ROM that will run on both Windows-based and Macintosh PCs.

To use any of these files, simply double-click the filename to open.

MINIMUM SYSTEM REQUIREMENTS

To access the contents of the CD-ROM, you must have at minimum the following components on your Windows-based or Macintosh PC:

Windows

- CD-ROM drive
- Pentium-class processor
- Microsoft Windows
- 64MB RAM
- Microsoft Word 97/98 or later
- Microsoft PowerPoint 97 or later
- Microsoft Excel 97 or later

Macintosh

- CD-ROM drive
- PowerPC processor
- Apple Mac OS 9.0 or later
- 64MB RAM
- Microsoft Word 98 or later
- Microsoft PowerPoint 97 or later
- Microsoft Excel 97 or later

RUN

To run the *Handbook for HIPAA-HITECH Security* CD-ROM, follow these steps:

Windows

1. Insert the CD into your CD-ROM drive.
2. If AutoPlay is enabled, the CD will open automatically to reveal five folders: Timeline and Budget, Risk Analysis, Administrative Controls, Physical Controls, and Technical Controls.
3. Double-click any of the five folders that appear in the CD window to reveal its contents.
4. Double-click any filename to open that file. You may customize and re-save each file to fit the needs of your individual practice.

If AutoPlay is not enabled and the CD-ROM does not open automatically, follow these steps:

1. Select the icon that designates your CD drive that appears on your desktop or in the My Computer window (select Start > My Computer) and double-click to display its contents. You should see five folders: Timeline and Budget, Risk Analysis, Administrative Controls, Physical Controls, and Technical Controls.
2. Double-click any of the five folders that appear in the CD window to reveal its contents.
3. Double-click any filename to open that file. You may customize and re-save each file to fit the needs of your individual practice.

Macintosh

1. Insert the CD into your CD-ROM drive.
2. Double-click the icon that appears on your desktop to open the CD-ROM and display its contents. You should see five folders: Timeline and Budget, Risk Analysis, Administrative Controls, Physical Controls, and Technical Controls.
3. Double-click any of the five folders that appear in the CD window to reveal its contents.
4. Double-click any filename to open that file. You may customize and re-save each file to fit the needs of your individual practice.

INDEX